Elements of Literature

First Course

W9-BYG-022

The Holt Reader

- **Respond to and Analyze Texts**
- **Apply Reading Skills**
- **Develop Vocabulary and Practice Fluency**

HOLT, RINEHART AND WINSTON

A Harcourt Education Company

Orlando • **Austin** • New York • San Diego • Toronto • London

Staff Credits

Executive Editor: Juliana Koenig

Senior Editor: Amy E. Fleming

Project Editor: Steve Oelenberger

Copyediting: Michael Neibergall, *Copyediting Manager;* Kristen Azzara, Mary Malone, *Copyediting Supervisors;* Christine Altgelt, Elizabeth Dickson, Leora Harris, Anne Heausler, Kathleen Scheiner, *Senior Copyeditors;* Emily Force, Julia Thomas Hu, Nancy Shore, *Copyeditors*

Project Administration: Marie Price, *Managing Editor;* Elizabeth LaManna, *Associate Managing Editor;* Janet Jenkins, *Senior Editorial Coordinator;* Christine Degollado, Betty Gabriel, Mark Koenig, Erik Netcher, *Editorial Coordinators*

Permissions: Ann Farrar, *Senior Permissions Editor;* Sally Garland, Susan Lowrance, *Permissions Editors*

Design: Betty Mintz, Richard Metzger, *Design Directors;* Chris Smith, *Senior Designer*

Series Design: Proof Positive/Farrowlyne Associates, Inc.

Production: Beth Prevelige, *Senior Production Manager;* Carol Trammel, *Production Manager;* Myles Gorospe, *Production Assistant*

Photo Research: Proof Positive/Farrowlyne Associates, Inc.

Manufacturing: Shirley Cantrell, *Manufacturing Supervisor;* Mark McDonald, *Inventory Analyst;* Amy Borseth, *Manufacturing Coordinator*

Cover

Photo Credit: (inset) *Boats at Fishbeach* by James Fitzgerald. Oil on canvasboard. Courtesy of Dan Broeckelmann and Krista Lisajus.

Requests for permission to make copies of any part of the work should be mailed to the following address: Permissions Department, Holt, Rinehart and Winston, 10801 N. MoPac Expressway, Building 3, Austin, Texas 78759-5415.

Printed in the United States of America
ISBN 0-03-068391-2

2 3 4 5 6 179 07 06 05 04

Contents

viii   Contents

To the Student

A Book for You

....

A book is like a garden carried in the pocket.
—Chinese Proverb

....

The more you put into reading, the more you get out of it. This book is designed to do just that—help you interact with the selections you read by marking them up, asking your own questions, taking notes, recording your own ideas, and responding to the questions of others.

A Book Designed for Your Success

The Holt Reader goes hand in hand with *Elements of Literature.* It is designed to help you interact with the selections and master the language arts skills.

The book has two parts, each of which follows a simple format:

Part 1   Reading Literature

To help you master how to respond to, analyze, evaluate, and interpret literature, *The Holt Reader* provides—

For each collection:
- The academic vocabulary you need to know to master the literary skills for the collection, defined for ready reference and use.
- Two selections from the corresponding collection in *Elements of Literature,* reprinted in an interactive format to support and guide your reading.
- A new selection for you to read and respond to, enabling you to apply and extend your skills and build toward independence.

For each selection:
- A Before You Read page that preteaches the literary focus and provides a reading skill to help you understand the selection.
- A Vocabulary Development page or section that preteaches selection vocabulary and provides a vocabulary skill to use while reading the prose selections.
- Literature printed in an interactive format to guide your reading and help you respond to the text.
- A Skills Practice graphic organizer that helps you understand the literary focus of the selection.
- A Skills Review page that helps you practice vocabulary and assess your understanding of the selection you've just read.

Part 2   Reading Informational Texts

To help you master how to read informational texts, this book contains—

- The academic vocabulary you need to know to understand informational reading skills, defined for ready reference and use.
- New informational selections in interactive format to guide your reading and help you respond to the text.
- A Before You Read page that preteaches a reading skill to help you comprehend the selection. Selection vocabulary is also pretaught on this page.
- A Skills Practice graphic organizer that helps you understand the reading focus of the selection.
- A Skills Review page that helps you practice vocabulary and assess your understanding of the selection you've just read.

A Book for Your Own Thoughts and Feelings

Reading is about *you*. It is about connecting your thoughts and feelings to the thoughts and feelings of the writer. Make this book your own. The more you give of yourself to your reading, the more you will get out of it. We encourage you to write in it. Jot down how you feel about the selection. Question the text. Note details you think need to be cleared up or topics you would like to learn more about.

A Walk Through the Book

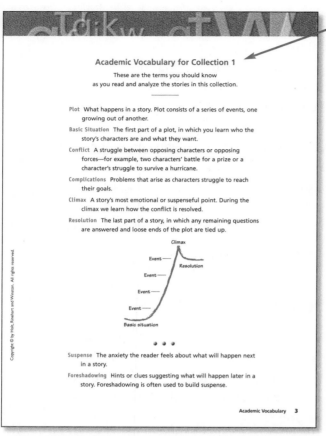

Academic Vocabulary
Academic vocabulary refers to the language of books, tests, and formal writing. Each collection begins with the terms, or academic language, you need to know to master the skills for that collection.

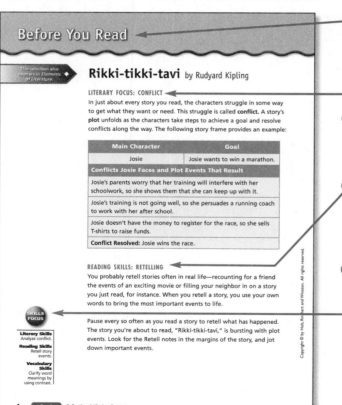

Before You Read
Previewing what you will learn builds success. This page tells you what the selection is about and prepares you to read it.

Literary Focus
This feature introduces the literary focus for the selection.

Reading Skills
This feature provides a reading skill for you to apply to the selection. It ties into and supports the literary focus.

Language Arts Skills
The skills covered with the selection are listed here.

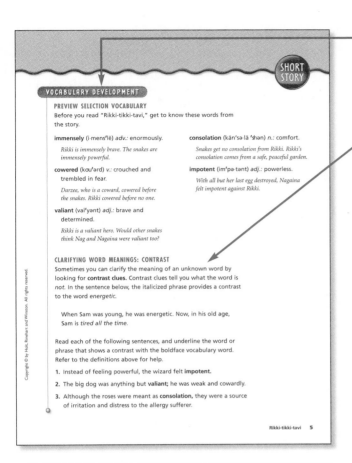

Vocabulary Development

Vocabulary words for the selection are pretaught. Each entry gives the pronunciation and definition of the word as well as a context sentence.

Vocabulary Skills

When you read, you not only have to recognize words but also decode them and determine meaning. This feature introduces a vocabulary skill to use to understand words in the selection.

Side-Column Notes

Each selection is accompanied by notes in the side column that guide your interaction with the selection. Many notes ask you to underline or circle in the text itself. Others provide lines on which you can write your responses to questions.

Types of Notes

The different types of notes throughout the selection help you—
• Focus on literary elements
• Apply the reading skill
• Apply the vocabulary skill
• Think critically about the selection
• Develop word knowledge
• Build vocabulary
• Build fluency

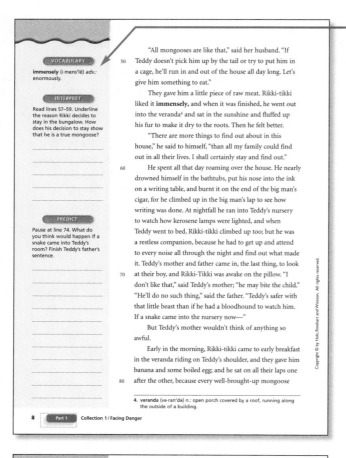

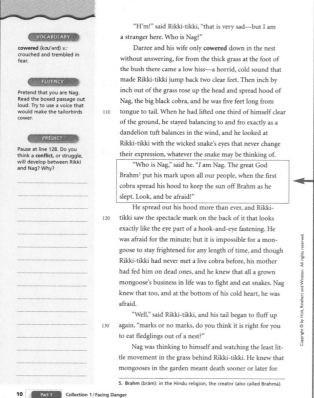

Vocabulary

The vocabulary words that were pretaught are defined in the side column and set in boldface in the selection, allowing you to see them in context.

Fluency

Successful readers are able to read fluently—clearly, easily, quickly, and without word identification problems. In most selections, you'll be given an opportunity to practice and improve your fluency.

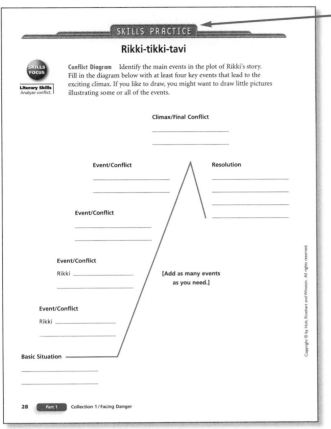

SKILLS PRACTICE

Rikki-tikki-tavi

SKILLS FOCUS

Literary Skills
Analyze conflict.

Conflict Diagram Identify the main events in the plot of Rikki's story. Fill in the diagram below with at least four key events that lead to the exciting climax. If you like to draw, you might want to draw little pictures illustrating some or all of the events.

Climax/Final Conflict

_____

_____

Event/Conflict

_____

_____

Resolution

_____

_____

Event/Conflict

_____

_____

Event/Conflict

Rikki _____

_____

[Add as many events
as you need.]

Event/Conflict

Rikki _____

_____

Basic Situation —

_____

_____

_____

Skills Review

Rikki-tikki-tavi

VOCABULARY AND COMPREHENSION

A. Clarifying Word Meanings: Contrast Choose three words from the Word Bank. Provide a contrast for each word by describing what it is *not*.

Word Bank
immensely
cowered
valiant
consolation
impotent

1. _____

_____

2. _____

_____

3. _____

_____

B. Reading Comprehension Answer each question below.

1. How does Rikki-tikki-tavi come to live with the family? _____

_____

_____

2. Why do Nag and Nagaina enter the house? _____

_____

_____

3. How does Rikki-tikki-tavi save Teddy's life? _____

_____

_____

SKILLS FOCUS

Vocabulary Skills
Clarify word meanings by using contrast.

Skills Practice

Graphic organizers help reinforce your understanding of the literary focus in a highly visual and creative way.

Skills Review: Vocabulary

Test your knowledge of the selection vocabulary and the vocabulary skill by completing this short activity.

Reading Comprehension

This feature allows you to see how well you've understood the selection you have just read.

Part One

Reading Literature

Facing Danger

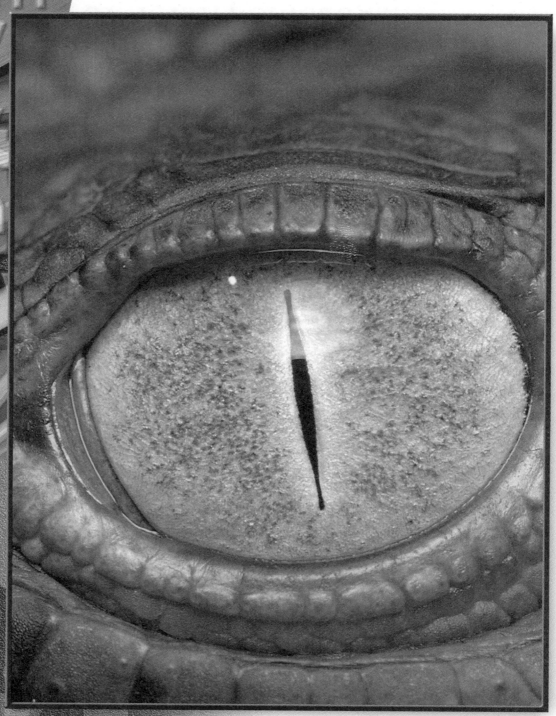

Digital Vision.

Academic Vocabulary for Collection 1

These are the terms you should know
as you read and analyze the stories in this collection.

———————

Plot What happens in a story. Plot consists of a series of events, one growing out of another.

Basic Situation The first part of a plot, in which you learn who the story's characters are and what they want.

Conflict A struggle between opposing characters or opposing forces—for example, two characters' battle for a prize or a character's struggle to survive a hurricane.

Complications Problems that arise as characters struggle to reach their goals.

Climax A story's most emotional or suspenseful point. During the climax we learn how the conflict is resolved.

Resolution The last part of a story, in which any remaining questions are answered and loose ends of the plot are tied up.

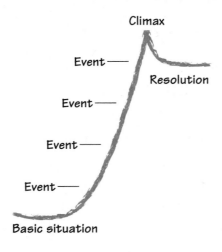

Suspense The anxiety the reader feels about what will happen next in a story.

Foreshadowing Hints or clues suggesting what will happen later in a story. Foreshadowing is often used to build suspense.

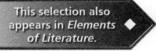

Rikki-tikki-tavi by Rudyard Kipling

LITERARY FOCUS: CONFLICT

In just about every story you read, the characters struggle in some way to get what they want or need. This struggle is called **conflict.** A story's **plot** unfolds as the characters take steps to achieve a goal and resolve conflicts along the way. The following story frame provides an example:

Main Character	Goal
Josie	Josie wants to win a marathon.
Conflicts Josie Faces and Plot Events That Result	
Josie's parents worry that her training will interfere with her schoolwork, so she shows them that she can keep up with it.	
Josie's training is not going well, so she persuades a running coach to work with her after school.	
Josie doesn't have the money to register for the race, so she sells T-shirts to raise funds.	
Conflict Resolved: Josie wins the race.	

READING SKILLS: RETELLING

You probably retell stories often in real life—recounting for a friend the events of an exciting movie or filling your neighbor in on a story you just read, for instance. When you retell a story, you use your own words to bring the most important events to life.

Pause every so often as you read a story to retell what has happened. The story you're about to read, "Rikki-tikki-tavi," is bursting with plot events. Look for the Retell notes in the margins of the story, and jot down important events.

SKILLS FOCUS

Literary Skills
Analyze conflict.

Reading Skills
Retell story events.

Vocabulary Skills
Clarify word meanings by using contrast.

VOCABULARY DEVELOPMENT

PREVIEW SELECTION VOCABULARY

Before you read "Rikki-tikki-tavi," get to know these words from the story.

immensely (i·mens′lē) *adv.:* enormously.

> *Rikki is immensely brave. The snakes are immensely powerful.*

cowered (kou′ərd) *v.:* crouched and trembled in fear.

> *Darzee, who is a coward, cowered before the snakes. Rikki cowered before no one.*

valiant (val′yənt) *adj.:* brave and determined.

> *Rikki is a valiant hero. Would other snakes think Nag and Nagaina were valiant too?*

consolation (kän′sə·lā′shən) *n.:* comfort.

> *Snakes get no consolation from Rikki. Rikki's consolation comes from a safe, peaceful garden.*

impotent (im′pə·tənt) *adj.:* powerless.

> *With all but her last egg destroyed, Nagaina felt impotent against Rikki.*

CLARIFYING WORD MEANINGS: CONTRAST

Sometimes you can clarify the meaning of an unknown word by looking for **contrast clues.** Contrast clues tell you what the word is *not.* In the sentence below, the italicized phrase provides a contrast to the word *energetic.*

> When Sam was young, he was energetic. Now, in his old age, Sam is *tired all the time.*

Read each of the following sentences, and underline the word or phrase that shows a contrast with the boldface vocabulary word. Refer to the definitions above for help.

1. Instead of feeling powerful, the wizard felt **impotent.**

2. The big dog was anything but **valiant;** he was weak and cowardly.

3. Although the roses were meant as **consolation,** they were a source of irritation and distress to the allergy sufferer.

Rikki-tikki-tavi

Rudyard Kipling

> **BACKGROUND: Literature and Social Studies**
>
> This story takes place in India many years ago, at a time when the British ruled that huge country. The family in this story lives in a cantonment (kan·tän′mənt), which is a kind of army base. The father is in the British army. This story is about a conflict between two deadly snakes and a brave little mongoose—a creature that looks something like a weasel or a large squirrel.

IDENTIFY

Circle the names of the characters introduced in the first paragraph. What sets Rikki apart from the other characters?

_____

_____

_____

_____

_____

_____

_____

_____

This is the story of the great war that Rikki-tikki-tavi fought single-handed, through the bathrooms of the big bungalow[1] in Segowlee cantonment.[2] Darzee, the tailorbird, helped him, and Chuchundra, the muskrat, who never comes out into the middle of the floor but always creeps round by the wall, gave him advice; but Rikki-tikki did the real fighting.

He was a mongoose, rather like a little cat in his fur and his tail but quite like a weasel in his head and his

10 habits. His eyes and the end of his restless nose were pink; he could scratch himself anywhere he pleased with any leg, front or back, that he chose to use; he could fluff up his tail till it looked like a bottlebrush, and his war cry as he scuttled through the long grass was *Rikk-tikk-tikki-tikki-tchk!*

One day, a high summer flood washed him out of the burrow where he lived with his father and mother and carried him, kicking and clucking, down a roadside ditch. He

VISUALIZE

Re-read lines 8–14. Underline three details that help you picture Rikki.

1. **bungalow** *n.:* in India, a low, one-storied house, named after a type of house found in Bengal, a region of South Asia.
2. **Segowlee** (sē·gou′lē) **cantonment:** British army post in Segowlee (now Segauli), India.

found a little wisp of grass floating there and clung to it till he lost his senses. When he revived, he was lying in the hot sun in the middle of a garden path, very draggled[3] indeed, and a small boy was saying: "Here's a dead mongoose. Let's have a funeral."

"No," said his mother; "let's take him in and dry him. Perhaps he isn't really dead."

They took him into the house, and a big man picked him up between his finger and thumb and said he was not dead but half choked; so they wrapped him in cotton wool and warmed him over a little fire, and he opened his eyes and sneezed.

"Now," said the big man (he was an Englishman who had just moved into the bungalow), "don't frighten him, and we'll see what he'll do."

It is the hardest thing in the world to frighten a mongoose, because he is eaten up from nose to tail with curiosity. The motto of all the mongoose family is "Run and find out," and Rikki-tikki was a true mongoose. He looked at the cotton wool, decided that it was not good to eat, ran all round the table, sat up and put his fur in order, scratched himself, and jumped on the small boy's shoulder.

"Don't be frightened, Teddy," said his father. "That's his way of making friends."

"Ouch! He's tickling under my chin," said Teddy.

Rikki-tikki looked down between the boy's collar and neck, snuffed at his ear, and climbed down to the floor, where he sat rubbing his nose.

"Good gracious," said Teddy's mother, "and that's a wild creature! I suppose he's so tame because we've been kind to him."

3. **draggled** v. used as adj.: wet and muddy, as if from being dragged around.

RETELL

Pause at line 29. Explain how Rikki gets to the bungalow.

_____

_____

_____

_____

_____

_____

_____

_____

_____

_____

IDENTIFY

Pause at line 39, and circle the motto of the mongoose family. List three things that Rikki does to live up to the motto.

_____

_____

_____

_____

_____

_____

_____

_____

immensely (i·mens'lē) *adv.:* enormously.

Read lines 57–59. Underline the reason Rikki decides to stay in the bungalow. How does his decision to stay show that he is a true mongoose?

_____

_____

_____

_____

_____

Pause at line 74. What do you think would happen if a snake came into Teddy's room? Finish Teddy's father's sentence.

_____

_____

_____

_____

_____

_____

_____

_____

_____

"All mongooses are like that," said her husband. "If
50   Teddy doesn't pick him up by the tail or try to put him in
a cage, he'll run in and out of the house all day long. Let's
give him something to eat."

They gave him a little piece of raw meat. Rikki-tikki
liked it **immensely,** and when it was finished, he went out
into the veranda[4] and sat in the sunshine and fluffed up
his fur to make it dry to the roots. Then he felt better.

"There are more things to find out about in this
house," he said to himself, "than all my family could find
out in all their lives. I shall certainly stay and find out."

60   He spent all that day roaming over the house. He nearly
drowned himself in the bathtubs, put his nose into the ink
on a writing table, and burnt it on the end of the big man's
cigar, for he climbed up in the big man's lap to see how
writing was done. At nightfall he ran into Teddy's nursery
to watch how kerosene lamps were lighted, and when
Teddy went to bed, Rikki-tikki climbed up too; but he was
a restless companion, because he had to get up and attend
to every noise all through the night and find out what made
it. Teddy's mother and father came in, the last thing, to look
70   at their boy, and Rikki-Tikki was awake on the pillow. "I
don't like that," said Teddy's mother; "he may bite the child."
"He'll do no such thing," said the father. "Teddy's safer with
that little beast than if he had a bloodhound to watch him.
If a snake came into the nursery now—"

But Teddy's mother wouldn't think of anything so
awful.

Early in the morning, Rikki-tikki came to early breakfast
in the veranda riding on Teddy's shoulder, and they gave him
banana and some boiled egg; and he sat on all their laps one
80   after the other, because every well-brought-up mongoose

---

4. **veranda** (və·ran'də) *n.:* open porch covered by a roof, running along
    the outside of a building.

A bungalow in India.

always hopes to be a house mongoose someday and have rooms to run about in; and Rikki-tikki's mother (she used to live in the General's house at Segowlee) had carefully told Rikki what to do if ever he came across white men.

Then Rikki-tikki went out into the garden to see what was to be seen. It was a large garden, only half cultivated, with bushes, as big as summerhouses, of Marshal Niel roses; lime and orange trees; clumps of bamboos; and thickets of high grass. Rikki-tikki licked his lips. "This is a 90 splendid hunting ground," he said, and his tail grew bottle-brushy at the thought of it, and he scuttled up and down the garden, snuffing here and there till he heard very sorrowful voices in a thorn bush. It was Darzee, the tailorbird, and his wife. They had made a beautiful nest by pulling two big leaves together and stitching them up the edges with fibers and had filled the hollow with cotton and downy fluff. The nest swayed to and fro as they sat on the rim and cried.

"What is the matter?" asked Rikki-tikki.

100 "We are very miserable," said Darzee. "One of our babies fell out of the nest yesterday and Nag ate him."

INFER

Re-read lines 77–84. Underline the lines that show how the family members feel about animals.

VISUALIZE

Underline the details that help you picture the garden **setting** (lines 85–98).

Notes

"H'm!" said Rikki-tikki, "that is very sad—but I am a stranger here. Who is Nag?"

Darzee and his wife only **cowered** down in the nest without answering, for from the thick grass at the foot of the bush there came a low hiss—a horrid, cold sound that made Rikki-tikki jump back two clear feet. Then inch by inch out of the grass rose up the head and spread hood of Nag, the big black cobra, and he was five feet long from tongue to tail. When he had lifted one third of himself clear of the ground, he stayed balancing to and fro exactly as a dandelion tuft balances in the wind, and he looked at Rikki-tikki with the wicked snake's eyes that never change their expression, whatever the snake may be thinking of.

"Who is Nag," said he. "*I* am Nag. The great God Brahm[5] put his mark upon all our people, when the first cobra spread his hood to keep the sun off Brahm as he slept. Look, and be afraid!"

He spread out his hood more than ever, and Rikki-tikki saw the spectacle mark on the back of it that looks exactly like the eye part of a hook-and-eye fastening. He was afraid for the minute; but it is impossible for a mongoose to stay frightened for any length of time, and though Rikki-tikki had never met a live cobra before, his mother had fed him on dead ones, and he knew that all a grown mongoose's business in life was to fight and eat snakes. Nag knew that too, and at the bottom of his cold heart, he was afraid.

"Well," said Rikki-tikki, and his tail began to fluff up again, "marks or no marks, do you think it is right for you to eat fledglings out of a nest?"

Nag was thinking to himself and watching the least little movement in the grass behind Rikki-tikki. He knew that mongooses in the garden meant death sooner or later for

5. **Brahm** (bräm): in the Hindu religion, the creator (also called Brahma).

him and his family, but he wanted to get Rikki-tikki off his guard. So he dropped his head a little and put it on one side.

"Let us talk," he said. "You eat eggs. Why should not I eat birds?"

140   "Behind you! Look behind you!" sang Darzee.

Rikki-tikki knew better than to waste time in staring. He jumped up in the air as high as he could go, and just under him whizzed by the head of Nagaina, Nag's wicked wife. She had crept up behind him as he was talking, to make an end of him; and he heard her savage hiss as the stroke missed. He came down almost across her back, and if he had been an old mongoose, he would have known that then was the time to break her back with one bite; but he was afraid of the terrible lashing return stroke of the

150 cobra. He bit, indeed, but did not bite long enough, and he jumped clear of the whisking tail, leaving Nagaina torn and angry.

"Wicked, wicked Darzee!" said Nag, lashing up as high as he could reach toward the nest in the thorn bush; but Darzee had built it out of reach of snakes, and it only swayed to and fro.

Rikki-tikki felt his eyes growing red and hot (when a mongoose's eyes grow red, he is angry), and he sat back on his tail and hind legs like a little kangaroo, and looked all

160 round him, and chattered with rage. But Nag and Nagaina had disappeared into the grass. When a snake misses its stroke, it never says anything or gives any sign of what it means to do next. Rikki-tikki did not care to follow them, for he did not feel sure that he could manage two snakes at once. So he trotted off to the gravel path near the house and sat down to think. It was a serious matter for him. If you read the old books of natural history, you will find they

RETELL

Re-read lines 138–166. Retell what happens between Rikki and the snakes.

"He was a mongoose, rather like a little cat in his fur and tail but quite like a weasel in his head and his habits."

say that when the mongoose fights the snake and happens to get bitten, he runs off and eats some herb that cures

170   him. That is not true. The victory is only a matter of quickness of eye and quickness of foot—snake's blow against the mongoose's jump—and as no eye can follow the motion of a snake's head when it strikes, this makes things much more wonderful than any magic herb. Rikki-tikki knew he was a young mongoose, and it made him all the more pleased to think that he had managed to escape a blow from behind. It gave him confidence in himself, and when Teddy came running down the path, Rikki-tikki was ready to be petted. But just as Teddy was stooping, something

180   wriggled a little in the dust and a tiny voice said: "Be careful. I am Death!" It was Karait, the dusty brown snakeling that lies for choice on the dusty earth; and his bite is as dangerous as the cobra's. But he is so small that nobody thinks of him, and so he does the more harm to people.

Rikki-tikki's eyes grew red again, and he danced up to Karait with the peculiar rocking, swaying motion that he had inherited from his family. It looks very funny, but it is so perfectly balanced a gait[6] that you can fly off from it at any angle you please; and in dealing with snakes this is an advantage. If Rikki-tikki had only known, he was doing a much more dangerous thing than fighting Nag, for Karait is so small and can turn so quickly that unless Rikki bit him close to the back of the head, he would get the return stroke in his eye or his lip. But Rikki did not know; his eyes were all red, and he rocked back and forth, looking for a good place to hold. Karait struck out, Rikki jumped sideways and tried to run in, but the wicked little dusty gray head lashed within a fraction of his shoulder, and he had to jump over the body, and the head followed his heels close.

Teddy shouted to the house: "Oh, look here! Our mongoose is killing a snake," and Rikki-tikki heard a scream from Teddy's mother. His father ran out with a stick, but by the time he came up, Karait had lunged out once too far, and Rikki-tikki had sprung, jumped on the snake's back, dropped his head far between his forelegs, bitten as high up the back as he could get hold, and rolled away. That bite paralyzed Karait, and Rikki-tikki was just going to eat him up from the tail, after the custom of his family at dinner, when he remembered that a full meal makes a slow mongoose, and if he wanted all his strength and quickness ready, he must keep himself thin. He went away for a dust bath under the castor-oil bushes, while Teddy's father beat the dead Karait. "What is the use of that?" thought Rikki-tikki; "I have settled it all"; and then Teddy's mother picked him up from the dust and hugged him, crying that he had saved Teddy from death, and Teddy's father said that he was a providence,[7] and Teddy looked on with big, scared eyes.

---

6. **gait** (gāt) *n.:* way of walking or running.
7. **providence** (präv′ə·dens) *n.:* favor or gift from God or nature.

IDENTIFY

Re-read lines 180–199. Underline the passages that tell why Karait is more dangerous than the cobras.

RETELL

Retell what happens during Rikki's **conflict** with Karait (lines 179–213).

_____
_____
_____
_____
_____
_____
_____
_____
_____
_____

INTERPRET

Re-read the dialogue between Rikki and Chuchundra in lines 237–258. Underline at least two or three lines that create a feeling of **suspense,** or uncertainty.

IDENTIFY

What does Rikki hear when the house is "as still as still" (line 259)? What does he think it is?

_____
_____
_____
_____
_____
_____

Rikki-tikki was rather amused at all the fuss, which, of course, he did not understand. Teddy's mother might just 220 as well have petted Teddy for playing in the dust. Rikki was thoroughly enjoying himself.

That night at dinner, walking to and fro among the wineglasses on the table, he might have stuffed himself three times over with nice things; but he remembered Nag and Nagaina, and though it was very pleasant to be patted and petted by Teddy's mother and to sit on Teddy's shoulder, his eyes would get red from time to time, and he would go off into his long war cry of *Rikk-tikk-tikki-tikki-tchk!*

Teddy carried him off to bed and insisted on Rikki-230 tikki's sleeping under his chin. Rikki-tikki was too well bred to bite or scratch, but as soon as Teddy was asleep, he went off for his nightly walk round the house, and in the dark he ran up against Chuchundra, the muskrat, creeping round by the wall. Chuchundra is a brokenhearted little beast. He whimpers and cheeps all night, trying to make up his mind to run into the middle of the room; but he never gets there.

"Don't kill me," said Chuchundra, almost weeping. "Rikki-tikki, don't kill me!"

"Do you think a snake killer kills muskrats?" said 240 Rikki-tikki scornfully.

"Those who kill snakes get killed by snakes," said Chuchundra, more sorrowfully than ever. "And how am I to be sure that Nag won't mistake me for you some dark night?"

"There's not the least danger," said Rikki-tikki, "but Nag is in the garden, and I know you don't go there."

"My cousin Chua, the rat, told me—" said Chuchundra, and then he stopped.

"Told you what?"

250 "H'sh! Nag is everywhere, Rikki-tikki. You should have talked to Chua in the garden."

"I didn't—so you must tell me. Quick, Chuchundra, or I'll bite you!"

Chuchundra sat down and cried till the tears rolled off his whiskers. "I am a very poor man," he sobbed. "I never had spirit enough to run out into the middle of the room. H'sh! I mustn't tell you anything. Can't you *hear*, Rikki-tikki?"

Rikki-tikki listened. The house was as still as still, but he thought he could just catch the faintest *scratch-scratch* in the world—a noise as faint as that of a wasp walking on a windowpane—the dry scratch of a snake's scales on brickwork.

"That's Nag or Nagaina," he said to himself, "and he is crawling into the bathroom sluice.[8] You're right, Chuchundra; I should have talked to Chua."

He stole off to Teddy's bathroom, but there was nothing there, and then to Teddy's mother's bathroom. At the bottom of the smooth plaster wall there was a brick pulled out to make a sluice for the bathwater, and as Rikki-tikki stole in by the masonry[9] curb where the bath is put, he heard Nag and Nagaina whispering together outside in the moonlight.

"When the house is emptied of people," said Nagaina to her husband, "*he* will have to go away, and then the garden will be our own again. Go in quietly, and remember that the big man who killed Karait is the first one to bite. Then come out and tell me, and we will hunt for Rikki-tikki together."

"But are you sure that there is anything to be gained by killing the people?" said Nag.

"Everything. When there were no people in the bungalow, did we have any mongoose in the garden? So long as

---

8. **sluice** (slo͞os) *n.*: drain.
9. **masonry** *n.* used as *adj.*: something built of stone or brick.

260

270

280

RETELL

Explain how Nag and Nagaina plan to regain control of the garden (lines 274–279).

_____

_____

_____

_____

_____

_____

_____

PREDICT

Pause at line 279. Do you think Nag and Nagaina's plan of attack will work? Why or why not?

_____

_____

_____

_____

_____

_____

_____

the bungalow is empty, we are king and queen of the garden; and remember that as soon as our eggs in the melon bed hatch (as they may tomorrow), our children will need room and quiet."

"I had not thought of that," said Nag. "I will go, but there is no need that we should hunt for Rikki-tikki afterward. I will kill the big man and his wife, and the child if I can, and come away quietly. Then the bungalow will be empty, and Rikki-tikki will go."

Rikki-tikki tingled all over with rage and hatred at this, and then Nag's head came through the sluice, and his five feet of cold body followed it. Angry as he was, Rikki-tikki was very frightened as he saw the size of the big cobra. Nag coiled himself up, raised his head, and looked into the bathroom in the dark, and Rikki could see his eyes glitter.

"Now, if I kill him here, Nagaina will know; and if I fight him on the open floor, the odds are in his favor. What am I to do?" said Rikki-tikki-tavi.

Nag waved to and fro, and then Rikki-tikki heard him drinking from the biggest water jar that was used to fill the bath. "That is good," said the snake. "Now, when Karait was killed, the big man had a stick. He may have that stick still, but when he comes in to bathe in the morning, he will not have a stick. I shall wait here till he comes. Nagaina—do you hear me?—I shall wait here in the cool till daytime."

There was no answer from outside, so Rikki-tikki knew Nagaina had gone away. Nag coiled himself down, coil by coil, round the bulge at the bottom of the water jar, and Rikki-tikki stayed still as death. After an hour he began to move, muscle by muscle, toward the jar. Nag was asleep, and Rikki-tikki looked at his big back, wondering which would be the best place for a good hold. "If I don't break his back at the first jump," said Rikki, "he can still fight; and

"I am Nag. . . . Look, and be afraid!"

PREDICT

Pause at line 319. What do you think will happen between Rikki and Nag? Give at least one reason for your answer.

_____

_____

_____

_____

_____

_____

_____

_____

_____

_____

_____

_____

_____

_____

_____

_____

_____

_____

_____

_____

_____

_____

_____

_____

if he fights—O Rikki!" He looked at the thickness of the neck below the hood, but that was too much for him; and a bite near the tail would only make Nag savage.

320 "It must be the head," he said at last, "the head above the hood; and when I am once there, I must not let go."

Then he jumped. The head was lying a little clear of the water jar, under the curve of it; and as his teeth met, Rikki braced his back against the bulge of the red earthenware to hold down the head. This gave him just one second's purchase,[10] and he made the most of it. Then he was battered to and fro as a rat is shaken by a dog—to and fro on the floor, up and down, and round in great circles, but his eyes were red and he held on as the body cartwhipped over 330 the floor, upsetting the tin dipper and the soap dish and the flesh brush, and banged against the tin side of the bath. As he held, he closed his jaws tighter and tighter, for he made sure[11] he would be banged to death, and for the honor of his family, he preferred to be found with his teeth locked.

---

10. **purchase** _n.:_ firm hold.
11. **made sure:** here, felt sure.

INTERPRET

Re-read lines 320–339. Write down three or four words that describe Rikki's personality.

_____

_____

_____

_____

_____

_____

INTERPRET

What does Rikki mean when he says that Nagaina will be "worse than five Nags" (line 351)?

_____

_____

_____

_____

_____

_____

_____

_____

_____

He was dizzy, aching, and felt shaken to pieces, when something went off like a thunderclap just behind him; a hot wind knocked him senseless and red fire singed his fur. The big man had been wakened by the noise and had fired both barrels of a shotgun into Nag just behind the hood.

340 Rikki-tikki held on with his eyes shut, for now he was quite sure he was dead; but the head did not move, and the big man picked him up and said: "It's the mongoose again, Alice; the little chap has saved *our* lives now." Then Teddy's mother came in with a very white face and saw what was left of Nag, and Rikki-tikki dragged himself to Teddy's bedroom and spent half the rest of the night shaking himself tenderly to find out whether he really was broken into forty pieces, as he fancied.

When morning came, he was very stiff but well pleased

350 with his doings. "Now I have Nagaina to settle with, and she will be worse than five Nags, and there's no knowing when the eggs she spoke of will hatch. Goodness! I must go and see Darzee," he said.

Without waiting for breakfast, Rikki-tikki ran to the thorn bush, where Darzee was singing a song of triumph at the top of his voice. The news of Nag's death was all over the garden, for the sweeper had thrown the body on the rubbish heap.

"Oh, you stupid tuft of feathers!" said Rikki-tikki

360 angrily. "Is this the time to sing?"

"Nag is dead—is dead—is dead!" sang Darzee. "The **valiant** Rikki-tikki caught him by the head and held fast. The big man brought the bang-stick, and Nag fell in two pieces! He will never eat my babies again."

"All that's true enough, but where's Nagaina?" said Rikki-tikki, looking carefully round him.

"Nagaina came to the bathroom sluice and called for Nag," Darzee went on; "and Nag came out on the end of a

stick—the sweeper picked him up on the end of a stick and
370 threw him upon the rubbish heap. Let us sing about the
great, the red-eyed Rikki-tikki!" and Darzee filled his throat
and sang.

"If I could get up to your nest, I'd roll your babies
out!" said Rikki-tikki. "You don't know when to do the
right thing at the right time. You're safe enough in your
nest there, but it's war for me down here. Stop singing a
minute, Darzee."

"For the great, beautiful Rikki-tikki's sake I will stop,"
said Darzee. "What is it, O Killer of the terrible Nag?"

380 "Where is Nagaina, for the third time?"

"On the rubbish heap by the stables, mourning for
Nag. Great is Rikki-tikki with the white teeth."

"Bother[12] my white teeth! Have you ever heard where
she keeps her eggs?"

"In the melon bed, on the end nearest the wall, where
the sun strikes nearly all day. She hid them there weeks
ago."

"And you never thought it worthwhile to tell me? The
end nearest the wall, you said?"

390 "Rikki-tikki, you are not going to eat her eggs?"

"Not eat exactly; no. Darzee, if you have a grain of
sense, you will fly off to the stables and pretend that your
wing is broken and let Nagaina chase you away to this
bush. I must get to the melon bed, and if I went there now,
she'd see me."

Darzee was a featherbrained little fellow who could
never hold more than one idea at a time in his head, and
just because he knew that Nagaina's children were born
in eggs like his own, he didn't think at first that it was
400 fair to kill them. But his wife was a sensible bird, and
she knew that cobra's eggs meant young cobras later on;

---

12. **bother** *interj.:* here, never mind.

IDENTIFY

Re-read lines 361–384. Circle the words that Darzee uses to describe Rikki. Then, underline two things Rikki wants to learn from Darzee.

PREDICT

Rikki asks where Nagaina keeps her eggs (lines 383–384). What do you think Rikki will do with Nagaina's eggs?

_____

_____

_____

_____

_____

_____

_____

_____

_____

_____

_____

IDENTIFY

The narrator calls Darzee's wife "a sensible bird" (line 400). Read on, and underline what she does that is sensible.

_____

_____

_____

_____

_____

_____

_____

_____

_____

_____

Darzee, a featherbrained little fellow.

VOCABULARY

consolation (kän′sə·lā′shən)
n.: comfort.

INTERPRET

What does Nagaina mean
when she says that "the boy
in the house will lie very
still" (line 418)? What does
she plan to do to Teddy?

_____

_____

_____

_____

_____

so she flew off from the nest and left Darzee to keep the babies warm and continue his song about the death of Nag. Darzee was very like a man in some ways.

   She fluttered in front of Nagaina by the rubbish heap and cried out, "Oh, my wing is broken! The boy in the house threw a stone at me and broke it." Then she fluttered more desperately than ever.

410   Nagaina lifted up her head and hissed, "You warned Rikki-tikki when I would have killed him. Indeed and truly, you've chosen a bad place to be lame in." And she moved toward Darzee's wife, slipping along over the dust.

   "The boy broke it with a stone!" shrieked Darzee's wife.

   "Well! It may be some **consolation** to you when you're dead to know that I shall settle accounts with the boy. My husband lies on the rubbish heap this morning, but before night the boy in the house will lie very still. What is the use of running away? I am sure to catch you. Little fool,
420   look at me!"

Darzee's wife knew better than to do *that,* for a bird who looks at a snake's eyes gets so frightened that she cannot move. Darzee's wife fluttered on, piping sorrowfully and never leaving the ground, and Nagaina quickened her pace.

Rikki-tikki heard them going up the path from the stables, and he raced for the end of the melon patch near the wall. There, in the warm litter above the melons, very cunningly hidden, he found twenty-five eggs about the size of a bantam's[13] eggs but with whitish skins instead of shells.

430 "I was not a day too soon," he said, for he could see the baby cobras curled up inside the skin, and he knew that the minute they were hatched, they could each kill a man or a mongoose. He bit off the tops of the eggs as fast as he could, taking care to crush the young cobras, and turned over the litter from time to time to see whether he had missed any. At last there were only three eggs left, and Rikki-tikki began to chuckle to himself, when he heard Darzee's wife screaming:

"Rikki-tikki, I led Nagaina toward the house, and she 440 has gone into the veranda, and—oh, come quickly—she means killing!"

Rikki-tikki smashed two eggs, and tumbled backward down the melon bed with the third egg in his mouth, and scuttled to the veranda as hard as he could put foot to the ground. Teddy and his mother and father were there at early breakfast, but Rikki-tikki saw that they were not eating anything. They sat stone still, and their faces were white. Nagaina was coiled up on the matting by Teddy's chair, within easy striking distance of Teddy's bare leg, and 450 she was swaying to and fro, singing a song of triumph.

"Son of the big man that killed Nag," she hissed, "stay still. I am not ready yet. Wait a little. Keep very still, all you

INFER

Why do you think Rikki takes the last egg with him to the veranda (line 444)?

---

13. **bantam's:** small chicken's.

three! If you move, I strike, and if you do not move, I strike. Oh, foolish people, who killed my Nag!"

Teddy's eyes were fixed on his father, and all his father could do was to whisper, "Sit still, Teddy. You mustn't move. Teddy, keep still."

Then Rikki-tikki came up and cried: "Turn round, Nagaina; turn and fight!"

460   "All in good time," said she, without moving her eyes. "I will settle my account with *you* presently. Look at your friends, Rikki-tikki. They are still and white. They are afraid. They dare not move, and if you come a step nearer, I strike."

"Look at your eggs," said Rikki-tikki, "in the melon bed near the wall. Go and look, Nagaina!"

The big snake turned half round and saw the egg on the veranda. "Ah-h! Give it to me," she said.

Rikki-tikki put his paws one on each side of the egg, 470   and his eyes were blood-red. "What price for a snake's egg? For a young cobra? For a young king cobra? For the last— the very last of the brood? The ants are eating all the others down by the melon bed."

Nagaina spun clear round, forgetting everything for the sake of the one egg; and Rikki-tikki saw Teddy's father shoot out a big hand, catch Teddy by the shoulder, and drag him across the little table with the teacups, safe and out of reach of Nagaina.

"Tricked! Tricked! Tricked! *Rikk-tck-tck!*" chuckled 480   Rikki-tikki. "The boy is safe, and it was I—I—I—that caught Nag by the hood last night in the bathroom." Then he began to jump up and down, all four feet together, his head close to the floor. "He threw me to and fro, but he could not shake me off. He was dead before the big man blew him in two. I did it! *Rikki-tikki-tck-tck!* Come then,

Nagaina. Come and fight with me. You shall not be a widow long."

Nagaina saw that she had lost her chance of killing Teddy, and the egg lay between Rikki-tikki's paws. "Give me the egg, Rikki-tikki. Give me the last of my eggs, and I will go away and never come back," she said, lowering her hood.

"Yes, you will go away, and you will never come back; for you will go to the rubbish heap with Nag. Fight, widow! The big man has gone for his gun! Fight!"

Rikki-tikki was bounding all round Nagaina, keeping just out of reach of her stroke, his little eyes like hot coals. Nagaina gathered herself together and flung out at him. Rikki-tikki jumped up and backwards. Again and again and again she struck, and each time her head came with a whack on the matting of the veranda and she gathered herself together like a watch spring. Then Rikki-tikki

490

500

Dr. E. R. Degginger/Color-Pic, Inc.

Chuchundra, a brokenhearted little beast.

INTERPRET

Do you believe Nagaina when she says that she'll go away and never come back (lines 490–491)? Why or why not?

_____

_____

_____

_____

_____

_____

_____

_____

_____

_____

_____

_____

_____

_____

_____

_____

_____

_____

_____

_____

_____

danced in a circle to get behind her, and Nagaina spun round to keep her head to his head, so that the rustle of her tail on the matting sounded like dry leaves blown along by the wind.

He had forgotten the egg. It still lay on the veranda, and Nagaina came nearer and nearer to it, till at last, while Rikki-tikki was drawing breath, she caught it in her mouth, turned to the veranda steps, and flew like an arrow down 510 the path, with Rikki-tikki behind her. When the cobra runs for her life, she goes like a whiplash flicked across a horse's neck. Rikki-tikki knew that he must catch her or all the trouble would begin again. She headed straight for the long grass by the thorn bush, and as he was running, Rikki-tikki heard Darzee still singing his foolish little song of triumph. But Darzee's wife was wiser. She flew off her nest as Nagaina came along and flapped her wings about Nagaina's head. If Darzee had helped, they might have turned her, but Nagaina only lowered her hood and went on. Still, the 520 instant's delay brought Rikki-tikki up to her, and as she plunged into the rat hole where she and Nag used to live, his little white teeth were clenched on her tail and he went down with her—and very few mongooses, however wise and old they may be, care to follow a cobra into its hole. It was dark in the hole, and Rikki-tikki never knew when it might open out and give Nagaina room to turn and strike at him. He held on savagely and stuck out his feet to act as brakes on the dark slope of the hot, moist earth. Then the grass by the mouth of the hole stopped waving, and Darzee 530 said: "It is all over with Rikki-tikki! We must sing his death song. Valiant Rikki-tikki is dead! For Nagaina will surely kill him underground."

So he sang a very mournful song that he made up on the spur of the minute, and just as he got to the most touching part, the grass quivered again, and Rikki-tikki, covered with dirt, dragged himself out of the hole leg by leg, licking his whiskers. Darzee stopped with a little shout. Rikki-tikki shook some of the dust out of his fur and sneezed. "It is all over," he said. "The widow will never

540 come out again." And the red ants that live between the grass stems heard him and began to troop down one after another to see if he had spoken the truth.

Rikki-tikki curled himself up in the grass and slept where he was—slept and slept till it was late in the afternoon, for he had done a hard day's work.

"Now," he said, when he awoke, "I will go back to the house. Tell the Coppersmith, Darzee, and he will tell the garden that Nagaina is dead."

The Coppersmith is a bird who makes a noise exactly

550 like the beating of a little hammer on a copper pot; and the reason he is always making it is because he is the town crier to every Indian garden and tells all the news to everybody who cares to listen. As Rikki-tikki went up the path, he heard his "attention" notes like a tiny dinner gong and then the steady "*Ding-dong-tock! Nag is dead—dong! Nagaina is dead! Ding-dong-tock!*" That set all the birds in the garden singing and the frogs croaking, for Nag and Nagaina used to eat frogs as well as little birds.

When Rikki got to the house, Teddy and Teddy's

560 mother (she looked very white still, for she had been fainting) and Teddy's father came out and almost cried over him; and that night he ate all that was given him till he could eat no more and went to bed on Teddy's shoulder, where Teddy's mother saw him when she came to look late at night.

"He saved our lives and Teddy's life," she said to her husband. "Just think, he saved all our lives."

Pause at line 542. What do you think happened to Nagaina's last egg?

_____

_____

_____

_____

_____

_____

_____

_____

_____

_____

_____

_____

_____

_____

_____

_____

_____

_____

Rikki-tikki knew that he must catch Nagaina or all the trouble would begin again.

> **INTERPRET**
>
> In lines 572–573, the narrator says, "Rikki-tikki had a right to be proud of himself, but he did not grow too proud." What do you think keeps Rikki from becoming too proud?
>
> _____
>
> _____
>
> _____
>
> _____
>
> _____
>
> _____
>
> _____
>
> _____
>
> _____
>
> _____
>
> _____

Rikki-tikki woke up with a jump, for the mongooses are light sleepers.

570 "Oh, it's you," said he. "What are you bothering for? All the cobras are dead; and if they weren't, I'm here."

Rikki-tikki had a right to be proud of himself, but he did not grow too proud, and he kept that garden as a mongoose should keep it, with tooth and jump and spring and bite, till never a cobra dared show its head inside the walls.

Darzee's Chant

Sung in honor of Rikki-tikki-tavi

Singer and tailor am I—
　　Doubled the joys that I know—
580 Proud of my lilt[14] to the sky,
　　Proud of the house that I sew.
Over and under, so weave I my music—
　　so weave I the house that I sew.

---

14. **lilt** *n.*: song.

Sing to your fledglings[15] again,

    Mother, O lift up your head!

Evil that plagued us is slain,

    Death in the garden lies dead.

Terror that hid in the roses is **impotent**—

    flung on the dunghill and dead!

590   Who has delivered us, who?

    Tell me his nest and his name.

Rikki, the valiant, the true,

    Tikki, with eyeballs of flame—

Rikk-tikki-tikki, the ivory-fanged,

    the hunter with eyeballs of flame!

Give him the Thanks of the Birds,

    Bowing with tail feathers spread,

Praise him with nightingale words—

    Nay, I will praise him instead.

600   Hear! I will sing you the praise of the

    bottle-tailed Rikki with eyeballs of red!

(Here Rikki-tikki interrupted, so the rest of the song is lost.)

---

15. fledglings (flej′liŋz) *n.:* baby birds.

VOCABULARY

impotent (im′pə·tənt) *adj.:* powerless.

IDENTIFY

Pause at the end of Darzee's chant. How would you describe Darzee's attitude toward Rikki?

_____

_____

_____

_____

_____

_____

_____

EXTEND

From what you know of Rikki's relationship with Darzee, what do you think Rikki might have said as he interrupted him?

_____

_____

_____

_____

_____

_____

Rikki-tikki-tavi

SKILLS FOCUS

Literary Skills
Analyze conflict.

Conflict Diagram   Identify the main events in the plot of Rikki's story. Fill in the diagram below with at least four key events that lead to the exciting climax. If you like to draw, you might want to draw little pictures illustrating some or all of the events.

Climax/Final Conflict

_____

_____

Event/Conflict

_____

_____

Resolution

_____

_____

_____

_____

Event/Conflict

_____

_____

Event/Conflict

Rikki _____

_____

**[Add as many events
as you need.]**

Event/Conflict

Rikki _____

_____

Basic Situation

_____

_____

Skills Review

Rikki-tikki-tavi

VOCABULARY AND COMPREHENSION

A. Clarifying Word Meanings: Contrast Choose three words from the Word Bank. Provide a contrast for each word by describing what it is *not*.

Word Bank

immensely

cowered

valiant

consolation

impotent

1. _____

_____

2. _____

_____

3. _____

_____

B. Reading Comprehension Answer each question below.

1. How does Rikki-tikki-tavi come to live with the family? _____

_____

_____

2. Why do Nag and Nagaina enter the house? _____

_____

_____

3. How does Rikki-tikki-tavi save Teddy's life? _____

_____

_____

SKILLS FOCUS

Vocabulary Skills
Clarify word meanings by using contrast.

Three Skeleton Key by George G. Toudouze

LITERARY FOCUS: SUSPENSE AND FORESHADOWING

A "page turner" is an exciting book; you're so eager to find out what happens that you read page after page, finding it hard to put the book down. One key ingredient in page turners is **suspense**—the feeling of uncertainty that propels you to keep reading. To create suspense, writers may create an eerie setting or withhold information from readers to keep you guessing.

To build suspense, writers sometimes plant clues in their stories. These clues hint at what might happen later. The use of such clues or hints is called **foreshadowing.**

I have a funny feeling about this place . . .

READING SKILLS: MAKING PREDICTIONS

Which of the following types of predictions have you made recently: the outcome of a baseball game? which of your classmates will become class president? what inventions will come about over the next few years? Making predictions is part of participating in life. Likewise, you participate more fully in a story when you make predictions about it. To make predictions when you read:

- Pay attention to what the narrator tells you about story characters and their situations.
- Make predictions, or guesses, about what will happen.
- Read on to find out if your predictions were on target.

SKILLS FOCUS

Literary Skills
Understand suspense.

Reading Skills
Make predictions.

Vocabulary Skills
Clarify word meanings by using examples.

VOCABULARY DEVELOPMENT

PREVIEW SELECTION VOCABULARY

The following words appear in "Three Skeleton Key." Take time to preview these words before you begin the story.

hordes (hôrdz) *n.:* large, moving crowds.

The rats swam ashore in hordes.

receding (ri·sēd′iŋ) *v.* used as *adj.:* moving back.

At first the ship came toward us, but then it drifted off in the receding waters.

fathom (fa*th*′əm) *v.:* understand.

The lighthouse keepers couldn't fathom the rats' nasty reaction.

edible (ed′ə·bəl) *adj.:* fit to be eaten.

The rats thought the men were edible.

derisive (di·rī′siv) *adj.:* scornful and ridiculing.

The rats peered with derisive eyes at the terrified men.

CLARIFYING WORD MEANINGS: EXAMPLES

Sometimes you can figure out the meaning of an unfamiliar word by looking in the text for examples of what it is. Words and phrases, such as *for example, for instance, like, such as, in this case,* and *as if,* sometimes signal that an example will follow.

Read each passage below, and underline the example provided for each boldface word.

1. **Hordes** of people went to the concert. In this case, there were literally thousands of music lovers crowding the stadium.

2. We just could not **fathom** the reason for his actions. For example, the more we thought, the more we were puzzled.

3. The guest asked if the food was **edible,** as if the spaghetti and meatballs were going to poison her!

Three Skeleton Key

George G. Toudouze

PREDICT

Pause at line 4. What kind of story might this be?

_____

_____

_____

WORD STUDY

Key (kē), in line 11, means "island." The words *cay* and *quay* are alternate forms of *key*.

IDENTIFY

Re-read lines 11–20. What **foreshadowing** clues does the writer give here? Circle them. What do those clues hint at?

_____

_____

_____

My most terrifying experience? Well, one does have a few in thirty-five years of service in the Lights, although it's mostly monotonous, routine work—keeping the light in order, making out the reports.

When I was a young man, not very long in the service, there was an opening in a lighthouse newly built off the coast of Guiana, on a small rock twenty miles or so from the mainland. The pay was high, so in order to reach the sum I had set out to save before I married, I volunteered
10 for service in the new light.

Three Skeleton Key, the small rock on which the light stood, bore a bad reputation. It earned its name from the story of the three convicts who, escaping from Cayenne in a stolen dugout canoe, were wrecked on the rock during the night, managed to escape the sea, but eventually died of hunger and thirst. When they were discovered, nothing remained but three heaps of bones, picked clean by the birds. The story was that the three skeletons, gleaming with phosphorescent[1] light, danced over the small rock,
20 screaming. . . .

But there are many such stories and I did not give the warnings of the old-timers at the *Île-de-Seine*[2] a second

---

1. **phosphorescent** (fäs′fə·res′ənt) *adj.:* glowing.
2. ***Île-de-Seine*** (ēl də sen′).

"Three Skeleton Key" by George G. Toudouze from *Esquire,* January 1937. Copyright 1937 by Hearst Communications, Inc. All rights reserved. Esquire is a trademark of Hearst Magazines Property, Inc. Reproduced by permission of **Esquire Magazine.**

thought. I signed up, boarded ship, and in a month I was installed at the light.

Picture a gray, tapering cylinder,[3] welded to the solid black rock by iron rods and concrete, rising from a small island twenty-odd miles from land. It lay in the midst of the sea, this island, a small, bare piece of stone, about one hundred fifty feet long, perhaps forty wide. Small, barely large enough for a man to walk about and stretch his legs at low tide.

This is an advantage one doesn't find in all lights, however, for some of them rise sheer from the waves, with no room for one to move save within the light itself. Still, on our island, one must be careful, for the rocks were treacherously smooth. One misstep and down you would fall into the sea—not that the risk of drowning was so great, but the waters about our island swarmed with huge sharks, who kept an eternal patrol around the base of the light.

Still, it was a nice life there. We had enough provisions to last for months, in the event that the sea should become too rough for the supply ship to reach us on schedule. During the day we would work about the light, cleaning the rooms, polishing the metalwork and the lens and reflector of the light itself, and at night we would sit on the gallery and watch our light, a twenty-thousand-candlepower lantern, swinging its strong white bar of light over the sea from the top of its hundred-twenty-foot tower. Some days, when the air would be very clear, we could see the land, a threadlike line to the west. To the east, north, and south stretched the ocean. Landsmen, perhaps, would soon have tired of that kind of life, perched on a small island off the coast of South America for eighteen weeks until one's turn for leave ashore came around. But we liked it there, my two

---

3. **tapering cylinder:** tube shape that gradually narrows toward one end; in this case, toward the top.

PREDICT

Pause at line 39. What do you think might happen later in the story, based on the information you just read?

_____

_____

_____

_____

_____

_____

_____

_____

_____

_____

_____

_____

_____

_____

_____

_____

_____

_____

_____

_____

_____

_____

fellow tenders and myself—so much so that for twenty-two months on end, with the exception of shore leaves, I was greatly satisfied with the life on Three Skeleton Key.

60   I had just returned from my leave at the end of June, that is to say, midwinter in that latitude, and had settled down to the routine with my two fellow keepers, a Breton[4] by the name of Le Gleo and the head keeper, Itchoua, a Basque[5] some dozen years or so older than either of us.

    Eight days went by as usual; then on the ninth night after my return, Itchoua, who was on night duty, called Le Gleo and me, sleeping in our rooms in the middle of the tower, at two in the morning. We rose immediately and, climbing the thirty or so steps that led to the gallery, stood beside our chief.

70   Itchoua pointed, and following his finger, we saw a big three-master, with all sail set, heading straight for the light. A queer course, for the vessel must have seen us; our light lit her with the glare of day each time it passed over her.

    Now, ships were a rare sight in our waters, for our light was a warning of treacherous reefs, barely hidden under the surface and running far out to sea. Consequently we were always given a wide berth, especially by sailing vessels, which cannot maneuver as readily as steamers.

    No wonder that we were surprised at seeing this three-master heading dead for us in the gloom of early morning. I

80 had immediately recognized her lines, for she stood out plainly, even at the distance of a mile, when our light shone on her.

    She was a beautiful ship of some four thousand tons, a fast sailer that had carried cargoes to every part of the world, plowing the seas unceasingly. By her lines she was identified as Dutch built, which was understandable, as Paramaribo and Dutch Guiana are very close to Cayenne.

---

4. **Breton** (bret'’n): person from Brittany, a region of northern France.
5. **Basque** (bask): Basques are people living in the Pyrenees, a mountain range in France and Spain.

Watching her sailing dead for us, a white wave boiling under her bows, Le Gleo cried out:

"What's wrong with her crew? Are they all drunk or insane? Can't they see us?"

Itchoua nodded soberly and looked at us sharply as he remarked: "See us? No doubt—if there *is* a crew aboard!"

"What do you mean, chief?" Le Gleo had started, turned to the Basque. "Are you saying that she's the *Flying Dutchman*?"[6]

His sudden fright had been so evident that the older man laughed:

"No, old man, that's not what I meant. If I say that no one's aboard, I mean she's a derelict."[7]

Then we understood her queer behavior. Itchoua was right. For some reason, believing her doomed, her crew had abandoned her. Then she had righted herself and sailed on, wandering with the wind.

The three of us grew tense as the ship seemed about to crash on one of our numerous reefs, but she suddenly lurched with some change of the wind, the yards[8] swung around, and the derelict came clumsily about and sailed dead away from us.

In the light of our lantern she seemed so sound, so strong, that Itchoua exclaimed impatiently:

"But why the devil was she abandoned? Nothing is smashed, no sign of fire—and she doesn't sail as if she were taking water."

Le Gleo waved to the departing ship:

"Bon voyage!" he smiled at Itchoua and went on. "She's leaving us, chief, and now we'll never know what—"

---

6. **Flying Dutchman:** fabled Dutch ghost ship whose captain is said to be condemned to sail the seas until Judgment Day. Seeing the *Flying Dutchman* is supposed to bring bad luck.
7. **derelict** (der'ə·likt') *n.:* here, abandoned ship.
8. **yards** *n.:* in nautical terms, rods fastened across the masts to support the sails.

INFER

Pause at line 90. What might have happened to the ship's crew?

_____

_____

_____

_____

_____

_____

_____

IDENTIFY

Skim lines 78–108, and circle the word *dead* each time it appears. What effect does this repetition have on you, the reader?

_____

_____

_____

_____

_____

_____

_____

INTERPRET

Pause at line 123. Throughout the story the writer speaks of the mysterious ship as if it were alive. In what way does this use of personification create **suspense**?

_____

_____

_____

_____

_____

_____

_____

_____

_____

_____

_____

_____

_____

_____

_____

_____

_____

_____

_____

_____

_____

"No, she's not!" cried the Basque. "Look! She's turning!"

As if obeying his words, the derelict three-master stopped, came about, and headed for us once more. And
120 for the next four hours the vessel played around us— zigzagging, coming about, stopping, then suddenly lurching forward. No doubt some freak of current and wind, of which our island was the center, kept her near us.

Then suddenly the tropic dawn broke, the sun rose, and it was day, and the ship was plainly visible as she sailed past us. Our light extinguished, we returned to the gallery with our glasses[9] and inspected her.

The three of us focused our glasses on her poop[10] and saw, standing out sharply, black letters on the white back-
130 ground of a life ring, the stenciled name "*Cornelius de Witt,* Rotterdam."

We had read her lines correctly: She was Dutch. Just then the wind rose and the *Cornelius de Witt* changed course, leaned to port, and headed straight for us once more. But this time she was so close that we knew she would not turn in time.

"Thunder!" cried Le Gleo, his Breton soul aching at seeing a fine ship doomed to smash upon a reef, "she's going to pile up! She's gone!"
140 I shook my head:

"Yes, and a shame to see that beautiful ship wreck herself. And we're helpless."

There was nothing we could do but watch. A ship sailing with all sail spread, creaming the sea with her forefoot as she runs before the wind, is one of the most beautiful sights in the world—but this time I could feel the tears stinging in my eyes as I saw this fine ship headed for her doom.

---

9. **glasses** *n.:* here, binoculars.
10. **poop** *n.:* in nautical terms, the stern (back) deck of a ship.

All this time our glasses were riveted on her and we suddenly cried out together:

150   "The rats!"

Now we knew why this ship, in perfect condition, was sailing without her crew aboard. They had been driven out by the rats. Not those poor specimens of rats you see ashore, barely reaching the length of one foot from their trembling noses to the tip of their skinny tails, wretched creatures that dodge and hide at the mere sound of a footfall.

No, these were ships' rats, huge, wise creatures, born on the sea, sailing all over the world on ships, transferring to other, larger ships as they multiply. There is as much difference between the rats of the land and these maritime rats as between a fishing smack[11] and an armored cruiser.

160

The rats of the sea are fierce, bold animals. Large, strong, and intelligent, clannish and seawise, able to put the best of mariners to shame with their knowledge of the sea, their uncanny ability to foretell the weather.

And they are brave, these rats, and vengeful. If you so much as harm one, his sharp cry will bring **hordes** of his fellows to swarm over you, tear you, and not cease until your flesh has been stripped from the bones.

11. **smack** *n.:* here, small sailboat.

hordes (hôrdz) *n.:* large, moving crowds.

PREDICT

Pause at line 169. Predict what role the rats may play later in the story.

_____

_____

_____

_____

_____

_____

_____

_____

_____

_____

_____

170   The ones on this ship, the rats of Holland, are the worst, superior to other rats of the sea as their brethren are to the land rats. There is a well-known tale about these animals.

    A Dutch captain, thinking to protect his cargo, brought aboard his ship not cats but two terriers, dogs trained in the hunting, fighting, and killing of vicious rats. By the time the ship, sailing from Rotterdam, had passed the Ostend light, the dogs were gone and never seen again. In twenty-four hours they had been overwhelmed, killed, and eaten by the rats.

180   At times, when the cargo does not suffice,[12] the rats attack the crew, either driving them from the ship or eating them alive. And studying the *Cornelius de Witt*, I turned sick, for her small boats were all in place. She had not been abandoned.

    Over her bridge, on her deck, in the rigging, on every visible spot, the ship was a writhing mass—a starving army coming toward us aboard a vessel gone mad!

    Our island was a small spot in that immense stretch of sea. The ship could have grazed us or passed to port or
190 starboard with its ravening[13] cargo—but no, she came for us at full speed, as if she were leading the regatta at a race, and impaled herself on a sharp point of rock.

    There was a dull shock as her bottom stove in,[14] then a horrible crackling as the three masts went overboard at once, as if cut down with one blow of some gigantic sickle. A sighing groan came as the water rushed into the ship; then she split in two and sank like a stone.

    But the rats did not drown. Not these fellows! As much at home in the sea as any fish, they formed ranks in the

CLARIFY

Re-read lines 180–187. What happened to the ship's crew?

12. **suffice** (sə·fīs′) *v.:* provide enough.
13. **ravening** (rav′ə·niŋ) *adj.:* greedily searching for animals to kill for food. A more common related word is *ravenous* (rav′ə·nəs), meaning "wildly, greedily hungry."
14. **stove in:** caved in.

200 water, heads lifted, tails stretched out, paws paddling. And
half of them, those from the forepart of the ship, sprang
along the masts and onto the rocks in the instant before she
sank. Before we had time even to move, nothing remained
of the three-master save some pieces of wreckage floating
on the surface and an army of rats covering the rocks left
bare by the **receding** tide.

　Thousands of heads rose, felt the wind, and we were
scented, seen! To them we were fresh meat, after possible
weeks of starving. There came a scream, composed of innu-
210 merable screams, sharper than the howl of a saw attacking
a bar of iron, and in the one motion, every rat leaped to
attack the tower!

　We barely had time to leap back, close the door leading
onto the gallery, descend the stairs, and shut every window
tightly. Luckily the door at the base of the light, which we
never could have reached in time, was of bronze set in
granite and was tightly closed.

　The horrible band, in no measurable time, had swarmed
up and over the tower as if it had been a tree, piled on the
220 embrasures[15] of the windows, scraped at the glass with thousands of claws, covered the lighthouse with a furry mantle,
and reached the top of the tower, filling the gallery and piling
atop the lantern.

　Their teeth grated as they pressed against the glass of
the lantern room, where they could plainly see us, though
they could not reach us. A few millimeters of glass, luckily
very strong, separated our faces from their gleaming, beady
eyes, their sharp claws and teeth. Their odor filled the
tower, poisoned our lungs, and rasped our nostrils with a
230 pestilential, nauseating smell. And there we were, sealed
alive in our own light, prisoners of a horde of starving rats.

---

15. **embrasures** (em·brā′zhərz) *n.*: slanted openings.

VOCABULARY

receding (ri·sēd′iŋ) *v.* used as *adj.*: moving back.

IDENTIFY

Pause at line 212. What has just happened to increase your feeling of **suspense**?

INTERPRET

Underline the words and phrases in lines 224–231 that appeal to your senses of sight, smell, and hearing. Why might the writer have chosen to describe the rats in such detail?

_____

_____

_____

_____

_____

_____

_____

_____

_____

_____

_____

Read the boxed passage aloud several times. The first time read slowly, for sense. Then, experiment with the tone of your voice and its volume to bring the vivid passage to life for your listeners. Note: The letter combination of *ph* in *phosphorescent* is pronounced "f".

VOCABULARY

fathom (fath'əm) *v.*: understand; get to the bottom of.

Fathom is also a noun meaning "a length of six feet." A fathom is a unit of measure for depth of water.

That first night, the tension was so great that we could not sleep. Every moment, we felt that some opening had been made, some window given way, and that our horrible besiegers were pouring through the breach. The rising tide, chasing those of the rats which had stayed on the bare rocks, increased the numbers clinging to the walls, piled on the balcony—so much so that clusters of rats clinging to one another hung from the lantern and the gallery.

240   With the coming of darkness we lit the light and the turning beam completely maddened the beasts. As the light turned, it successively blinded thousands of rats crowded against the glass, while the dark side of the lantern room gleamed with thousands of points of light, burning like the eyes of jungle beasts in the night.

All the while we could hear the enraged scraping of claws against the stone and glass, while the chorus of cries was so loud that we had to shout to hear one another. From time to time, some of the rats fought among themselves and a dark cluster would detach itself, falling into the sea like a ripe fruit from a tree. Then we would see phosphorescent streaks as triangular fins slashed the water—sharks, permanent guardians of our rock, feasting on our jailers.

The next day we were calmer and amused ourselves teasing the rats, placing our faces against the glass which separated us. They could not **fathom** the invisible barrier which separated them from us, and we laughed as we watched them leaping against the heavy glass.

260   But the day after that, we realized how serious our position was. The air was foul; even the heavy smell of oil within our stronghold could not dominate the fetid odor of the beasts massed around us. And there was no way of admitting fresh air without also admitting the rats.

The morning of the fourth day, at early dawn, I saw the wooden framework of my window, eaten away from the outside, sagging inwards. I called my comrades and the three of us fastened a sheet of tin in the opening, sealing it tightly. When we had completed that task, Itchoua turned to us and said dully:

270   "Well—the supply boat came thirteen days ago, and she won't be back for twenty-nine." He pointed at the white metal plate sealing the opening through the granite. "If that gives way"—he shrugged—"they can change the name of this place to Six Skeleton Key."

The next six days and seven nights, our only distraction was watching the rats whose holds were insecure fall a hundred and twenty feet into the maws of the sharks—but they were so many that we could not see any diminution in their numbers.

280   Thinking to calm ourselves and pass the time, we attempted to count them, but we soon gave up. They moved incessantly, never still. Then we tried identifying them, naming them.

Stephen Dalton/Photo Researchers.

PREDICT

Pause at line 274. Do you think the three lighthouse keepers will die? Will they change the name of the island to Six Skeleton Key? Explain.

WORD STUDY

Re-read the sentence in lines 281–282, and look for a context clue that helps you define *incessantly*. Underline the clue. What does *incessantly* mean?

One of them, larger than the others, who seemed to lead them in their rushes against the glass separating us, we named "Nero";[16] and there were several others whom we had learned to distinguish through various peculiarities.

But the thought of our bones joining those of the convicts was always in the back of our minds. And the gloom 290 of our prison fed these thoughts, for the interior of the light was almost completely dark, as we had had to seal every window in the same fashion as mine, and the only space that still admitted daylight was the glassed-in lantern room at the very top of the tower.

Then Le Gleo became morose and had nightmares in which he would see the three skeletons dancing around him, gleaming coldly, seeking to grasp him. His maniacal, raving descriptions were so vivid that Itchoua and I began seeing them also.

300 It was a living nightmare, the raging cries of the rats as they swarmed over the light, mad with hunger; the sickening, strangling odor of their bodies—

True, there is a way of signaling from lighthouses. But to reach the mast on which to hang the signal, we would have to go out on the gallery where the rats were.

There was only one thing left to do. After debating all of the ninth day, we decided not to light the lantern that night. This is the greatest breach of our service, never committed as long as the tenders of the light are alive; for the 310 light is something sacred, warning ships of danger in the night. Either the light gleams a quarter-hour after sundown, or no one is left alive to light it.

Well, that night, Three Skeleton Light was dark, and all the men were alive. At the risk of causing ships to crash on our reefs, we left it unlit, for we were worn out—going mad!

---

16. **Nero** (nir′ō): emperor of Rome (A.D. 54–68) known for his cruelty.

At two in the morning, while Itchoua was dozing in his room, the sheet of metal sealing his window gave way. The chief had just time enough to leap to his feet and cry for help, the rats swarming over him.

320   But Le Gleo and I, who had been watching from the lantern room, got to him immediately, and the three of us battled with the horde of maddened rats which flowed through the gaping window. They bit, we struck them down with our knives—and retreated.

We locked the door of the room on them, but before we had time to bind our wounds, the door was eaten through and gave way, and we retreated up the stairs, fighting off the rats that leaped on us from the knee-deep swarm.

330   I do not remember, to this day, how we ever managed to escape. All I can remember is wading through them up the stairs, striking them off as they swarmed over us; and then we found ourselves, bleeding from innumerable bites, our clothes shredded, sprawled across the trapdoor in the floor of the lantern room—without food or drink. Luckily, the trapdoor was metal, set into the granite with iron bolts.

The rats occupied the entire light beneath us, and on the floor of our retreat lay some twenty of their fellows, who had gotten in with us before the trapdoor closed and whom we
340   had killed with our knives. Below us, in the tower, we could hear the screams of the rats as they devoured everything **edible** that they found. Those on the outside squealed in reply and writhed in a horrible curtain as they stared at us through the glass of the lantern room.

Itchoua sat up and stared silently at his blood trickling from the wounds on his limbs and body and running in thin streams on the floor around him. Le Gleo, who was in as bad a state (and so was I, for that matter), stared at

PREDICT

Pause at line 319. The window that had been keeping the rats out just gave way. What will happen next?

_____

_____

_____

_____

_____

_____

IDENTIFY

In lines 320–329, the **suspense** builds. What unanswered question is going through your mind at this point?

_____

_____

_____

_____

_____

_____

_____

VOCABULARY

edible (ed′ə·bəl) *adj.*: fit to be eaten.

the chief and me vacantly, started as his gaze swung to the
350 multitude of rats against the glass, then suddenly began
laughing horribly:

"Hee! Hee! The Three Skeletons! Hee! Hee! The Three
Skeletons are now *six* skeletons! *Six* skeletons!"

He threw his head back and howled, his eyes glazed, a
trickle of saliva running from the corners of his mouth and
thinning the blood flowing over his chest. I shouted to him
to shut up, but he did not hear me, so I did the only thing
I could to quiet him—I swung the back of my hand across
his face.

360 The howling stopped suddenly, and his eyes swung
around the room; then he bowed his head and began weeping softly, like a child.

Our darkened light had been noticed from the mainland, and as dawn was breaking, the patrol was there to
investigate the failure of our light. Looking through my
binoculars, I could see the horrified expression on the faces
of the officers and crew when, the daylight strengthening,
they saw the light completely covered by a seething mass of
rats. They thought, as I afterwards found out, that we had
370 been eaten alive.

But the rats had also seen the ship or had scented the
crew. As the ship drew nearer, a solid phalanx[17] left the
light, plunged into the water, and swimming out, attempted
to board her. They would have succeeded, as the ship was
hove to;[18] but the engineer connected his steam to a hose
on the deck and scalded the head of the attacking column,
which slowed them up long enough for the ship to get
under way and leave the rats behind.

Then the sharks took part. Belly up, mouths gaping,
380 they arrived in swarms and scooped up the rats, sweeping

CLARIFY

Re-read lines 363–378. Why
didn't the officers on the
patrol ship stay and rescue
the keepers?

---

17. **phalanx** (fā′laŋks′) *n.:* closely packed group. A phalanx is an ancient
     military formation, and the word still has warlike connotations.
18. **hove to:** stopped by being turned into the wind.

© CORBIS.

through them like a sickle through wheat. That was one day that sharks really served a useful purpose.

The remaining rats turned tail, swam to the shore, and emerged dripping. As they neared the light, their comrades greeted them with shrill cries, with what sounded like a **derisive** note predominating. They answered angrily and mingled with their fellows. From the several tussles that broke out, it seemed as if they resented being ridiculed for their failure to capture the ship.

390   But all this did nothing to get us out of our jail. The small ship could not approach but steamed around the light at a safe distance, and the tower must have seemed fantastic, some weird, many-mouthed beast hurling defiance at them.

Finally, seeing the rats running in and out of the tower through the door and the windows, those on the ship decided that we had perished and were about to leave when Itchoua, regaining his senses, thought of using the light as a signal. He lit it and, using a plank placed and withdrawn before the

VOCABULARY

derisive (di·rī′siv) *adj.*: scornful and ridiculing.

Notes

CLARIFY

Re-read lines 399–401. What does Itchoua do to signal that he and the other keepers are still alive?

_____

_____

_____

_____

_____

_____

_____

_____

400 beam to form the dots and dashes, quickly sent out our story to those on the vessel.

Our reply came quickly. When they understood our position—how we could not get rid of the rats, Le Gleo's mind going fast, Itchoua and myself covered with bites, cornered in the lantern room without food or water—they had a signalman send us their reply.

His arms swinging like those of a windmill, he quickly spelled out:

"Don't give up, hang on a little longer! We'll get you out

410 of this!"

Then she turned and steamed at top speed for the coast, leaving us little reassured.

She was back at noon, accompanied by the supply ship, two small coast guard boats, and the fireboat—a small squadron. At twelve-thirty the battle was on.

After a short reconnaissance,[19] the fireboat picked her way slowly through the reefs until she was close to us, then turned her powerful jet of water on the rats. The heavy stream tore the rats from their places and hurled them screaming into

420 the water, where the sharks gulped them down. But for every ten that were dislodged, seven swam ashore, and the stream could do nothing to the rats within the tower. Furthermore, some of them, instead of returning to the rocks, boarded the fireboat, and the men were forced to battle them hand to hand. They were true rats of Holland, fearing no man, fighting for the right to live!

Nightfall came, and it was as if nothing had been done; the rats were still in possession. One of the patrol boats stayed by the island; the rest of the flotilla[20] departed for

430 the coast. We had to spend another night in our prison. Le Gleo was sitting on the floor, babbling about skeletons,

---

19. **reconnaissance** (ri·kän′ə·səns) *n.*: exploratory survey or examination.
20. **flotilla** (flō·til′ə) *n.*: small fleet of boats.

and as I turned to Itchoua, he fell unconscious from his wounds. I was in no better shape and could feel my blood flaming with fever.

Somehow the night dragged by, and the next afternoon I saw a tug, accompanied by the fireboat, come from the mainland with a huge barge in tow. Through my glasses, I saw that the barge was filled with meat.

Risking the treacherous reefs, the tug dragged the
440 barge as close to the island as possible. To the last rat, our besiegers deserted the rock, swam out, and boarded the barge reeking with the scent of freshly cut meat. The tug dragged the barge about a mile from shore, where the fireboat drenched the barge with gasoline. A well-placed incendiary shell from the patrol boat set her on fire.

The barge was covered with flames immediately, and the rats took to the water in swarms, but the patrol boat bombarded them with shrapnel from a safe distance, and the sharks finished off the survivors.

450 A whaleboat from the patrol boat took us off the island and left three men to replace us. By nightfall we were in the hospital in Cayenne. What became of my friends?

Well, Le Gleo's mind had cracked and he was raving mad. They sent him back to France and locked him up in an asylum, the poor devil! Itchoua died within a week; a rat's bite is dangerous in that hot, humid climate, and infection sets in rapidly.

As for me—when they fumigated the light and repaired the damage done by the rats, I resumed my service
460 there. Why not? No reason why such an incident should keep me from finishing out my service there, is there?

Besides—I told you I liked the place—to be truthful, I've never had a post as pleasant as that one, and when my time came to leave it forever, I tell you that I almost wept as Three Skeleton Key disappeared below the horizon.

PREDICT

Pause at line 438. What will the rescuers do with the barge loaded with meat?

_____

_____

_____

_____

_____

_____

_____

_____

CONNECT

In lines 453–460, we find out what happened to the three men following the incident. Were any of your predictions on target? Explain.

_____

_____

_____

_____

_____

_____

_____

_____

_____

Three Skeleton Key

Literary Skills
Analyze the use of suspense and foreshadowing.

Steps to Suspense   To create suspense, writers may create eerie settings, drop hints about possible story outcomes, and introduce exciting plot complications. Skim through "Three Skeleton Key" and the notes you took. Then, on the steps below, describe ways George G. Toudouze, the story's writer, kept you in suspense.

Step 5:

_____

_____

_____

Step 4:

_____

_____

_____

Step 3:

_____

_____

_____

Step 2:

_____

_____

_____

Step 1:

_____

_____

_____

Skills Review

Three Skeleton Key

VOCABULARY AND COMPREHENSION

A. Clarifying Word Meanings: Examples   Choose three words from the Word Bank. Then, write a sentence or two in which you give an example of each.

1. _____

   _____

2. _____

   _____

3. _____

   _____

B. Reading Comprehension   Answer each question below.

1. Where does the story take place? _____

   _____

   _____

2. How do the rats get onto the island? _____

   _____

   _____

3. How do the rescuers get the rats away from the lighthouse? _____

   _____

   _____

SKILLS FOCUS

Vocabulary Skills
Clarify word meanings by using examples.

The Monkey and the Crocodile

retold by A. K. Ramanujan

LITERARY FOCUS: PLOT

When you get ready to read a story, you expect to find out about characters and the things they do or things that happen to them. This series of events is called a **plot.** A plot can be broken down into parts.

Basic situation: Here, you learn who the characters are and what they want.

Events: The story's main character takes steps to resolve a conflict—something that is preventing him or her from reaching a goal.

Climax: This is the high point of the story, when we find out how the conflict will be resolved.

Resolution: This is the last part of the story, when the loose ends of the plot are tied up.

READING SKILLS: RETELLING

When you retell a story, you use your own words to describe what happened. Retellings help you to identify events that move the story's plot forward. You can also use retelling to make sure you understand what's happening in a story. As you read "The Monkey and the Crocodile," pause from time to time to retell what has happened.

SKILLS FOCUS

Literary Skills
Recognize elements of plot.

Reading Skills
Retell story events.

Vocabulary Skills
Clarify word meanings by using restatement.

VOCABULARY DEVELOPMENT

PREVIEW SELECTION VOCABULARY

Preview these words from "The Monkey and the Crocodile" before you begin to read.

relish (rel′ish) *n.:* enjoyment.

The apples were delicious, and the monkey ate them with great relish.

sulked (sulkt) *v.:* showed disappointment or displeasure by withdrawing; moped.

When the crocodile's wife didn't get her way, she sulked.

conscience (kän′shəns) *n.:* inner sense of right and wrong.

The crocodile's conscience wouldn't allow him to bring his friend home to be eaten.

clambered (klam′bərd) *v.:* climbed by using both hands and feet.

With hands and feet moving quickly, the monkey clambered up the tree to safety.

CLARIFYING WORD MEANINGS: RESTATEMENT

You're probably familiar with the phrase "in other words . . ." People use that phrase to signal they are going to restate something in simpler words. Writers use restatement, too. They do so to make the meanings of difficult words or terms more clear. In the passage below, for example, the meaning of *villa* is given in a restatement following the term.

Nestled high in the mountains was the **villa** of the Fontaine family. If you squinted you could just make out the red-tiled roof of the country house among the trees.

Words or statements that provide restatements often appear near the difficult word.

The Monkey and the Crocodile

retold by A. K. Ramanujan

Digital Vision.

DECODING TIP

One way you can deal with unfamiliar words is by looking for familiar words within the new word. What two words do you find in the word *plentiful* (line 2)?

_____

_____

_____

_____

_____

VOCABULARY

relish (rel'ish) *n.:* enjoyment.

On the banks of the Ganges, a monkey lived in a rose-apple tree. The rose-apples were delicious and plentiful. While he was eating them with obvious **relish** one day, a crocodile came out of the river, and the monkey threw down a few rose-apples and said, "These are the best rose-apples in the world. They taste like nectar." The crocodile chomped on them and found them truly wonderful. The monkey and the crocodile became friends, and the crocodile took to visiting the monkey every day to eat the fruit of that

10 wonderful tree and to talk in its shade.

One day the crocodile went home and took some of the fruit to his wife. "These are wonderful. They taste like nectar. Where did you get them?" asked the wife.

"The Monkey and the Crocodile" (Kannada/Tamil) from *Folktales from India: A Selection of Oral Tales from Twenty-two Languages,* selected and edited by A. K. Ramanujan. Copyright © 1991 by A. K. Ramanujan. Reproduced by permission of **Pantheon Books, a division of Random House, Inc.**

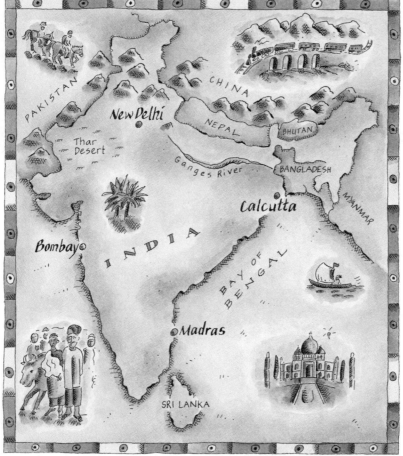

© Jennifer Thermes/Getty Images.

He said, "From a tree on the banks of the Ganges."

"But you can't climb the tree. Did you pick them up from the sands?"

"No, I've a new friend who lives in the tree, a monkey. He throws them down for me and we talk."

20 "Oh, that's why you've been coming home late! A monkey that lives on such fruit must have such sweet flesh. His heart must taste like heaven. I'd love to eat it," said the crocodile wife.

The crocodile didn't like the turn the conversation was taking. "How can you talk like that? He's my friend! He's like a brother-in-law to you."

But the wife **sulked** and said, "I want his heart. Why are you so taken with this monkey? Is it a he or a she? Bring

Notes _____

_____

_____

_____

_____

_____

_____

_____

_____

_____

_____

_____

_____

_____

(**IDENTIFY**)

Re-read lines 19–25. What **conflict** does the crocodile face?

_____

_____

_____

_____

_____

_____

_____

_____

(**VOCABULARY**)

sulked (sulkt) *v.:* showed resentment or dissatisfaction by withdrawing; moped.

© Brand X Pictures/Photo 24.

me his heart, or hers, which is even better. Or else I'll starve myself to death."

30   The crocodile tried his best to talk her out of her jealousy and ill-will, but he couldn't. He agreed to bring the monkey home on his back for a meal, as it were.

Next day, he invited the monkey to go home with him. "My wife has heard so much about you. She loved the rose-apples. She wants you to come home with me. If you come down from the tree and sit on my back, I'll take you there."

The monkey said, "You are a crocodile and live in the water. I can't even swim. I'll drown and die."

40   "Oh no, I'll take you carefully on my back. We don't live in the water. We live on a dry, sunny island in the middle of the river. Come with me. You'll enjoy it."

The monkey was persuaded and came down. He brought handfuls of rose-apples for the crocodile's wife. As the crocodile swam through the river, he felt terribly guilty. His **conscience** wouldn't allow him to take his friend home and let his wife make a meal of his heart, without at least telling him what he was doing. So he said, "I haven't been quite straight with you. My wife sent me today to bring you

50 home because she wants to eat your heart. That's what she wants, and I couldn't go against her wishes."

"Oh is that what she wants? My heart! Why didn't you tell me this before? I would have been happy to bring it down and give it to your wife," said the monkey.

"What do you mean?" asked the crocodile.

"I don't carry my heart around with me. I usually leave it in the tree when I come down. Let's go back and I'll give it to you."

The crocodile turned around and swam back to the

60 bank. The monkey quickly jumped off his back and **clambered** up the tree to safety.

Copyright © by Holt, Rinehart and Winston. All rights reserved.

VOCABULARY

conscience (kän′shəns) *n.:* inner sense of right and wrong.

clambered (klam′bərd) *v.:* climbed by using both hands and feet.

RETELL

When you reach line 61, describe how the conflict is finally **resolved.**

_____

_____

_____

_____

_____

_____

_____

_____

_____

_____

_____

_____

_____

_____

The Monkey and the Crocodile

SKILLS FOCUS

Literary Skills
Analyze plot.

Plot Storyboard   A storyboard is a "map" of a movie. It contains frames with drawings that show what is happening in each scene. For example, the first frame of a storyboard for "The Monkey and the Crocodile" might show the monkey throwing rose-apples to the crocodile. The caption under it might say, "The monkey and the crocodile become friends."

Create your own storyboard of "The Monkey and the Crocodile." In each frame, draw a scene. Write a description of each scene below your drawings.

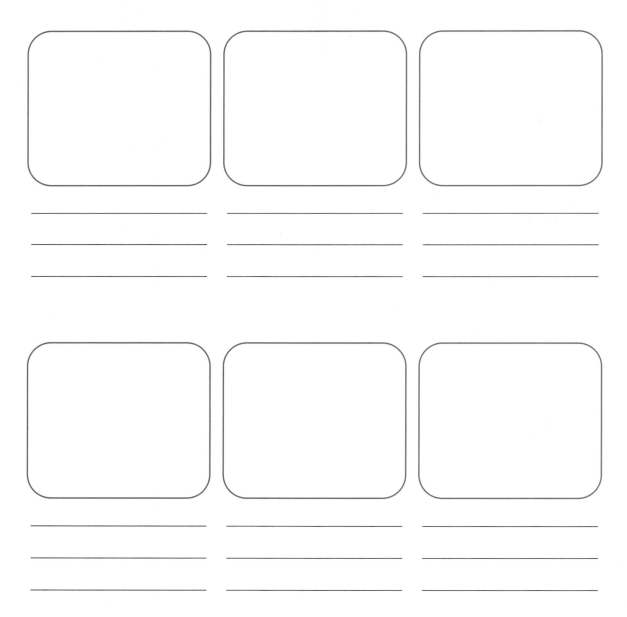

Skills Review

The Monkey and the Crocodile

VOCABULARY AND COMPREHENSION

A. Clarifying Word Meanings: Restatement   Read each passage below, and underline the restatement of each boldface word.

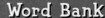
1. The crocodile's wife **sulked** when she didn't get her way. When his wife looked unhappy, the crocodile always got nervous.

2. The delicious rose apples were eaten by the animals with **relish,** with great enjoyment.

3. The monkey quickly **clambered** up his tree to safety. His awkward climbing method—using both his hands and feet—delighted the watching children.

4. The crocodile's **conscience** led him to tell the monkey about his wife's plan. That inner voice, the voice that told the crocodile right from wrong, saved the life of his monkey friend.

B. Reading Comprehension   Answer each question below.

1. Who are the characters in the story? _____

_____

_____

2. What do the crocodile and his wife disagree about? _____

_____

_____

3. What happens at the end of the story? Does the monkey get eaten?

_____

_____

_____

SKILLS FOCUS

Vocabulary Skills
Clarify word meanings by using restatement.

Characters:
Living Many Lives

Academic Vocabulary for Collection 2

These are the terms you should know
as you read and analyze the stories in this collection.

_____

Character A person or an animal who takes part in the action of a story.

Characterization The way a writer tells you about character. Typically you learn about characters by observing their appearance and actions, "listening" to what they have to say, reading about their thoughts and feelings, and paying attention to how other characters react to them.

Direct Characterization Statements in a story that tell you directly what a character is like. Example: "Although Jason was tough, he was able to make friends easily."

Indirect Characterization Showing rather than telling what a character is like. You must observe the character and make your own conclusions about the character.

Character Trait A quality that can't be seen in a character. Character traits are revealed through a character's appearance, words, actions, thoughts, and effects on other characters.

Motivation The reasons characters do the things they do. Feelings, needs, wishes, and pressures from other story characters are all forces that can motivate a character.

Mother and Daughter by Gary Soto

LITERARY FOCUS: CHARACTER TRAITS

What's your best friend like? funny? a little impatient? a neat freak? The words you choose to describe your friend also describe his or her character traits. **Character traits** are the qualities that are revealed by a character's appearance, spoken words, actions, and thoughts. Character traits are also revealed by how a character affects other characters in the story.

Use the space below to list some character traits of your favorite book or television character.

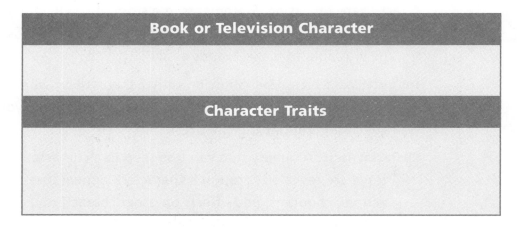

Book or Television Character
Character Traits

READING SKILLS: MAKING INFERENCES

Imagine that you are eating lunch in your backyard. You leave your sandwich on the picnic table and go to the house for a glass of water. When you return to your lunch, your sandwich is gone and your dog has peanut butter on his nose. What do you think happened? You can use the evidence you have to make an **inference,** or educated guess, that your dog swiped your sandwich. In the same way you can use story details to make inferences about characters in a story.

As you read "Mother and Daughter," collect story details to help you make inferences about the characters.

SKILLS FOCUS

Literary Skills
Understand character traits.

Reading Skills
Make inferences.

Vocabulary Skills
Understand word origins.

VOCABULARY DEVELOPMENT

PREVIEW SELECTION VOCABULARY

Take a few minutes to preview these words before you begin to read "Mother and Daughter."

matinees (mat'·n·āz') *n.:* afternoon performances of a play or a movie.

> *Yollie and her mother got along well enough to go to matinees together at the local theater almost every Saturday afternoon.*

antics (an'tiks) *n.:* playful or silly acts.

> *People who witnessed Mrs. Moreno's antics couldn't help laughing.*

meager (mē'gər) *adj.:* slight; small amount.

> *Mrs. Moreno remembers that her parents worked hard for their meager salaries.*

sophisticated (sə·fis'tə·kāt'id) *adj.:* worldly; elegant and refined.

> *Yollie admired the way sophisticated people in New York dressed.*

tirade (tī'rād') *n.:* long, scolding speech.

> *Yollie felt bad about her angry tirade against her mom.*

UNDERSTANDING WORD ORIGINS

A word's **etymology** (et'ə·mäl'ə·jē) tells you what language the word comes from and how the word has developed through different languages over many years. An etymology is usually listed in brackets or parentheses after the word itself in a dictionary. Definitions of symbols and abbreviations in the front or back of the dictionary will help you read the etymology. For example, this common symbol, "<," means "comes from" or "derived from."

Take a look at the etymology of *student* to understand the word's history. As you read the story that follows, look for sidenotes that help explain the etymology of words.

Etymology	Meaning
student < L *studere*, to study	*Student* comes from the Latin word *studere*, which means "to study."

Mother and Daughter

Gary Soto

Yollie's mother, Mrs. Moreno, was a large woman who wore a muumuu and butterfly-shaped glasses. She liked to water her lawn in the evening and wave at low-riders, who would stare at her behind their smoky sunglasses and laugh. Now and then a low-rider from Belmont Avenue would make his car jump and shout *"Mamacita!"* But most of the time they just stared and wondered how she got so large.

Mrs. Moreno had a strange sense of humor. Once, Yollie and her mother were watching a late-night movie 10 called *They Came to Look.* It was about creatures from the underworld who had climbed through molten lava to walk the earth. But Yollie, who had played soccer all day with the kids next door, was too tired to be scared. Her eyes closed but sprang open when her mother screamed, "Look, Yollie! Oh, you missed a scary part. The guy's face was all ugly!"

Orion Press/Black Sheep.

But Yollie couldn't keep her eyes open. They fell shut again and stayed shut, even when her mother screamed and slammed a heavy palm on the arm of her chair.

"Mom, wake me up when the movie's over so I can go to bed," mumbled Yollie.

"OK, Yollie, I wake you," said her mother through a mouthful of popcorn.

But after the movie ended, instead of waking her daughter, Mrs. Moreno laughed under her breath, turned the TV and lights off, and tiptoed to bed. Yollie woke up in the middle of the night and didn't know where she was. For a moment she thought she was dead. Maybe something from the underworld had lifted her from her house and carried her into the earth's belly. She blinked her sleepy eyes, looked around at the darkness, and called, "Mom? Mom, where are you?" But there was no answer, just the throbbing hum of the refrigerator.

Finally, Yollie's grogginess cleared and she realized her mother had gone to bed, leaving her on the couch. Another of her little jokes.

But Yollie wasn't laughing. She tiptoed into her mother's bedroom with a glass of water and set it on the nightstand next to the alarm clock. The next morning, Yollie woke to screams. When her mother reached to turn off the alarm, she had overturned the glass of water.

Yollie burned her mother's morning toast and gloated. "Ha! Ha! I got you back. Why did you leave me on the couch when I told you to wake me up?"

Despite their jokes, mother and daughter usually got along. They watched bargain **matinees** together, and played croquet in the summer and checkers in the winter. Mrs. Moreno encouraged Yollie to study hard because she wanted her daughter to be a doctor. She bought Yollie a desk, a

INFER

Re-read lines 21–22. What can you learn about Mrs. Moreno from the way she speaks?

_____

_____

_____

RETELL

Re-read lines 23–32. What has happened to Yollie?

_____

_____

_____

COMPARE & CONTRAST

Pause at line 43. Think about Yollie's response to her mother's practical joke. What **character trait** do Yollie and Mrs. Moreno have in common?

_____

_____

_____

VOCABULARY

matinees (mat″n·āz′) *n.:* afternoon performances of a play or a movie.

Matinee is from the French *matin,* meaning "morning."

_____

_____

_____

_____

_____

_____

_____

_____

_____

_____

_____

_____

_____

_____

_____

_____

_____

antics (an′tiks) *n.:* playful or
silly acts.

50 typewriter, and a lamp that cut glare so her eyes would not
grow tired from hours of studying.

Yollie was slender as a tulip, pretty, and one of the
smartest kids at Saint Theresa's. She was captain of crossing
guards, an altar girl, and a whiz in the school's monthly
spelling bees.

"Tienes que estudiar mucho," Mrs. Moreno said every
time she propped her work-weary feet on the hassock. "You
have to study a lot, then you can get a good job and take
care of me."

60 "Yes, Mama," Yollie would respond, her face buried in
a book. If she gave her mother any sympathy, she would
begin her stories about how she had come with her family
from Mexico with nothing on her back but a sack with
three skirts, all of which were too large by the time she
crossed the border because she had lost weight from not
having enough to eat.

Everyone thought Yollie's mother was a riot. Even the
nuns laughed at her **antics.** Her brother Raul, a nightclub
owner, thought she was funny enough to go into show
business.

Orion Press/Black Sheep.

70　　　But there was nothing funny about Yollie needing a new outfit for the eighth-grade fall dance. They couldn't afford one. It was late October, with Christmas around the corner, and their dented Chevy Nova had gobbled up almost one hundred dollars in repairs.

　　　"We don't have the money," said her mother, genuinely sad because they couldn't buy the outfit, even though there was a little money stashed away for college. Mrs. Moreno remembered her teenage years and her hardworking parents, who picked grapes and oranges, and chopped beets
80　and cotton for **meager** pay around Kerman. Those were the days when "new clothes" meant limp and out-of-style dresses from Saint Vincent de Paul.

　　　The best Mrs. Moreno could do was buy Yollie a pair of black shoes with velvet bows and fabric dye to color her white summer dress black.

　　　"We can color your dress so it will look brand-new," her mother said brightly, shaking the bottle of dye as she ran hot water into a plastic dish tub. She poured the black liquid into the tub and stirred it with a pencil. Then, slowly
90　and carefully, she lowered the dress into the tub.

　　　Yollie couldn't stand to watch. She *knew* it wouldn't work. It would be like the time her mother stirred up a batch of molasses for candy apples on Yollie's birthday. She'd dipped the apples into the goo and swirled them and seemed to taunt Yollie by singing *"Las Mañanitas"* to her. When she was through, she set the apples on wax paper. They were hard as rocks and hurt the kids' teeth. Finally, they had a contest to see who could break the apples open by throwing them against the side of the house. The apples
100　shattered like grenades, sending the kids scurrying for cover, and in an odd way the birthday party turned out to be a success. At least everyone went home happy.

VOCABULARY

meager (mē′gər) *adj.:* slight; small amount.

Meager is derived from the Latin *macer,* meaning "lean" or "thin."

INFER

Pause at line 82. Why do you think Mrs. Moreno is genuinely sad that she cannot afford a new dress for Yollie?

_____

_____

_____

IDENTIFY

What does Mrs. Moreno do to give Yollie a "new" dress (lines 86–90)?

_____

_____

_____

RETELL

Pause at line 102. What happened at the birthday party that Yollie is remembering?

_____

_____

_____

VOCABULARY

sophisticated (sə·fis′tə·kāt′id) *adj.*: worldly; elegant and refined.

This word is derived from the Greek *sophistēs,* meaning "wise man."

IDENTIFY

Pause at line 112. Why is the dance so important to Yollie?

_____

_____

_____

_____

_____

IDENTIFY

Underline the details in lines 121–128 that bring the scene to life.

WORD STUDY

Re-read lines 125–128. Circle the context clues that help you understand the word *jitterbugged.* Based on those clues, what do you think the jitterbug is?

_____

_____

_____

_____

_____

To Yollie's surprise, the dress came out shiny black. It looked brand-new and **sophisticated,** like what people in New York wear. She beamed at her mother, who hugged Yollie and said, "See, what did I tell you?"

The dance was important to Yollie because she was in love with Ernie Castillo, the third-best speller in the class. She bathed, dressed, did her hair and nails, and primped

110 until her mother yelled, "All right already." Yollie sprayed her neck and wrists with Mrs. Moreno's Avon perfume and bounced into the car.

Mrs. Moreno let Yollie out in front of the school. She waved and told her to have a good time but behave herself, then roared off, blue smoke trailing from the tail pipe of the old Nova.

Yollie ran into her best friend, Janice. They didn't say it, but each thought the other was the most beautiful girl at the dance; the boys would fall over themselves asking them

120 to dance.

The evening was warm but thick with clouds. Gusts of wind picked up the paper lanterns hanging in the trees and swung them, blurring the night with reds and yellows. The lanterns made the evening seem romantic, like a scene from a movie. Everyone danced, sipped punch, and stood in knots of threes and fours, talking. Sister Kelly got up and jitterbugged with some kid's father. When the record ended, students broke into applause.

Janice had her eye on Frankie Ledesma, and Yollie,
130 who kept smoothing her dress down when the wind picked up, had her eye on Ernie. It turned out that Ernie had his mind on Yollie, too. He ate a handful of cookies nervously, then asked her for a dance.

"Sure," she said, nearly throwing herself into his arms.

They danced two fast ones before they got a slow one. As they circled under the lanterns, rain began falling, lightly at first. Yollie loved the sound of the raindrops ticking against the leaves. She leaned her head on Ernie's shoulder, though his sweater was scratchy. He felt warm and tender. Yollie could
140 tell that he was in love, and with her, of course. The dance continued successfully, romantically, until it began to pour.

"Everyone, let's go inside—and, boys, carry in the table and the record player," Sister Kelly commanded.

The girls and boys raced into the cafeteria. Inside, the girls, drenched to the bone, hurried to the restrooms to brush their hair and dry themselves. One girl cried because her velvet dress was ruined. Yollie felt sorry for her and helped her dry the dress off with paper towels, but it was no use. The dress was ruined.

150 Yollie went to a mirror. She looked a little gray now that her mother's makeup had washed away but not as bad as some of the other girls. She combed her damp hair, careful not to pull too hard. She couldn't wait to get back to Ernie.

Yollie bent over to pick up a bobby pin, and shame spread across her face. A black puddle was forming at her feet. Drip, black drip. Drip, black drip. The dye was falling from her dress like black tears. Yollie stood up. Her dress was now the color of ash. She looked around the room. The other girls, unaware of Yollie's problem, were busy

PREDICT

Pause at line 141. How might the rain affect Yollie's evening?

_____

_____

_____

_____

_____

INFER

Re-read lines 147–149. Underline the details that help reveal one of Yollie's **character traits**. What trait do Yollie's feelings and actions reveal?

_____

_____

_____

_____

_____

IDENTIFY CAUSE & EFFECT

Pause at line 156. What causes the black puddle to form at Yollie's feet?

_____

_____

_____

_____

_____

CONNECT

Pause at line 165. Does Yollie have good reason to be ashamed of her dress? If this happened to you, would you be embarrassed or just laugh it off?

_____

_____

_____

_____

_____

_____

_____

_____

_____

_____

_____

_____

160 grooming themselves. What could she do? Everyone would laugh. They would know she dyed an old dress because she couldn't afford a new one. She hurried from the restroom with her head down, across the cafeteria floor and out the door. She raced through the storm, crying as the rain mixed with her tears and ran into twig-choked gutters.

When she arrived home, her mother was on the couch eating cookies and watching TV.

"How was the dance, *m'ija*? Come watch the show with me. It's really good."

170 Yollie stomped, head down, to her bedroom. She undressed and threw the dress on the floor.

> Her mother came into the room. "What's going on? What's all the racket, baby?"
>
> "The dress. It's cheap! It's no good!" Yollie kicked the dress at her mother and watched it land in her hands. Mrs. Moreno studied it closely but couldn't see what was wrong. "What's the matter? It's just a bit wet."
>
> "The dye came out, that's what."
>
> Mrs. Moreno looked at her hands and saw the grayish
180 dye puddling in the shallow lines of her palms. Poor baby, she thought, her brow darkening as she made a sad face.

WORD STUDY

M'ija (line 168) is Spanish for "my daughter."

FLUENCY

Re-read the boxed passage several times, and try to "hear" the characters' voices. Then, read the passage aloud. Vary the tone and volume of your voice to distinguish the narrator from Yollie and her mother.

She wanted to tell her daughter how sorry she was, but she knew it wouldn't help. She walked back to the living room and cried.

The next morning, mother and daughter stayed away from each other. Yollie sat in her room turning the pages of an old *Seventeen,* while her mother watered her plants with a Pepsi bottle.

"Drink, my children," she said loud enough for Yollie
190 to hear. She let the water slurp into pots of coleus and cacti. "Water is all you need. My daughter needs clothes, but I don't have no money."

Yollie tossed her *Seventeen* on her bed. She was embarrassed at last night's **tirade.** It wasn't her mother's fault that they were poor.

When they sat down together for lunch, they felt awkward about the night before. But Mrs. Moreno had made a fresh stack of tortillas and cooked up a pan of *chile verde,* and that broke the ice. She licked her thumb and smacked
200 her lips.

"You know, honey, we gotta figure a way to make money," Yollie's mother said. "You and me. We don't have to be poor. Remember the Garcias. They made this stupid little tool that fixes cars. They moved away because they're rich. That's why we don't see them no more."

"What can we make?" asked Yollie. She took another tortilla and tore it in half.

"Maybe a screwdriver that works on both ends? Something like that." The mother looked around the room
210 for ideas, but then shrugged. "Let's forget it. It's better to get an education. If you get a good job and have spare time then maybe you can invent something." She rolled her tongue over her lips and cleared her throat. "The county fair hires people. We can get a job there. It will be here next week."

INFER

Pause at the end of line 184. Underline the words that tell you what Mrs. Moreno is thinking, what she looks like, and what she is doing. What **character traits** do these details reveal?

_____

_____

_____

WORD STUDY

Pause at line 190. A coleus is a type of plant in the mint family. The word *coleus* comes from the Greek word *koleos,* which means "a sheath." Part of the coleus plant's flower looks like it has a sheath, or covering, around it. *Cacti* is the plural form of *cactus,* a desert plant.

VOCABULARY

tirade (tī'rād') *n.:* long, scolding speech.

Tirade comes from the Italian word *tirare,* meaning "to draw or shoot."

INTERPRET

Re-read lines 201–214. What do Mrs. Moreno's words reveal about her personality and her outlook on life?

_____

_____

_____

_____

_____

_____

_____

_____

_____

_____

_____

_____

_____

_____

_____

_____

_____

_____

_____

_____

_____

_____

_____

_____

Yollie hated the idea. What would Ernie say if he saw her pitching hay at the cows? How could she go to school smelling like an armful of chickens? "No, they wouldn't hire us," she said.

The phone rang. Yollie lurched from her chair to
220 answer it, thinking it would be Janice wanting to know why she had left. But it was Ernie wondering the same thing. When he found out she wasn't mad at him, he asked if she would like to go to a movie.

"I'll ask," Yollie said, smiling. She covered the phone with her hand and counted to ten. She uncovered the receiver and said, "My mom says it's OK. What are we going to see?"

After Yollie hung up, her mother climbed, grunting, onto a chair to reach the top shelf in the hall closet. She wondered why she hadn't done it earlier. She reached
230 behind a stack of towels and pushed her chubby hand into the cigar box where she kept her secret stash of money.

"I've been saving a little money every month," said Mrs. Moreno. "For you, _m'ija._" Her mother held up five twenties, a blossom of green that smelled sweeter than flowers on that Saturday. They drove to Macy's and bought a blouse, shoes, and a skirt that would not bleed in rain or any other kind of weather.

Orion Press/Black Sheep.

Mother and Daughter

Character Traits Chart   Writers bring characters to life by describing how the characters look, talk, act, and think. Sometimes a writer directly describes a character's traits. For example, a writer might tell you that so-and-so is kind, sympathetic, or tough. Often, however, you have to make inferences about the characters based on details the writer provides.

SKILLS FOCUS

Literary Focus
Analyze character traits.

Select one of the characters from "Mother and Daughter," and complete this chart with details you find in the story. Then, review those details and list the character's traits in the box.

Character:

Character Traits

Appearance

Speech

Actions

Thoughts and Feelings

Other Characters' Reactions

Skills Review

Mother and Daughter

VOCABULARY AND COMPREHENSION

A. Word Origins   The partial etymologies given below tell the story of three of the Word Bank words. Select the vocabulary word that matches each etymology, and write the word in the blank provided.

1. < G *sophistēs,* meaning "wise man" _____

2. < Fr *matin,* "morning" _____

3. < L *macer,* "lean; thin" _____

B. Reading Comprehension   Answer each question below.

1. What is Mrs. Moreno's personality like? _____

_____

_____

2. Why is Yollie upset about the upcoming dance? _____

_____

_____

3. Why does Yollie leave the dance early? _____

_____

_____

4. What does Mrs. Moreno do to cheer Yollie up after the dance?

_____

_____

_____

SKILLS FOCUS

Vocabulary Skills
Understand word origins.

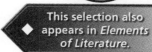
A Rice Sandwich by Sandra Cisneros

LITERARY FOCUS: THE NARRATOR

A **narrator** is the teller of a story. When you begin reading a story, look for clues about who the narrator is. A narrator who observes the action and is not a story character is called an **omniscient** (äm·nish′ənt) **narrator.** This type of narrator can tell you about the thoughts and feelings of all the story characters.

A **first-person narrator,** on the other hand, *is* a story character. A first-person narrator participates directly in the story's action. If the storyteller tells the whole tale using first-person pronouns such as *I, me,* and *mine,* then you know that you're reading a story told by a first-person narrator.

Identify the type of narrator in each of these passages.

Passage	Narrator	
"I am not diving off this cliff," I said as we approached the top. Then I saw all the kids lined up to jump, and I gathered my courage.	Omniscient First Person	❐ ❐
The math test was extremely hard. Roz began to wish she had studied. Cora got stuck on item 3 and couldn't finish.	Omniscient First Person	❐ ❐

READING SKILLS: MAKING INFERENCES

Stories told by a first-person narrator usually give you a lot of information about the character who is narrating the story. However, it is still important for you to take part in the story by making your own inferences, educated guesses, about the characters. Use these tips to make inferences about Esperanza, the narrator of "A Rice Sandwich."

- Pay close attention to what Esperanza says and does.
- Observe the way other characters respond to Esperanza.
- Examine what you learn about Esperanza's thoughts.
- Think about how Esperanza is like, or not like, people you know.

SKILLS FOCUS

Literary Skills
Understand the narrator.

Reading Skills
Make inferences.

A Rice Sandwich

Sandra Cisneros

WORD STUDY

A canteen (line 2) is a place where food or drink can be obtained. *Canteen* comes from the French *cantine* and the Italian *cantina,* both of which mean "wine cellar" or "vault."

IDENTIFY

Re-read lines 1–9. Underline the clues that hint at who the **narrator** is. Describe what you know about the narrator so far.

_____

_____

_____

_____

The special kids, the ones who wear keys around their necks, get to eat in the canteen. The canteen! Even the name sounds important. And these kids at lunch time go there because their mothers aren't home or home is too far away to get to.

My home isn't far but it's not close either, and somehow I got it in my head one day to ask my mother to make me a sandwich and write a note to the principal so I could eat in the canteen too.

10 Oh no, she says pointing the butter knife at me as if I'm starting trouble, no sir. Next thing you know everybody will be wanting a bag lunch—I'll be up all night cutting bread into little triangles, this one with mayonnaise, this one with mustard, no pickles on mine, but mustard on one side please. You kids just like to invent more work for me.

> But Nenny says she doesn't want to eat at school—ever—because she likes to go home with her best friend Gloria who lives across the schoolyard. Gloria's mama has a big color T.V. and all they do is watch cartoons. Kiki and
>
> 20 Carlos, on the other hand, are patrol boys. They don't want to eat at school either. They like to stand out in the cold especially if it's raining. They think suffering is good for you ever since they saw that movie "300 Spartans."

I'm no Spartan[1] and hold up an anemic[2] wrist to prove it. I can't even blow up a balloon without getting dizzy. And besides, I know how to make my own lunch. If I ate at school there'd be less dishes to wash. You would see me less and less and like me better. Every day at noon my chair would be empty. Where is my favorite daughter you would

30 cry, and when I came home finally at 3 p.m. you would appreciate me.

Okay, okay, my mother says after three days of this. And the following morning I get to go to school with my mother's letter and a rice sandwich because we don't have lunch meat.

Mondays or Fridays, it doesn't matter, mornings always go by slow and this day especially. But lunch time came finally and I got to get in line with the stay-at-school kids. Everything is fine until the nun who knows all the canteen

40 kids by heart looks at me and says: you, who sent you here? And since I am shy, I don't say anything, just hold out my hand with the letter. This is no good, she says, till Sister Superior gives the okay. Go upstairs and see her. And so I went.

I had to wait for two kids in front of me to get hollered at, one because he did something in class, the other because he didn't. My turn came and I stood in front of the big desk

---

1. **Spartan:** hardy, disciplined person, like the Spartans of ancient Greece.
2. **anemic** (ə·nē′mik) *adj.:* pale and weak.

FLUENCY

In the boxed passage of text, the writer uses a technique that allows you to "hear" what the main character is thinking. Read the paragraph aloud several times, striving for smooth delivery and a tone of voice that conveys the main character's state of mind.

CLARIFY

In this short, **first-person narrative** the author writes in present tense and does not always tell you who is speaking or to whom she is speaking. Re-read lines 24–31. Underline words or phrases that help you figure out who the writer is speaking to.

INFER

Pause at line 35. Think about what the narrator brings to lunch and why. What can you infer about the narrator from that detail?

_____

_____

_____

_____

_____

IDENTIFY

Re-read lines 36–44. Circle the words that tell you what kind of school the writer attends.

with holy pictures under the glass while the Sister Superior read my letter. It went like this:

50 Dear Sister Superior,

Please let Esperanza eat in the lunch room because she lives too far away and she gets tired. As you can see she is very skinny. I hope to God she does not faint.

Thanking you,
Mrs. E. Cordero.

You don't live far, she says. You live across the boulevard. That's only four blocks. Not even. Three maybe. Three long blocks away from here. I bet I can see your house from my
60 window. Which one? Come here. Which one is your house?

And then she made me stand up on a box of books and point. That one? she said pointing to a row of ugly 3-flats, the ones even the raggedy men are ashamed to go into. Yes, I nodded even though I knew that wasn't my house and started to cry. I always cry when nuns yell at me, even if they're not yelling.

Then she was sorry and said I could stay—just for today, not tomorrow or the day after—you go home. And I said yes and could I please have a Kleenex—I had to blow
70 my nose.

In the canteen, which was nothing special, lots of boys and girls watched while I cried and ate my sandwich, the bread already greasy and the rice cold.

A Rice Sandwich

Narrator Detector   By now you know that "A Rice Sandwich" is narrated by the main character, Esperanza. But how did you find out? The story gives you clues in the form of first-person pronouns that Esperanza uses to refer to herself. Re-read lines 32–35 to find all four clues. Write those pronouns on the lines below. Then, tell how you learned the narrator's name.

Literary Skills
Analyze the narrator.

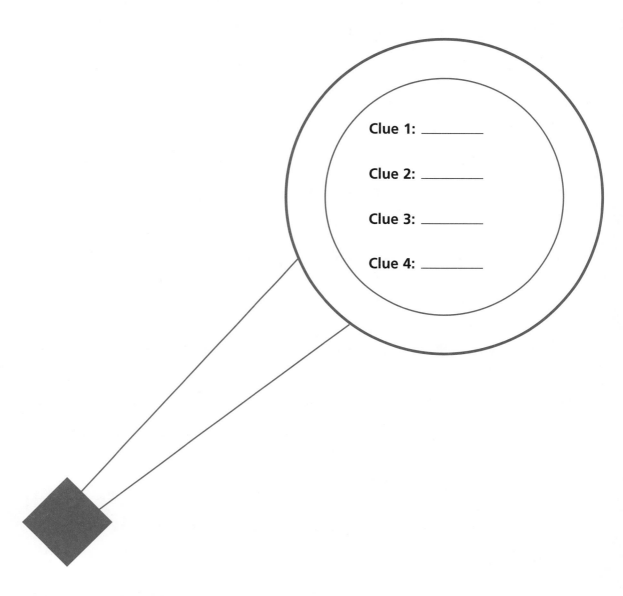

Clue 1: _____

Clue 2: _____

Clue 3: _____

Clue 4: _____

Where in the story did you find the narrator's name?

_____

_____

Skills Review

A Rice Sandwich

COMPREHENSION

Reading Comprehension   Answer each question below.

1. Who is the narrator of "A Rice Sandwich"?

_____

_____

_____

_____

2. Which students eat in the school's canteen?

_____

_____

_____

_____

3. How does Esperanza persuade her mother to write the note so she can eat in the canteen too?

_____

_____

_____

_____

4. Does Esperanza enjoy eating in the canteen? Explain.

_____

_____

_____

_____

Learning to Float by Veronica Chambers

LITERARY FOCUS: CHARACTER TRAITS

We learn about characters in many different ways. Sometimes a writer will tell us directly what a character is like; for example, "Tommy had a cruel streak." More often, however, writers allow us to find out for ourselves what a character is like by describing his or her appearance, speech, thoughts, actions, and effect on other characters.

As you read "Learning to Float," look for details that help bring its main character, Marisol, to life.

READING SKILLS: MAKING PREDICTIONS

One of the pleasures of reading is jumping right into a story and getting to know some new people as their story unfolds. You are about to meet Marisol, a young girl from Brooklyn, in the story that follows. Pause from time to time as you read to think over Marisol's situation. Then, try to predict how she will deal with life's unexpected twists and turns. (A prediction is a guess based on what you know about life and people.) Keep in mind that although not all your predictions will turn out to be correct, half the fun of reading a story is being surprised at how things turn out. If any of your predictions prove to be incorrect, simply adjust them as you go on.

As you read, you may want to fill out a chart like this one:

My Prediction	What Really Happened

SKILLS FOCUS

Literary Skills
Identify character traits.

Reading Skills
Make predictions.

Vocabulary Skills
Use context clues.

VOCABULARY DEVELOPMENT

PREVIEW SELECTION VOCABULARY

Get to know these words before you read "Learning to Float."

registered (rej′is·tərd) *v.:* signed up; enrolled.

Marisol was a little nervous when she registered for school.

immersion (i·mur′zhən) *n.:* act of being totally absorbed in studies or a culture.

The guidance counselor said immersion is the best way to learn a language.

plunged (plunjd) *v.:* threw oneself into a place or situation.

When I first plunged into the swimming pool, I struggled to stay afloat.

instinct (in′stiŋkt′) *n.:* inborn tendency to behave in a certain way.

Magda's father taught us that floating is a natural instinct.

USING CONTEXT CLUES

When you come across an unfamiliar word, you can often figure out its meaning by using **context clues.** In the examples below, the italicized passages provide context clues for the boldface words. Look for these types of context clues in "Learning to Float." They will help you figure out the meanings of unfamiliar words and phrases.

RESTATEMENT: "You are **loco**. Absolutely *crazy*!"

DEFINITION: **Tortillas,** *flat, round bread that is grilled,* taste delicious.

EXAMPLE: Marisol marveled at the **exotic** foods. *Mango, papaya, and plantains* were not at all common where she lived.

CONTRAST: Unlike her mother, who was **fluent** in Spanish, Marisol *spoke very little of that language.*

from Marisol and Magdalena

Learning to Float

Veronica Chambers

BEFORE YOU READ

Here are some details you should know before you read this story, which is part of a novel titled *Marisol and Magdalena.*

- Panama is a small country located in Central America. Spanish is the main language spoken there. *Abuela* means "grandmother" in Spanish.
- Marisol is a teenager from Brooklyn, New York. Her best friend there is Magdalena, or Magda. Marisol is sent by her mother to Panama to visit her grandmother (Abuela) for a year. Marisol's mother hopes that Marisol will learn more about Panama.

Abuela woke me up early. "We have to go to the market," she said, shaking me gently. "We don't have all day."

"*Abuela, please,*" I begged. "Five more minutes."

"Forget about it," she said, flipping on the lights and turning on the clock radio full blast. "I hope you like pancakes."

I sat up in the bed, groggy but hungry. "With blueberries?" I asked.

"You're in Panama," Abuela said, laughing. "Bananas or

10 coconut?"

Banana pancakes? Coconut pancakes? They both sounded pretty strange. "Can I get them mixed together?" I asked.

"Definitely," she said. "Now don't take all day in the shower."

IDENTIFY

Pause at line 10. What do you know about the narrator so far?

_____

_____

_____

INFER

Re-read lines 7–10, and underline the names of fruits. What do you know about these fruits? How does Marisol's choice show that she has not been in Panama before?

_____

_____

FLUENCY

Take the role of Marisol or Abuela, and read and act out the boxed passage with another student. Underline the words that you will emphasize or say in a louder voice.

PREDICT

Pause at line 31. Do you think Abuela will move to America? Explain.

I picked up the neatly folded pink towel that Abuela laid on my bed.

"You know, Mami was worried that you might be too poor to have an extra towel," I said.

20 "I can afford extra towels," Abuela said, waving her hand as if to dismiss the idea. "My retirement check isn't much, but I manage."

"Why don't you move to America?" I asked. "You could live with me and Mami."

"Why don't you move to Panama?" Abuela asked, placing her hand on her hip.

"I just *did*," I reminded her.

Abuela didn't say anything at first. She looked at me with a faraway look in her eye, then she nodded her head.

30 "I guess that's true," she said, smiling. "Now, don't be all day in the shower."

My banana-coconut pancakes were delicious, the best I'd ever had. And by eight o'clock Abuela and I were out the door. The market wasn't a grocery store as I had imagined

it to be. It was more like a street fair, with people selling everything from spices to fruit and rice from stalls. Walking past the different *vendedores* selling their wares, I wondered if they could tell I was American. I was dressed in my favorite pair of jeans and my "Girls Rule" T-shirt. Most of

40 the other girls I saw wore brightly colored sundresses, like the one Ana had worn the day before.

When we stopped to buy rice or fruit, the vendors always greeted me in Spanish and expected me to understand. I did, for the most part, but I was still nervous about trying to use my Spanish. So when people spoke to me, I nodded and smiled.

"You're going to have to speak Spanish at some point," Abuela said. I was surprised that she had noticed that I wasn't talking.

50 "*La unica manera de mejorarse es practicando,*" Abuela said, taking my hand and leading me down another row of vendedores. "The only way you'll get better is to practice."

"You don't understand," I said. "At home people make fun of my Spanish."

"*People?*" Abuela asked, raising one eyebrow. "People like who?"

"Like Roxana and my friend Magda's brothers and sister."

"*No importa,*" Abuela said. "It doesn't matter now.

60 You'll be speaking like a native in no time at all. That is, if you speak. You've got to open your mouth and try."

We passed a stall where a woman was selling homemade cookies. "Can I have some?" I asked Abuela.

She just looked at me. "I don't know," she said. "Ask her."

I walked up to the woman's table and spoke slowly. "*Buenos días, señora.*"

DECODING TIP

Circle the word *vendors* (line 42). Then, find and circle the word printed in italics in the previous paragraph that looks almost like *vendors*. Read the words nearby that help explain its meaning. *Vendors* and *vendedores* have the same meaning. What does *vendors* mean?

_____

_____

_____

DECODING TIP

Circle the word *practicando* (line 50). Draw a line from this word to another word in the paragraph that resembles it. What might *practicando* mean?

_____

_____

INFER

Look through the part of the story you have read so far. Box words and phrases that reveal Marisol's problems with speaking Spanish. How would you feel in her place?

_____

_____

_____

_____

_____

registered (rej′is·tərd) *v.:*
signed up; enrolled.

Registered comes from the
Latin word *registrare,* which
means "record."

immersion (i·mur′zhən) *n.:*
act of being totally absorbed
in studies or a culture.

Immersion comes from the
Latin prefix *in–,* meaning
"into" and the Latin word
mergere, meaning "dip,
plunge into, or sink." In this
context, *immersion* means
"being completely absorbed
and surrounded by a new
culture and language" as if
being plunged into the "sea"
of the new culture.

Pause at line 94. Will Marisol
have a good day at school?
Explain.

_____

_____

_____

_____

_____

_____

_____

_____

_____

_____

_____

The lady smiled and asked me what I wanted. "*Buenos días, niña. Qué quieres?*"

70   "*Quiero dos galletes de chocolate,*" I said. "I want two chocolate cookies."

Just then, I felt a finger poke me in the back. "*No dices por favor?*" Abuela said.

"Please," I added.

The woman smiled again and handed me the cookies in a little plastic bag. I thanked her and we walked away.

"You spoke Spanish and no one laughed," Abuela said, raising her left eyebrow.

"No one laughed," I said, taking a bite of a cookie.

80   Two weeks later Abuela **registered** me for school. It was the first week of August and I couldn't help but feel that my summer vacation had been cut in half. At the school, Abuela and I met the guidance counselor, a woman named Mrs. Ortiz. She was beautiful—tall and dark skinned with wavy shoulder-length hair.

"All of your teachers speak English," Mrs. Ortiz explained. "They'll give you as much help as you need."

I looked at the printed schedule she had handed me. I was taking Spanish, English literature, and math in

90   the morning. Then science, history, gym, and art in the afternoon.

"Well, I think you're all set," Abuela said, standing up. "Make sure to meet Ana to walk home from school."

"Bye, Abuela," I said, smiling.

"This is really a terrific opportunity for you," Mrs. Ortiz said as we walked to my first class. "**Immersion** is the best way to learn a language. Maybe you could tutor one of

the students in English, and the student could tutor you in
Spanish. I'll talk to your homeroom teacher, Señora
100   Baptiste, about setting something up."

I started cracking my knuckles as soon as I walked
into my homeroom class with Mrs. Ortiz. Standing in
front of a classroom of total strangers was not my idea of
a good time.

"Class, I want you to meet Marisol Mayaguéz," Señora
Baptiste said.

It was strange hearing how Panamanian my name
sounded, when I didn't feel Panamanian at all. I stared
down at a square on the floor.

110   "You'll be fine," Mrs. Ortiz said. *"No te preocupes."*

At lunchtime I walked into the cafeteria. I just couldn't stop
cracking my knuckles. It was the most knuckle cracking I'd

Look for familiar English
word parts in the Spanish
sentence *No te preocupes*
(line 110). Underline the
word or word parts you
recognize. What does the
Spanish sentence mean?

_____

_____

_____

_____

_____

_____

_____

_____

_____

_____

_____

_____

_____

_____

_____

_____

_____

_____

_____

Use context clues to figure out the meaning of the Spanish sentence *Estás de moda* in line 123. Circle those clues. What does the phrase mean?

_____

_____

_____

_____

_____

What does *Nueva* in line 131 mean? Circle the context clue that states its meaning.

_____

Underline a familiar English word part in the Spanish phrase *Que significa* in line 141. Then circle a context clue that follows. What does the sentence mean?

_____

_____

_____

_____

_____

ever done and my fingers were starting to hurt. Then I saw Ana, waving to me.

"Marisol, *ven aca,*" Ana said. "I saved you a place at my table."

I was relieved that I wouldn't have to sit alone, but afraid to sit at a table where all the kids spoke nothing but Spanish.

120   Ana was wearing a blue sundress with white flowers all over it, the same orange sandals, and the same orange-tinted sunglasses.

"*Estás de moda,* Ana," I said. "You look great."

"Thanks," she said, standing up and giving a little spin. "I guess I'm stylish enough for America."

I wasn't sure about that, but I didn't say anything. Ana was my only chance at a new friend so far. I wasn't going to hurt her feelings by telling her that the girls I knew in New York would never wear an outfit like hers.

130   After school I met Ana, and we walked home together.

"Tell me all about Nueva York," Ana said as we walked down the tiny winding street. "Do you know how lucky you are to come from New York, the Big Apple? *Wow!*"

"Well, nobody in New York calls it the Big Apple," I said, laughing.

"Do you go to clubs every night?" Ana asked, talking as fast in English as she did in Spanish. "Do you meet lots of rock stars and famous people?"

"As if," I said, jumping down a hopscotch drawn on the

140   sidewalk. At least some things were the same in Panama.

"*As if,*" Ana repeated. "*Que significa* as if?"

"It means no way," I explained.

"So what do you do for fun?" Ana asked.

"Me and my best friend, Magda, we watch music videos and play punchball in the park," I said, shrugging. "Just regular stuff."

"Your regular stuff sounds *muy divertido* to me," Ana said.

"Do you have a best friend?" I asked as we crossed
150 the street. I knew where I was now. Abuela's apartment building was at the end of the block.

Ana scratched her arm and looked down. "I did have a best friend," she said quietly. "Her name was Digna. But she's not here anymore. She moved to Nicaragua to live with her father. I had to start the school year completely by myself."

I thought about Magda in New York. We were going to take Roberto Clemente Junior High School by storm this year—drill team, honor roll, everything. Now I was here
160 starting the school year completely by myself and Magda was there—in New York, without me.

"I'm glad you came to Panama," Ana said, opening the door to her apartment.

"Thanks, Ana," I said. I stood on the porch for a second. Looking out onto Panama City, the palm trees blowing in the wind.

I thought about the scene in *The Wizard of Oz*, when Dorothy says, "We're not in Kansas anymore, Toto." That was exactly how I felt, and I didn't even have a dog to tell it
170 to. I was in this on my own.

"Como te fue hoy?" Abuela asked, wiping her hands on her apron. "How'd it go today?"

"Not bad," I said, trying to smile. "Not bad at all."

"OK, we'll talk over *cena*," she said. "You go and relax."

PREDICT

Box the information about Ana's and Marisol's old friends. How are the girls' situations similar? Do you predict they will become friends? Why or why not?

_____

_____

_____

_____

_____

_____

_____

INFER

In line 167, underline Marisol's allusion, or reference, to a popular movie. What does she mean?

_____

_____

_____

_____

WORD STUDY

Underline the translation of *Como te fue hoy?* What does *cena* (line 174) probably mean?

_____

_____

INFER

Pause at line 188. What might the narrator be feeling? How do you know?

_____

_____

_____

_____

_____

_____

_____

_____

_____

_____

_____

_____

_____

_____

WORD STUDY

Tío (line 196) is the Spanish word for "uncle."

VOCABULARY

plunged (plunjd) *v.*: threw oneself into a place or situation.

I kept thinking about what Mrs. Ortiz had said, about how coming to Panama was an opportunity. She had said the best way to learn a language was through "immersion." It was a funny word—immersion. I kind of knew what it meant, but I had never heard anybody actually use the word in regular conversation.

I went into the living room, to the shelf where Abuela kept all her books. I pulled out the *American Heritage Dictionary* that I had spotted a few days before. I opened it and was surprised to see my mother's maiden name, Inez Velásquez, written in her same perfect handwriting.

This dictionary must have belonged to Mami when she was in school, I thought, and even though it was just a book, I held it to my chest for a second.

I sat on Abuela's old red couch, the couch filled with stuffing that had popped out on the side. I opened the dictionary and flipped to the I's. The word was listed under its root word—*immerse.* The definition read: IMMERSE— 1. TO PLUNGE INTO A FLUID. 2. TO BAPTIZE BY SUBMERGING IN WATER. 3. TO ABSORB, ENGROSS.

I thought about what I was doing last summer, at exactly this time. I was in New York, and Tío Ricardo, Magda's father, was teaching Magda and me how to swim at the Y. He insisted that all we had to do was jump into the cold water. Every day, he waited for us on the deep side of the pool and held out his arms as we **plunged** in. He let us struggle for a second, then pulled us up out of the water. Eventually, we stopped struggling and started to float.

Holding Mami's dictionary open on my lap, I closed my eyes and remembered how dark it had been underneath the water, how the pool water burned going up my nose, how the chlorine stung my eyes. Magda had been her usual fearless self, but I was so scared.

Sitting in Abuela's living room, I remembered when my arms and legs began to move in sync. It wasn't more than a dog paddle, but it was the first time that I actually didn't sink like a stone.

Panama—the language, the place, the people—was like that pool, only deeper and wider.

There were oceans that now separated me from everything and everyone I'd ever known. But Tío Ricardo had taught me that it was the body's natural **instinct** to float.

"Don't fight so hard to swim, *hija*," he had said when I splashed and splashed like my life depended on it.

"It'll come naturally," he said.

Now I was *immersed* again, plunged into this place that everyone in my family called home.

"I've jumped in. Tío Ricardo always said that's the hardest part," I whispered to myself as I put the dictionary back on the shelf. "Now let's see if I can swim."

instinct (in′stiŋkt′) *n.:* inborn tendency to behave in a certain way.

INFER

What do you think Marisol means in the last sentence of the story? How does that sentence help you explain the story's title, "Learning to Float"?

_____

_____

_____

_____

_____

_____

_____

_____

_____

_____

_____

_____

_____

_____

_____

Learning to Float

Literary Skills
Analyze
character traits.

Character Traits Chart   A **character trait** is a quality in a person that can't be seen. Generosity, kindness, and shyness are all character traits. We discover character traits by examining a character's appearance, speech, thoughts, actions, and their effect on other characters. Fill in the following chart with examples of Marisol's actions, words, thoughts, and so on. Then, list a character trait that each action or statement suggests or reveals.

Action/Statement/ Speech/Thoughts/ Effect on Other Characters	Action/Statement/ Speech/Thoughts/ Effect on Other Characters	Action/Statement/ Speech/Thoughts/ Effect on Other Characters

↓ ↓ ↓

Character Trait	Character Trait	Character Trait

Skills Review

Learning to Float

VOCABULARY AND COMPREHENSION

A. Using Context Clues Fill in the blanks with the correct Word Bank word. Use context clues in the paragraph to help you.

I (1) _____ for Chinese-language classes two weeks ago. I have never (2) _____ into something like this before. The work is intense: I am using the method called (3) _____, in which nothing but Chinese is spoken during the day. I feel as if I have an (4) _____ for language because I seem to be catching on quickly.

B. Reading Comprehension Answer each question below.

1. Who is Abuela? Where does she live? _____

_____

_____

2. Why does Marisol feel out of place at school? _____

_____

_____

3. Who is Ana? Who is Magda? _____

_____

_____

4. What has Marisol realized at the story's end? What does she hope to

find out? _____

_____

_____

Vocabulary Skills
Use context clues.

Living in the Heart

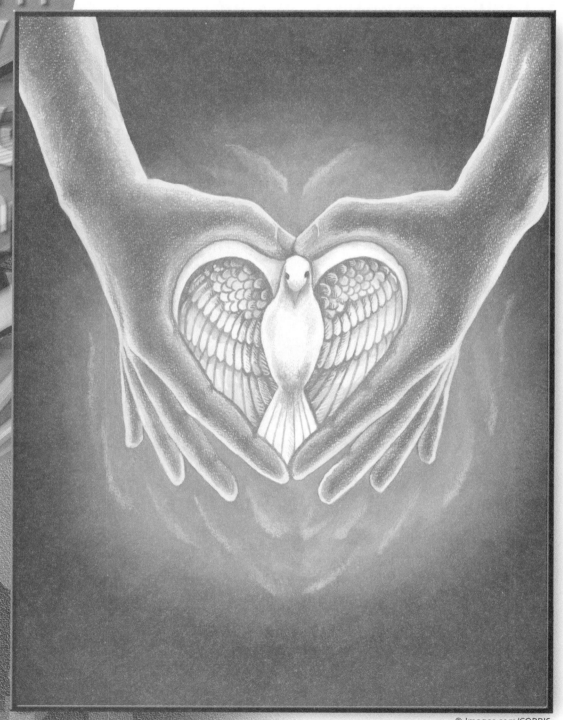

© Images.com/CORBIS.

Academic Vocabulary for Collection 3

These are the terms you should know
as you read and analyze the selections in this collection.

_____

Topic or Subject   What a story or poem is about. A story's topic may
be friendship, for example. A **theme** goes a step further and
comments on the topic; for example, "To be a good friend you
must like yourself first."

Theme   A truth about life revealed in a work of literature. Theme is
a key element of literature—of fiction, nonfiction, poetry, and
drama.

Recurring Theme   A theme that appears over and over again in literature. For example, a poem written in China one thousand years
ago may have the same theme as a story that was written just
last year. You may be familiar with recurring themes such as
"love is powerful" and "honesty is the best policy."

●   ●   ●

Narrative Poem   A poem that is written to tell a story. Like stories,
narrative poems have plots, characters, and settings.

This selection also appears in *Elements of Literature*. ◆

The Highwayman

by Alfred Noyes

LITERARY FOCUS: TOPIC VERSUS THEME

In the same way parents and teachers tell real-life stories to teach a lesson or make a point, writers often reveal insights about life through stories and poems. We call such insights **themes**. While a story's **topic** may be clear and easy to agree on, its theme is more open to interpretation. The theme is the idea the writer conveys *about* a topic.

NARRATIVE POEMS

A **narrative** is a story; a **narrative poem** tells a story. Most narrative poems, like most stories, have a plot, characters, setting, and theme. "The Highwayman," the narrative poem you're about to read, even contains dialogue—words spoken by characters.

READING SKILLS: MAKING PREDICTIONS

Have you ever read a real page turner, a book you just couldn't put down? What makes these books so gripping and fun to read is the element of suspense. Since we don't know what will happen next, we predict and then hungrily read further to see if we're right.

Use your powers of prediction as you read the classic poem "The Highwayman." You may want to record and track your predictions on a chart like this one:

Questions About What Will Happen	My Predictions	What Really Happens

SKILLS FOCUS

Literary Skills
Understand topic and theme; understand narrative poems.

Reading Skills
Make predictions.

The Highwayman

Alfred Noyes

> **BACKGROUND: Literature and Social Studies**
>
> The highwayman in this famous poem is a robber who lived in England in the 1700s. Highwaymen used to stop stagecoaches on the lonely moorlands of northern England and Scotland to rob the rich passengers of money and jewels. Some highwaymen were considered heroes by the Scots because they shared the money with the poor. Highwaymen were sometimes dashing, romantic figures who dressed in expensive clothes. The poem is based on a true story that the poet heard while he was on vacation in the part of England where highwaymen used to lie in wait for stagecoaches.

Part 1

The wind was a torrent of darkness among the gusty trees,
The moon was a ghostly galleon[1] tossed upon cloudy seas,
The road was a ribbon of moonlight over the purple moor,
And the highwayman came riding—
5   Riding—riding—
The highwayman came riding, up to the old inn door.

He'd a French cocked hat on his forehead, a bunch of lace
   at his chin,
A coat of the claret[2] velvet, and breeches of brown doeskin.
They fitted with never a wrinkle. His boots were up to
   the thigh.

VISUALIZE

Pause at line 6. Underline the words that help you picture the **setting**.

INFER

Read lines 7–12. Underline details that describe the highwayman's appearance. What can you infer about the highwayman from the way he dresses?

_____

_____

_____

_____

_____

---

1. **galleon** (gal'ē·ən) *n.*: large sailing ship.
2. **claret** (klar'it) *n.* used as *adj.*: purplish red, like claret wine.

The Haywain by John Constable (1776–1837).

A **narrative poem**, like any other narrative, contains a setting, characters, conflict, and plot. Pause at line 20. Circle the **major characters** in this narrative so far.

_____

_____

_____

_____

_____

_____

_____

_____

INFER

What does the description of Tim (lines 19–24) reveal about his **character**?

_____

_____

_____

_____

_____

_____

_____

10   And he rode with a jeweled twinkle,

    His pistol butts a-twinkle,

His rapier hilt[3] a-twinkle, under the jeweled sky.

Over the cobbles he clattered and clashed in the dark

    inn yard.

And he tapped with his whip on the shutters, but all was

    locked and barred.

He whistled a tune to the window, and who should be

15   waiting there

But the landlord's black-eyed daughter,

    Bess, the landlord's daughter,

Plaiting[4] a dark red love knot into her long black hair.

And dark in the dark old inn yard a stable wicket[5] creaked

Where Tim the ostler[6] listened. His face was white and

20   peaked.

---

3. rapier (rā′pē·ər) **hilt:** sword handle.

4. plaiting (plāt′iŋ) *v.* used as *adj.:* braiding.

5. wicket *n.:* small door or gate.

6. ostler (äs′lər) *n.:* person who takes care of horses; groom.

His eyes were hollows of madness, his hair like moldy hay,
But he loved the landlord's daughter,
    The landlord's red-lipped daughter,
Dumb as a dog he listened, and he heard the robber say—

25   "One kiss, my bonny sweetheart, I'm after a prize tonight,
But I shall be back with the yellow gold before the morning
    light;
Yet, if they press me sharply, and harry[7] me through the day,
Then look for me by moonlight,
    Watch for me by moonlight,
I'll come to thee by moonlight, though hell should bar
30   the way."

He rose upright in the stirrups. He scarce could reach
    her hand,
But she loosened her hair in the casement.[8] His face burnt
    like a brand
As the black cascade of perfume came tumbling over
    his breast;
And he kissed its waves in the moonlight,
35   (Oh, sweet black waves in the moonlight!)
Then he tugged at his rein in the moonlight, and galloped
    away to the west.

Part 2
He did not come in the dawning. He did not come at noon;
And out of the tawny sunset, before the rise of the moon,
When the road was a gypsy's ribbon, looping the
    purple moor,
40   A redcoat troop came marching—

---

7. **harry** *v.:* harass or push along.
8. **casement** *n.:* window that opens outward on hinges.

INFER

Pause at line 24. What person-to-person **conflict** might be suggested here? Who is on each side of the conflict?

_____

_____

_____

_____

_____

_____

IDENTIFY

Re-read lines 25–30. Underline the promise that the highwayman makes to the landlord's daughter. When does he say he will return?

_____

_____

_____

_____

_____

INFER

What is your impression of the highwayman's **character**? Find and circle words or passages in Part 1 that support your ideas.

PREDICT

Pause at line 48. What do you think will happen if the highwayman returns while the soldiers are still there?

_____

_____

_____

_____

_____

_____

_____

Marching—marching—
King George's men came marching, up to the old inn door.

They said no word to the landlord. They drank his ale
    instead.
But they gagged his daughter, and bound her, to the foot of
    her narrow bed.
Two of them knelt at her casement, with muskets at
45   their side!
There was death at every window;
        And hell at one dark window;
For Bess could see, through her casement, the road that _he_
    would ride.

They had tied her up to attention, with many a
    sniggering jest;
They had bound a musket beside her, with the muzzle
50   beneath her breast!
"Now, keep good watch!" and they kissed her. She heard the
    dead man say—
Look for me by moonlight;
    Watch for me by moonlight;
I'll come to thee by moonlight, though hell should bar
    the way!

She twisted her hands behind her; but all the knots
55   held good!
She writhed her hands till her fingers were wet with sweat
    or blood!
They stretched and strained in the darkness, and the hours
    crawled by like years,
Till, now, on the stroke of midnight,
    Cold, on the stroke of midnight,
The tip of one finger touched it! The trigger at least
60   was hers!

The tip of one finger touched it; she strove no more for
    the rest!
Up, she stood up to attention, with the muzzle beneath
    her breast.
She would not risk their hearing; she would not strive again;
For the road lay bare in the moonlight;
65   Blank and bare in the moonlight;
And the blood of her veins, in the moonlight, throbbed to
    her love's refrain.

INFER

Who is the dead man referred to in line 51? Why does the narrator call him a dead man?

_____

_____

_____

_____

_____

RETELL

Pause at line 66. Retell what has happened since the highwayman left the landlord's daughter (line 36).

_____

_____

_____

_____

_____

_____

_____

_____

_____

_____

_____

_____

_____

_____

_____

_____

_____

_____

_____

_____

_____

_____

_____

_____

_____

_____

_____

Tlot-tlot; tlot-tlot! Had they heard it? The horse hoofs
    ringing clear;
Tlot-tlot, tlot-tlot, in the distance? Were they deaf that they
    did not hear?
Down the ribbon of moonlight, over the brow of the hill,
70   The highwayman came riding,
        Riding, riding!
The redcoats looked to their priming![9] She stood up,
    straight and still.

Tlot-tlot, in the frosty silence! *Tlot-tlot,* in the echoing night!
Nearer he came and nearer. Her face was like a light!
Her eyes grew wide for a moment; she drew one last deep
75   breath,
Then her fingers moved in the moonlight,
        Her musket shattered the moonlight,
Shattered her breast in the moonlight and warned him—
    with her death.

He turned. He spurred to the west; he did not know
    who stood
Bowed, with her head o'er the musket, drenched with her
80   own blood!
Not till the dawn he heard it, his face grew gray to hear
How Bess, the landlord's daughter,
        The landlord's black-eyed daughter,
Had watched for her love in the moonlight, and died in the
    darkness there.

Back, he spurred like a madman, shouting a curse to
85   the sky,
With the white road smoking behind him and his rapier
    brandished high.

---

9. **priming** (prīm'iŋ) *n.:* explosive for firing a gun.

Blood-red were his spurs in the golden noon; wine-red was
    his velvet coat;
When they shot him down on the highway,
    Down like a dog on the highway,
And he lay in his blood on the highway, with the bunch of
90   lace at his throat.

And still of a winter's night, they say, when the wind is in
    the trees,
When the moon is a ghostly galleon tossed upon cloudy seas,
When the road is a ribbon of moonlight over the purple moor,
A highwayman comes riding—
95   *Riding—riding—*
A highwayman comes riding, up to the old inn door.

Over the cobbles he clatters and clangs in the dark inn yard;
He taps with his whip on the shutters, but all is locked
    and barred.
He whistles a tune to the window, and who should be
    waiting there
100 *But the landlord's black-eyed daughter,*
    Bess, the landlord's daughter,
Plaiting a dark red love knot into her long black hair.

INFER

Pause at line 90. Why does the highwayman return to the inn if he knows he might die there?

_____

_____

_____

_____

_____

FLUENCY

After you've read lines 91–102, practice them aloud until you can read smoothly and with expression. Decide how to read each line: loudly, softly, quickly, slowly, with sorrow, and so on. Look for ways to capture the powerful rhythm with your voice.

INTERPRET

Why do you think the poet included lines 91–101? What different feeling would you have about the poem if it ended at line 90?

_____

_____

_____

_____

_____

The Highwayman

SKILLS FOCUS

Literary Skills
Analyze topic and theme; understand narrative poems.

Theme Web "The Highwayman" is a **narrative poem** that tells a story about love, betrayal, and death. Complete the theme web below to help you analyze its **theme.** Fill in the side boxes first. Then, tell what you learned about "The Highwayman" by filling in the center box.

What I learned about Bess:

_____

_____

_____

What Bess's actions show about life:

_____

_____

_____

Theme

This poem showed me that

_____

_____

_____

_____

_____

_____

What I learned about the highwayman:

_____

_____

_____

What the highwayman's actions show about life:

_____

_____

_____

What I learned about Tim and the troops:

_____

_____

_____

What Tim's actions show about life:

_____

_____

_____

What I learned from the setting:

_____

_____

_____

What the setting contributes to the story:

_____

_____

_____

Skills Review

The Highwayman

COMPREHENSION

Reading Comprehension   Answer each question below.

1. Who does the highwayman ride to the inn to see?

   _____

   _____

   _____

2. Who overhears the highwayman talking to Bess?

   _____

   _____

   _____

3. Why do the redcoats come to the inn?

   _____

   _____

   _____

4. Why does Bess shoot herself?

   _____

   _____

   _____

5. What happens to the highwayman?

   _____

   _____

   _____

This selection also appears in *Elements of Literature.*

Echo and Narcissus

retold by Roger Lancelyn Green

LITERARY FOCUS: RECURRING THEMES

You can probably think of a story whose main character accomplishes something great against all odds. Chances are that you have also read a story about the power of love. Stories are told by people all over the world, and they've been told throughout history. No matter where or when in history we live, people share the same kinds of dreams, fears, and needs. That is why the same **themes**—insights about life—come up again and again in stories. A theme that occurs over and over in literature is called a **recurring theme.**

READING SKILLS: USING CONTEXT CLUES

All readers, even skilled ones, come across unfamiliar words from time to time. Skipping over these words may lead to confusion. Using a dictionary to look up every unfamiliar word you come across would soon become tiring and would slow down your reading. An easier way to figure out a word's meaning is to use **context clues,** the words and sentences that surround an unfamiliar word and help you understand what the unfamiliar word means.

As you read "Echo and Narcissus," use the questions below to help you figure out word meanings.

- Does the surrounding text give clues to the word's meaning?
- Is there a familiar word or word part within the unfamiliar word?
- How is the word used in the sentence?
- Does the meaning I've guessed make sense in the sentence?

SKILLS FOCUS

Literary Skills
Understand recurring themes.

Reading Skills
Use context clues.

Vocabulary Skills
Use context clues.

VOCABULARY DEVELOPMENT

PREVIEW SELECTION VOCABULARY

You may be unfamiliar with these words from "Echo and Narcissus."
Take a few minutes to preview the words before you begin to read.

detain (dē·tān′) *v.:* hold back; delay.

Echo was asked to detain Hera, so Hera's husband, Zeus, could wander about.

vainly (vān′lē) *adv.:* uselessly; without result.

Echo tried vainly to attract the young man's attention.

unrequited (un′ri·kwīt′id) *v.* used as *adj.:* not returned in kind.

Unfortunately, Echo's love was unrequited, for Narcissus loved only himself.

parched (pärcht) *v.* used as *adj.:* very hot and dry.

Narcissus's throat was parched, so he eagerly knelt to drink the cool water.

intently (in·tent′lē) *adv.:* with great concentration.

Narcissus gazed intently at his reflection in the pool.

USING CONTEXT CLUES

In the Reading Skills for this selection, you learned how to use **context clues** to figure out the meaning of unfamiliar words when you're reading. Context clues include *definitions, examples, restatements,* and *contrast words.* The chart below gives examples of context clues for one of your vocabulary words. The context clues are in italics.

Definition	My skin was **parched,** *dry and hot,* after the desert hike.
Example	The poor little dog must have been **parched.** He *drank his water thirstily.*
Restatement	The land was so **parched** that it wasn't fit for crops. The *dried out* soil would produce no grain this year.
Contrast	Our neighbor's lawn was **parched,** but we *watered ours regularly to keep it nice and green.*

ECHO AND NARCISSUS

retold by Roger Lancelyn Green

IDENTIFY

Pause at line 5. Underline two words that describe Echo. Circle the words that tell who Hera was.

IDENTIFY

Re-read lines 13–15. Underline the details that tell why Hera becomes angry with Echo.

VOCABULARY

detain (dē·tān') v.: hold back; delay.

INFER

Pause at line 19. Underline the punishment that Hera gives Echo. What does this punishment reveal about Hera's character?

_____

_____

_____

_____

_____

_____

Up on the wild, lonely mountains of Greece lived the Oreades,[1] the nymphs or fairies of the hills, and among them one of the most beautiful was called Echo. She was one of the most talkative, too, and once she talked too much and angered Hera, wife of Zeus, king of the gods.

When Zeus grew tired of the golden halls of Mount Olympus, the home of the immortal gods, he would come down to earth and wander with the nymphs on the mountains. Hera, however, was jealous and often came to see what he was doing. It seemed strange at first that she always met Echo, and that Echo kept her listening for hours on end to her stories and her gossip.

But at last Hera realized that Echo was doing this on purpose to **detain** her while Zeus went quietly back to Olympus as if he had never really been away.

"So nothing can stop you talking?" exclaimed Hera. "Well, Echo, I do not intend to spoil your pleasure. But from this day on, you shall be able only to repeat what other people say—and never speak unless someone else speaks first."

Hera returned to Olympus, well pleased with the punishment she had made for Echo, leaving the poor nymph to weep sadly among the rocks on the mountainside and speak only the words which her sisters and their friends shouted happily to one another.

She grew used to her strange fate after a while, but then a new misfortune befell her.

"Narcissus" (retitled "Echo and Narcissus") from *Tales the Muses Told* by Roger Lancelyn Green. Copyright © 1965 by Don Bolognese. Published by The Bodley Head. Reproduced by permission of **Random House UK Ltd.**

1. **Oreades** (ō'rē·ad'ēz).

There was a beautiful youth called Narcissus,[2] who was the son of a nymph and the god of a nearby river. He grew up in the plain of Thebes[3] until he was sixteen years old

30 and then began to hunt on the mountains toward the north where Echo and her sister Oreades lived.

As he wandered through the woods and valleys, many a nymph looked upon him and loved him. But Narcissus laughed at them scornfully, for he loved only himself.

Farther up the mountains Echo saw him. And at once her lonely heart was filled with love for the beautiful youth, so that nothing else in the world mattered but to win him.

Now she wished indeed that she could speak to him words of love. But the curse which Hera had placed upon

40 her tied her tongue, and she could only follow wherever he went, hiding behind trees and rocks, and feasting her eyes **vainly** upon him.

One day Narcissus wandered farther up the mountain than usual, and all his friends, the other Theban youths, were left far behind. Only Echo followed him, still hiding among the rocks, her heart heavy with unspoken love.

Presently Narcissus realized that he was lost, and hoping to be heard by his companions, or perhaps by some mountain shepherd, he called out loudly:

50 "Is there anybody here?"

"Here!" cried Echo.

Narcissus stood still in amazement, looking all around in vain. Then he shouted, even more loudly:

"Whoever you are, come to me!"

"Come to me!" cried Echo eagerly.

Still no one was visible, so Narcissus called again:

"Why are you avoiding me?"

---

2. **Narcissus** (när·sis′əs).
3. **Thebes** (thēbz).

WORD STUDY

Scornfully, in line 34, describes the way Narcissus laughed. Underline the **context clues** nearby that help you understand that *scornfully* means "in a way that shows contempt or disdain."

PREDICT

Pause at line 42. What do you think will happen when Echo and Narcissus meet?

_____

_____

_____

_____

_____

_____

_____

_____

_____

VOCABULARY

vainly (vān′lē) *adv.:* uselessly; without result.

FLUENCY

After you've read lines 50–65, practice reading this boxed passage aloud. Use different voices that fit the two characters and their situation.

INTERPRET

Pause at line 77. In your opinion, if Echo could speak normally, would Narcissus's opinion of her change? Explain why or why not.

_____

_____

_____

_____

_____

_____

_____

_____

_____

IDENTIFY

Re-read lines 79–83. Underline the words that tell who Aphrodite is.

IDENTIFY

Re-read lines 84–88. Underline the details that tell why Aphrodite decides to punish Narcissus. Circle the details that tell how she's going to punish him.

VOCABULARY

unrequited (un′ri·kwīt′id) *v.* used as *adj.*: not returned in kind.

Echo repeated his words, but with a sob in her breath, and Narcissus called once more:

60   "Come here, I say, and let us meet!"

"Let us meet!" cried Echo, her heart leaping with joy as she spoke the happiest words that had left her lips since the curse of Hera had fallen on her. And to make good her words, she came running out from behind the rocks and tried to clasp her arms about him.

But Narcissus flung the beautiful nymph away from him in scorn.

"Away with these embraces!" he cried angrily, his voice full of cruel contempt. "I would die before I would have

70   you touch me!"

"I would have you touch me!" repeated poor Echo.

"Never will I let you kiss me!"

"Kiss me! Kiss me!" murmured Echo, sinking down among the rocks, as Narcissus cast her violently from him and sped down the hillside.

"One touch of those lips would kill me!" he called back furiously over his shoulder.

"Kill me!" begged Echo.

And Aphrodite,[4] the goddess of love, heard her and

80   was kind to her, for she had been a true lover. Quietly and painlessly, Echo pined away and died. But her voice lived on, lingering among the rocks and answering faintly whenever Narcissus or another called.

"He shall not go unpunished for this cruelty," said Aphrodite. "By scorning poor Echo like this, he scorns love itself. And scorning love, he insults me. He is altogether eaten up with self-love . . . Well, he shall love himself and no one else, and yet shall die of **unrequited** love!"

---

4. **Aphrodite** (af′rə·dīt′ē).

It was not long before Aphrodite made good her threat, and in a very strange way. One day, tired after hunting, Narcissus came to a still, clear pool of water away up the mountainside, not far from where he had scorned Echo and left her to die of a broken heart.

With a cry of satisfaction, for the day was hot and cloudless, and he was **parched** with thirst, Narcissus flung himself down beside the pool and leaned forward to dip his face in the cool water.

What was his surprise to see a beautiful face looking up at him through the still waters of the pool. The moment he saw, he loved—and love was a madness upon him so that he could think of nothing else.

"Beautiful water nymph!" he cried. "I love you! Be mine!"

Desperately he plunged his arms into the water—but the face vanished and he touched only the pebbles at the

© Royalty-Free/CORBIS.

INFER

To whom is Narcissus speaking in lines 121–123?

_____

_____

_____

_____

_____

_____

_____

_____

IDENTIFY

"Echo and Narcissus" is an **origin myth,** a story that explains how something came to be. What two things in nature does this myth explain?

_____

_____

_____

_____

_____

_____

_____

bottom of the pool. Drawing out his arms, he gazed **intently** down and, as the water grew still again, saw once more the face of his beloved.

110   Poor Narcissus did not know that he was seeing his own reflection, for Aphrodite hid this knowledge from him—and perhaps this was the first time that a pool of water had reflected the face of anyone gazing into it.

Narcissus seemed enchanted by what he saw. He could not leave the pool, but lay by its side day after day looking at the only face in the world which he loved—and could not win—and pining just as Echo had pined.

Slowly Narcissus faded away, and at last his heart broke.

"Woe is me for I loved in vain!" he cried.

"I loved in vain!" sobbed the voice of Echo among

120   the rocks.

"Farewell, my love, farewell," were his last words, and Echo's voice broke and its whisper shivered into silence: "My love . . . farewell!"

So Narcissus died, and the earth covered his bones. But with the spring, a plant pushed its green leaves through the earth where he lay. As the sun shone on it, a bud opened and a new flower blossomed for the first time—a white circle of petals round a yellow center. The flowers grew and spread, waving in the gentle breeze which whispered among

130   them like Echo herself come to kiss the blossoms of the first Narcissus flowers.

© Royalty-Free/CORBIS.

Echo and Narcissus

Thematic Graph   Details in a story can point to its **theme.** For example, if each character in a story loses something, the theme might have something to say about how losses affect people.

One of the possible themes in "Echo and Narcissus" is stated below. Find six details in the story that support this theme. Write the supporting details in the boxes. Then, jot down other stories, poems, or films that have the same theme.

SKILLS FOCUS

Literary Skills
Analyze recurring themes.

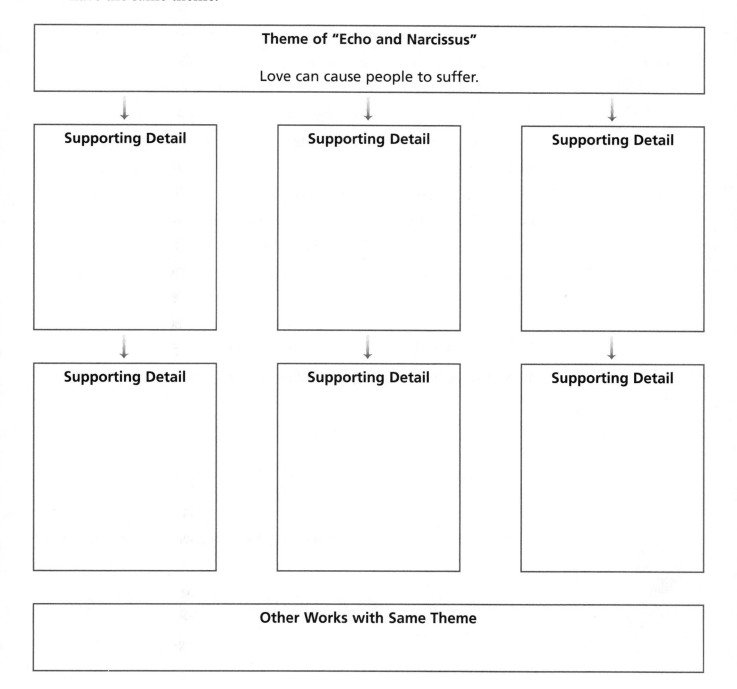

Theme of "Echo and Narcissus"

Love can cause people to suffer.

Supporting Detail

Supporting Detail

Supporting Detail

Supporting Detail

Supporting Detail

Supporting Detail

Other Works with Same Theme

Skills Review

Echo and Narcissus

VOCABULARY AND COMPREHENSION

Word Bank

detain

vainly

unrequited

parched

intently

A. Using Context Clues   Fill in the blanks of the paragraph below with words from the Word Bank. Use the context clues to help you.

Tom was asked to help (1) _____ Sacha after school. Sacha's friends were planning a surprise party and wanted him to arrive home later than usual. "Come on, Tom, I'm (2) _____ and need to get some water," said Sacha. Sacha had been in a bad mood lately, thinking that his feelings of friendship were (3) _____. After all, they had forgotten his birthday, hadn't they? Tom was (4) _____ trying to keep Sacha at school, but his efforts were wasted as Sacha raced home. Tom was just in time to see Sacha gazing (5) _____ at the crowd of friends gathered in his living room. "Thanks," he said with a gulp. "I thought you forgot all about me."

B. Reading Comprehension   Answer each question below.

1. Why does Hera punish Echo? What does she do to punish her?

   _____

   _____

2. Whom does Narcissus love? Whom does Echo love? _____

   _____

3. Why does Aphrodite make Narcissus fall in love with his own reflection?

   _____

4. According to this myth, what two reminders do we have today of

   Echo and Narcissus? _____

   _____

SKILLS FOCUS

Vocabulary Skills
Use context clues.

MYTH

Phaethon *retold by* Robert Graves

LITERARY FOCUS: THEMES AND RECURRING THEMES

Remember graduating from elementary school to middle school? You might have been a little sad to leave your old school, but you were probably also excited about moving to a new school. This is a life experience that students share around the world. These commonly shared experiences and feelings often form the bases of recurring themes. A **recurring theme** is an insight about life that is explored time and time again in literature and art. For example, in the fairy tale "Rumpelstiltskin" we learn that greed and bitterness can destroy lives. In *A Christmas Carol,* Dickens reveals a similar insight: Scrooge is a terrible person until he changes his greedy ways.

READING SKILLS: IDENTIFY CAUSE AND EFFECT

If you trained for a marathon in the same pair of running shoes every day for a year, what would happen? You'd probably injure your leg muscles and joints. The **cause** of the injuries is running in worn-out shoes. The **effect** of running in worn-out shoes is injuries.

These same kinds of cause-effect patterns can be found in stories you read. As you read "Phaethon," identify causes and effects. Ask yourself, "Why did this happen?" and "What happened because of this?" You might want to record the cause-effect patterns you find in a chart like this one.

Cause: Why did this happen?	Effect: What happened because of this?

SKILLS FOCUS

Literary Skills
Identify themes and recurring themes.

Reading Skills
Identify causes and effects.

Phaëthon

a Greek myth *retold by* Robert Graves

Helius's chariot.

IDENTIFY

Personification is a special kind of metaphor in which a nonhuman thing or quality is referred to as if it were human. In the first sentence, circle the name of the nonhuman thing that is personified as the Greek god Helius.

The Sun, whose name was Helius, owned a palace near Colchis in the Far East beyond the Black Sea. He was counted among the smaller gods, because his father had been a Titan. At cockcrow every morning, Helius harnessed four white horses to a fiery chariot—so bright that nobody could look at it without hurting his eyes—which he drove across the sky to another palace in the Far West, near the Elysian Fields.° There he unharnessed his team, and when they had grazed, loaded them and the chariot on a golden

10 ferryboat, in which he sailed, fast asleep, round the world

From "Phaëthon's Story" from *Greek Gods and Heroes* by Robert Graves. Copyright © 1957 by Robert Graves. Reproduced by permission of **Carcanet Press Limited.**

° **Elysian** (ē·lizh′ən) **Fields:** area of complete bliss; paradise.

by way of the Ocean Stream until he reached Colchis again. Helius enjoyed watching what went on in the world below, but he could never take a holiday from work.

> Phaethon, his eldest son, was constantly asking permission to drive the chariot. "Why not have a day in bed for a change, Father?" Helius always answered, "I must wait until you are a little older." Phaethon grew so impatient and bad-tempered—throwing stones at the palace windows, and pulling up the flowers in the garden—that at last
> 20 Helius said, "Very well, then, you may drive it tomorrow. But keep a firm hold of the reins. The horses are very spirited." Phaethon tried to show off before his younger sisters, and the horses, realizing that he did not know how to manage the reins, started plunging up and down. The Olympians felt icy cold one minute, and the next saw trees and grasses scorching from the heat. "Stop those stupid tricks, boy!" shouted Zeus.
>
> "My team is out of control, Your Majesty," gasped Phaethon.

30 Zeus, in disgust, threw a thunderbolt at Phaethon, and killed him. His body fell into the River Po. The little girls wept and wept. Zeus changed them to poplar trees.

FLUENCY

Read the boxed passage aloud, using different tones of voice for the three characters. You may want to use different colored highlighters to indicate dialogue.

IDENTIFY CAUSE & EFFECT

Pause at line 27. What caused the Olympians to feel these extremes of temperature?

_____

_____

_____

_____

_____

_____

INTERPRET

Circle a passage from the story that has special meaning to you. What do you think is the **theme**, or message, of this myth?

_____

_____

_____

_____

_____

Phaethon

Plot and Theme Map   One way to discover the **theme** of a story is to examine what happens and why. Draw the main story events from "Phaethon" in the boxes below. Explain the events on the lines provided. The first panel has been done for you.

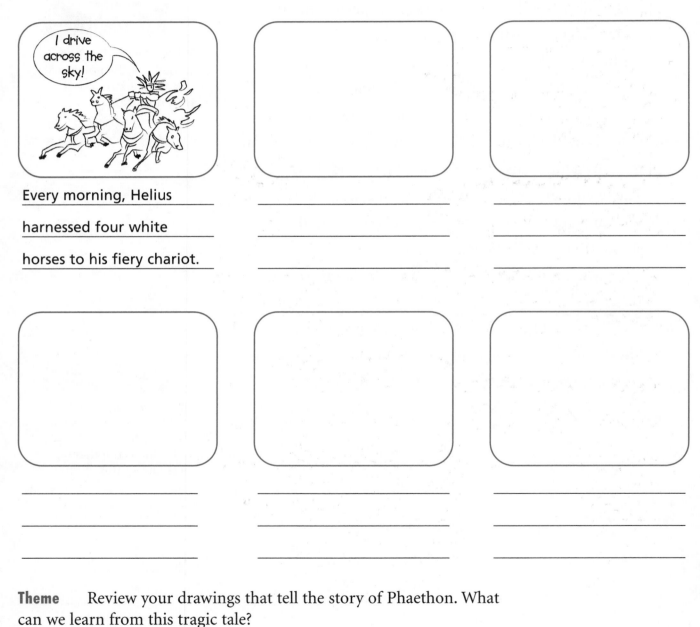

Every morning, Helius

harnessed four white

horses to his fiery chariot.

Theme   Review your drawings that tell the story of Phaethon. What can we learn from this tragic tale?

_____

_____

Skills Review

Phaethon

COMPREHENSION

Reading Comprehension   Answer each question below.

1. Who is Phaethon's father? What is his job?

_____

_____

_____

2. How does Phaethon persuade his father to let him drive the chariot?

_____

_____

_____

3. Why do the Olympians feel cold one minute and hot the next?

_____

_____

_____

4. Why does Zeus throw a thunderbolt at Phaethon?

_____

_____

_____

5. What becomes of Phaethon at the end of the story?

_____

_____

_____

Point of View:
Can You See It
My Way?

© Jeremy Browne/Getty Images.

Academic Vocabulary for Collection 4

These are the terms you should know
as you read and analyze the stories in this collection.

———

Narrator Character or voice who is narrating, or telling a story.

Point of View Vantage point from which a story is told. A story can be told from the point of view of one of its characters or from the point of view of an outsider, a person who simply observes the action.

Omniscient Point of View The all-knowing point of view, in which the narrator stands outside the action. This type of narrator can tell you everything about all the characters, even their most private thoughts.

First-Person Point of View When a story's character tells the story, we say the story is written from the first-person point of view. In this point of view we know only what the one character can tell us.

Third-Person Limited Point of View In this point of view, the narrator is not part of the story but has the ability to zoom in on the thoughts and feelings of just one story character.

• • •

Subjective Writing Type of writing in which the author shares his or her own feelings, thoughts, opinions, and judgments.

Objective Writing Unbiased writing that presents facts and figures rather than the writer's private feelings.

After Twenty Years by O. Henry

LITERARY FOCUS: OMNISCIENT POINT OF VIEW

The way a story is told depends on the **point of view,** or on *who* is telling the story. When the narrator of a story knows everything about everybody in a story, including their feelings, their pasts, and their futures, the story is being told from the **omniscient point of view.**

The paragraph below is written from the omniscient point of view. The column on the right helps you figure out why.

Story Passage	The narrator . . .
(1) The mountain climbers were overwhelmed with a sense of their own smallness. **(2)** Ravi recalled the feeling he got as a boy when his grandfather took him to see the elephants. **(3)** Ravi had conquered his fear of the elephants by riding on their backs, and **(4)** in two weeks he would stand atop the jagged ridge he now faced.	1. reveals characters' feelings 2. reveals a character's thoughts 3. reveals past events 4. reveals future events

READING SKILLS: MAKING PREDICTIONS

Nothing ruins a movie more than having someone who's seen it tell you what will happen next. Much of the fun of watching a movie or reading a story is **making predictions,** or guessing at what is going to happen.

Use the tips below to make predictions.

- Look for clues that **foreshadow,** or hint at, what will happen next.
- Predict possible outcomes. Guess where the writer is leading, and revise your predictions as you go.
- Base predictions on your personal experiences, including reading experiences.

SKILLS FOCUS

Literary Skills
Understand omniscient point of view.

Reading Skills
Make predictions.

Vocabulary Skills
Clarify word meanings by recognizing word parts.

VOCABULARY DEVELOPMENT

PREVIEW SELECTION VOCABULARY

Before beginning to read "After Twenty Years," take some time to preview these words:

habitual (hə·bich′ōō·əl) *adj.:* done or fixed by habit.

The officer made his habitual check of the buildings.

intricate (in′tri·kit) *adj.:* complicated; full of detail.

The officer twirled his club with intricate movements.

dismally (diz′məl·ē) *adv.:* miserably; gloomily.

People walked dismally through the rainy streets.

egotism (ē′gō·tiz′əm) *n.:* conceit; talking about oneself too much.

His egotism made him brag about his success.

simultaneously (sī′məl·tā′nē·əs·lē) *adv.:* at the same time.

Each man looked simultaneously at his friend's face.

CLARIFYING WORD MEANINGS: WORDS AND WORD PARTS

Many readers use strategies to figure out the meanings of unfamiliar words. One good strategy is to look for a word or word parts within the unfamiliar word for a clue to its meaning. Practice using this strategy as you read the story that follows. Here are some examples:

Unfamiliar Word	Meaning
un**controll**able	"not able to be controlled"
fashionista	"person who works in the fashion industry"
globalize	"organize or establish worldwide"

After Twenty Years

O. Henry

The policeman on the beat moved up the avenue impressively. The impressiveness was **habitual** and not for show, for spectators were few. The time was barely ten o'clock at night, but chilly gusts of wind with a taste of rain in them had well nigh depeopled the streets.

Trying doors as he went, twirling his club with many **intricate** and artful movements, turning now and then to cast his watchful eye down the pacific[1] thoroughfare, the officer, with his stalwart form and slight swagger, made a

10   fine picture of a guardian of the peace. The vicinity was one that kept early hours. Now and then you might see the lights of a cigar store or of an all-night lunch counter, but the majority of the doors belonged to business places that had long since been closed.

When about midway of a certain block, the policeman suddenly slowed his walk. In the doorway of a darkened hardware store a man leaned with an unlighted cigar in his mouth. As the policeman walked up to him, the man spoke up quickly.

20   "It's all right, officer," he said reassuringly. "I'm just waiting for a friend. It's an appointment made twenty years ago. Sounds a little funny to you, doesn't it? Well, I'll explain if you'd like to make certain it's all straight. About that long ago there used to be a restaurant where this store stands—'Big Joe' Brady's restaurant."

"Until five years ago," said the policeman. "It was torn down then."

---

1. **pacific** *adj.:* peaceful.

© Andy Sotiriou/Getty Images.

The man in the doorway struck a match and lit his
cigar. The light showed a pale, square-jawed face with keen
30 eyes and a little white scar near his right eyebrow. His scarf
pin was a large diamond, oddly set.

"Twenty years ago tonight," said the man, "I dined here
at 'Big Joe' Brady's with Jimmy Wells, my best chum and
the finest chap in the world. He and I were raised here in
New York, just like two brothers, together. I was eighteen
and Jimmy was twenty. The next morning I was to start for
the West to make my fortune. You couldn't have dragged
Jimmy out of New York; he thought it was the only place
on earth. Well, we agreed that night that we would meet
40 here again exactly twenty years from that date and time, no
matter what our conditions might be or from what distance
we might have to come. We figured that in twenty years
each of us ought to have our destiny worked out and our
fortunes made, whatever they were going to be."

IDENTIFY

Underline the words in lines
32–44 that tell about the
agreement Jimmy Wells and
the man in the doorway had
made twenty years earlier.
How old would Jimmy and
the man in the doorway be
when they met after twenty
years?

_____

_____

_____

_____

_____

_____

Notes _____

_____

_____

_____

_____

_____

_____

_____

PREDICT

Pause at line 72. Will Jimmy show up for the appointment? Explain your reasoning.

_____

_____

_____

_____

_____

_____

_____

_____

_____

_____

_____

_____

_____

_____

_____

_____

_____

_____

_____

_____

_____

"It sounds pretty interesting," said the policeman. "Rather a long time between meets, though, it seems to me. Haven't you heard from your friend since you left?"

"Well, yes, for a time we corresponded," said the other. "But after a year or two we lost track of each other. You see, the West is a pretty big proposition, and I kept hustling around over it pretty lively. But I know Jimmy will meet me here if he's alive, for he always was the truest, staunchest old chap in the world. He'll never forget. I came a thousand miles to stand in this door tonight, and it's worth it if my old partner turns up."

The waiting man pulled out a handsome watch, the lids of it set with small diamonds.

"Three minutes to ten," he announced. "It was exactly ten o'clock when we parted here at the restaurant door."

"Did pretty well out West, didn't you?" asked the policeman.

"You bet! I hope Jimmy has done half as well. He was a kind of plodder, though, good fellow as he was. I've had to compete with some of the sharpest wits going to get my pile. A man gets in a groove in New York. It takes the West to put a razor edge on him."

The policeman twirled his club and took a step or two.

"I'll be on my way. Hope your friend comes around all right. Going to call time on him sharp?"

"I should say not!" said the other. "I'll give him half an hour at least. If Jimmy is alive on earth, he'll be here by that time. So long, officer."

"Good night, sir," said the policeman, passing on along his beat, trying doors as he went.

There was now a fine, cold drizzle falling, and the wind had risen from its uncertain puffs into a steady blow. The few foot passengers astir in that quarter hurried **dismally**

VOCABULARY

dismally (diz′məl·ē) _adv._: miserably; gloomily.

and silently along with coat collars turned high and pocketed hands. And in the door of the hardware store the man
who had come a thousand miles to fill an appointment, uncertain almost to absurdity, with the friend of his youth, smoked his cigar and waited.

About twenty minutes he waited, and then a tall man in a long overcoat, with collar turned up to his ears, hurried across from the opposite side of the street. He went directly to the waiting man.

80

"Is that you, Bob?" he asked, doubtfully.

"Is that you, Jimmy Wells?" cried the man in the door.

"Bless my heart!" exclaimed the new arrival, grasping both the other's hands with his own. "It's Bob, sure as fate. I was certain I'd find you here if you were still in existence. Well, well, well!—twenty years is a long time. The old restaurant's gone, Bob; I wish it had lasted, so we could have had another dinner there. How has the West treated you, old man?"

90

"Bully;[2] it has given me everything I asked it for. You've changed lots, Jimmy. I never thought you were so tall by two or three inches."

"Oh, I grew a bit after I was twenty."

"Doing well in New York, Jimmy?"

100

"Moderately. I have a position in one of the city departments. Come on, Bob; we'll go around to a place I know of and have a good long talk about old times."

The two men started up the street, arm in arm. The man from the West, his **egotism** enlarged by success, was beginning to outline the history of his career. The other, submerged in his overcoat, listened with interest.

At the corner stood a drugstore, brilliant with electric lights. When they came into this glare, each of them turned **simultaneously** to gaze upon the other's face.

110

---

2. **bully** *interj.:* informal term meaning "very well."

FLUENCY

Imagine you're trying out for the part of narrator on a TV program presenting this story. Read the boxed passage aloud several times. Pause at each comma; stop at each period. Decide where to read slowly and where to speed up a little so you get the most meaning from the words. Practice until you can read this passage smoothly and effectively.

IDENTIFY

Re-read lines 96–98. What clues in this passage tell you that Bob may be in for a surprise? Underline them.

_____

_____

_____

_____

_____

_____

_____

_____

VOCABULARY

egotism (ē′gō·tiz′əm) *n.:* conceit; talking about oneself too much.

simultaneously (sī′məl·tā′nē·əs·lē) *adv.:* at the same time.

Underline the detail in lines 113–115 that proves to Bob he has been tricked.

Look back over the story and circle three clues **fore-shadowing** that Bob might be a criminal. Put an F next to each circle.

What is unexpected about the ending of the story? In your opinion, was it okay for Jimmy Wells to have his old friend Bob arrested? Tell why or why not.

_____

_____

_____

_____

_____

_____

_____

_____

_____

_____

_____

_____

_____

The man from the West stopped suddenly and released his arm.

"You're not Jimmy Wells," he snapped. "Twenty years is a long time, but not long enough to change a man's nose from a Roman to a pug."

"It sometimes changes a good man into a bad one," said the tall man. "You've been under arrest for ten minutes, 'Silky' Bob. Chicago thinks you may have dropped over our way and wires us she wants to have a chat with you. Going

120   quietly, are you? That's sensible. Now, before we go to the station, here's a note I was asked to hand to you. You may read it here at the window. It's from Patrolman Wells."

The man from the West unfolded the little piece of paper handed him. His hand was steady when he began to read, but it trembled a little by the time he had finished. The note was rather short.

Bob: I was at the appointed place on time. When you struck the match to light your cigar, I saw it was the face of the man wanted in Chicago. Somehow I couldn't do

130   it myself, so I went around and got a plainclothes man to do the job.

Jimmy

After Twenty Years

Point of View Questionnaire   This story is told by an **omniscient narrator** who knows all the story's secrets. Complete the questionnaire to examine the way the point of view affects the theme of "After Twenty Years."

Literary Skills
Analyze point of view.

---

1. What pronouns does the narrator use to describe the story's characters?

_____

_____

---

2. Does the narrator reveal the inner thoughts of any of the characters? Explain.

_____

_____

---

3. How might this story differ if it were told by the policeman? List at least three points of difference, including what you would know and what you would not know.

   • _____

   • _____

   • _____

---

4. How might this story be different if it were told from Silky Bob's point of view? List at least three points of difference, including what you would know and what you would not know.

   • _____

   • _____

   • _____

---

5. Think of the story's theme—what it reveals about life. How could a different point of view affect the theme?

_____

_____

Skills Review

After Twenty Years

VOCABULARY AND COMPREHENSION

A. Clarifying Word Meanings: Words and Word Parts Match words and definitions. Write the letter of the correct definition next to each word. Then, circle familiar word parts in the Word Bank words. (Not all words will contain familiar word parts.)

_____ **1.** habitual   **a.** miserably; gloomily

_____ **2.** intricate   **b.** at the same time

_____ **3.** dismally   **c.** done or fixed by habit; customary

_____ **4.** egotism   **d.** complicated; full of detail

_____ **5.** simultaneously   **e.** conceit; talking about oneself too much

B. Reading Comprehension Write **T** or **F** next to each statement to tell if it is true or false.

_____ **1.** The night was chilly, and the streets were empty.

_____ **2.** Jimmy and Bob had been writing to each other for twenty years.

_____ **3.** The two friends planned to meet at 10 P.M.

_____ **4.** Jimmy didn't want to leave New York.

_____ **5.** Bob didn't recognize Jimmy when he saw him.

SKILLS FOCUS

Vocabulary Skills
Clarify word meanings by recognizing word parts.

This selection also appears in *Elements of Literature.*

Names/Nombres by Julia Alvarez

LITERARY FOCUS: SUBJECTIVE OR OBJECTIVE POINT OF VIEW?

Nonfiction writing can be described in the following ways: **Subjective writing** expresses personal feelings, thoughts, opinions, and judgments of the writer. **Objective writing,** on the other hand, sticks to the facts. It presents information in an unbiased manner. Writers may combine subjective and objective details within the same text. It's your job to figure out which statements are subjective and which are objective.

Take a look at these passages, and identify them as examples of either subjective or objective writing.

Passage	Point of View	
McPhee Tower, built in 1949, burned to the ground Thursday morning. Investigators say the fire was caused by an electrical short in the building's wiring.	Subjective	❐
	Objective	❐
Although some would disagree with me, I have to say that science writing is the most rewarding career a person could choose. No other job can compare.	Subjective	❐
	Objective	❐

READING SKILLS: DISCOVERING THE MAIN IDEA

The **main idea** is the central idea that a writer wants you to remember. All the important ideas in a text should add up to the main idea. Sometimes the main idea is **implied,** or suggested, by details rather than clearly stated. In such cases, you must **infer,** or guess at, the main idea that the writer wants you to understand.

Use these tips to help you infer the main idea.
- Identify the important details.
- Think about the point that the details make.
- State the main idea in your own words.

SKILLS FOCUS

Literary Skills
Understand objective and subjective points of view.

Reading Skills
Find the main idea.

Vocabulary Skills
Clarify word meanings by using definitions.

VOCABULARY DEVELOPMENT

PREVIEW SELECTION VOCABULARY

You may be unfamiliar with these vocabulary words. Take a few minutes to preview the words before you read "Names/Nombres."

ethnicity (eth·nis′ə·tē) *n.:* common culture or nationality.

Julia's ethnicity was important to her friends.

exotic (eg·zät′ik) *adj.:* foreign; not native.

At her graduation party, Julia's family served exotic dishes.

heritage (her′ə·tij) *n.:* traditions that are passed along.

Julia remained proud of her Dominican heritage.

convoluted (kän′və·loot′id) *adj.:* complicated.

The grammar of a new language often seems convoluted.

CLARIFYING WORD MEANINGS: USING DEFINITIONS

If you look closely, you can sometimes find the definition of a difficult word right in the passage containing the word. Be on the lookout for such phrases as *in other words* and *that is* when looking for definitions in context.

The italicized passages in the following sentences provide definitions of the boldface words:

- My friends all wondered if I were an **immigrant.** They seemed sure I had *come to the United States from another country.*
- By Dominican custom my full name includes the **surnames,** *or last names,* of my father and mother for four generations back.
- My sister's name didn't **translate** into English; in other words, there was simply no way to *restate it in another language.*

Names / Nombres

Julia Alvarez

© Royalty-Free/CORBIS.

When we arrived in New York City, our names changed almost immediately. At Immigration, the officer asked my father, *Mister Elbures,* if he had anything to declare. My father shook his head no, and we were waved through. I was too afraid we wouldn't be let in if I corrected the man's pronunciation, but I said our name to myself, opening my mouth wide for the organ blast of the *a,* trilling my tongue for the drumroll of the *r, All-vah-rrr-es!* How could anyone get *Elbures* out of that orchestra of sound?

10   At the hotel my mother was Missus Alburest, and I was *little girl,* as in, "Hey, little girl, stop riding the elevator up and down. It's *not* a toy."

    When we moved into our new apartment building, the super called my father *Mister Alberase,* and the neighbors who became mother's friends pronounced her name *Jew-lee-ah* instead of *Hoo-lee-ah.* I, her namesake, was

> **INFER**
>
> Pause at line 9. How does Julia feel when the officer mispronounces her father's name?
>
> _____
> _____
> _____
> _____
> _____
> _____
> _____
> _____
> _____
> _____
> _____

IDENTIFY

Re-read lines 19–25. Describe how Julia and her mother react to Julia's new names.

_____

_____

_____

_____

_____

_____

_____

_____

IDENTIFY

Re-read lines 26–35. How does the author feel about being called Judy Alcatraz? Would you classify this essay as an example of **subjective writing** or **objective writing**? Explain.

_____

_____

_____

_____

_____

_____

_____

_____

known as *Hoo-lee-tah* at home. But at school I was *Judy* or *Judith*, and once an English teacher mistook me for *Juliet*.

It took a while to get used to my new names. I won-
20   dered if I shouldn't correct my teachers and new friends. But my mother argued that it didn't matter. "You know what your friend Shakespeare said, '*A rose by any other name would smell as sweet.*'"[1] My family had gotten into the habit of calling any famous author "my friend" because I had begun to write poems and stories in English class.

By the time I was in high school, I was a popular kid, and it showed in my name. Friends called me *Jules* or *Hey Jude*, and once a group of troublemaking friends my mother forbade me to hang out with called me *Alcatraz*. I was *Hoo-*
30   *lee-tah* only to Mami and Papi and uncles and aunts who came over to eat sancocho[2] on Sunday afternoons—old world folk whom I would just as soon go back to where they came from and leave me to pursue whatever mischief I wanted to in America. *JUDY ALCATRAZ*, the name on the "Wanted" poster would read. Who would ever trace her to me?

My older sister had the hardest time getting an Amer-ican name for herself because *Mauricia* did not translate into English. Ironically, although she had the most foreign-sounding name, she and I were the Americans in the family.
40   We had been born in New York City when our parents had first tried immigration and then gone back "home," too homesick to stay. My mother often told the story of how she had almost changed my sister's name in the hospital.

After the delivery, Mami and some other new mothers were cooing over their new baby sons and daughters and exchanging names and weights and delivery stories. My

---

1. **"A rose . . . as sweet":** Julia's mother is quoting from the play *Romeo and Juliet.*
2. **sancocho** (sän·kō′chō) *adj.:* stew of meats and fruit.

mother was embarrassed among the Sallys and Janes and Georges and Johns to reveal the rich, noisy name of *Mauricia,* so when her turn came to brag, she gave her baby's name as *Maureen.*

"Why'd ya give her an Irish name with so many pretty Spanish names to choose from?" one of the women asked.

My mother blushed and admitted her baby's real name to the group. Her mother-in-law had recently died, she apologized, and her husband had insisted that the first daughter be named after his mother, *Mauran.* My mother thought it the ugliest name she had ever heard, and she talked my father into what she believed was an improvement, a combination of *Mauran* and her own mother's name, *Felicia.*

"Her name is *Mao-ree-shee-ah,*" my mother said to the group of women.

"Why, that's a beautiful name," the new mothers cried. "*Moor-ee-sha, Moor-ee-sha,*" they cooed into the pink blanket. *Moor-ee-sha* it was when we returned to the States eleven years later. Sometimes, American tongues found even that mispronunciation tough to say and called her *Maria* or *Marsha* or *Maudy* from her nickname *Maury.* I pitied her. What an awful name to have to transport across borders!

My little sister, Ana, had the easiest time of all. She was plain *Anne*—that is, only her name was plain, for she turned out to be the pale, blond "American beauty" in the family. The only Hispanic thing about her was the affectionate nicknames her boyfriends sometimes gave her. *Anita,* or, as one goofy guy used to sing to her to the tune of the banana advertisement, *Anita Banana.*

Later, during her college years in the late sixties, there was a push to pronounce Third World[3] names correctly. I remember calling her long distance at her group house and a roommate answering.

---

3. **Third World:** developing countries of Latin America, Africa, and Asia.

IDENTIFY

Re-read lines 51–68. What point is the author making in this passage?

_____

_____

_____

_____

_____

_____

_____

FLUENCY

After you've read this passage about Mauricia's name, read it again aloud. See if you can make your voice show the feelings of Julia's mother and the other mothers. When you get to the different spellings of *Mauricia,* pronounce them the way they're spelled out.

_____

_____

_____

_____

_____

_____

IDENTIFY

Pause at line 83. How is Julia's sister Ana different from the others in the family? List two ways.

_____

_____

_____

_____

_____

_____

_____

IDENTIFY

Julia says that, at first, she wanted to be known by her correct Dominican name. Underline the details that tell why she changed her mind (lines 84–91).

_____

_____

_____

_____

_____

_____

_____

VOCABULARY

ethnicity (eth·nis′ə·tē) *n.*: common culture or nationality.

Julia Alvarez.

80   "Can I speak to Ana?" I asked, pronouncing her name the American way.

"Ana?" The man's voice hesitated. "Oh! You must mean *Ah-nah*!"

Our first few years in the States, though, **ethnicity** was not yet "in." Those were the blond, blue-eyed, bobby-sock years of junior high and high school before the sixties ushered in peasant blouses, hoop earrings, serapes.[4] My initial desire to be known by my correct Dominican name faded. I just wanted to be Judy and merge with the Sallys and Janes

90   in my class. But, inevitably, my accent and coloring gave me away. "So where are you from, Judy?"

"New York," I told my classmates. After all, I had been born blocks away at Columbia-Presbyterian Hospital.

"I mean, *originally*."

"From the Caribbean," I answered vaguely, for if I specified, no one was quite sure on what continent our island was located.

4. **serapes** (sə·rä′pēs) *n.*: woolen shawls worn in Latin American countries.

"Really? I've been to Bermuda. We went last April for spring vacation. I got the worst sunburn! So, are you from Portoriko?"

"No," I sighed. "From the Dominican Republic."

"Where's that?"

"South of Bermuda."

They were just being curious, I knew, but I burned with shame whenever they singled me out as a "foreigner," a rare, **exotic** friend.

"Say your name in Spanish, oh, please say it!" I had made mouths drop one day by rattling off my full name, which, according to Dominican custom, included my middle names, Mother's and Father's surnames for four generations back.

"Julia Altagracia María Teresa Álvarez Tavares Perello Espaillat Julia Pérez Rochet González." I pronounced it slowly, a name as chaotic with sounds as a Middle Eastern bazaar or market day in a South American village.

My Dominican **heritage** was never more apparent than when my extended family attended school occasions. For my graduation, they all came, the whole lot of aunts and uncles and the many little cousins who snuck in without tickets. They sat in the first row in order to better understand the Americans' fast-spoken English. But how could they listen when they were constantly speaking among themselves in florid-sounding[5] phrases, rococo[6] consonants, rich, rhyming vowels?

Introducing them to my friends was a further trial to me. These relatives had such complicated names and there were so many of them, and their relationships to myself were so **convoluted.** There was my Tía[7] Josefina, who was

---

5. **florid-sounding:** flowery; using fancy words.
6. **rococo** (rə·kō′kō) *adj.:* fancy. Rococo is an early-eighteenth-century style of art and architecture known for its fancy ornamentation.
7. **Tía** (tē′ä) *n.:* Spanish for "aunt." *Tío* is "uncle."

INTERPRET

Why do you think Julia deliberately misspells *Puerto Rico* (line 100)?

_____

_____

_____

VOCABULARY

exotic (eg·zät′ik) *adj.:* foreign; not native.

heritage (her′ə·tij) *n.:* traditions that are passed along.

convoluted (kän′və·loot′id) *adj.:* complicated.

INFER

In what way is Julia's family different from the families of her friends? How does she feel about the relatives who come to her graduation (lines 116–133)?

_____

_____

_____

_____

_____

_____

_____

not really an aunt but a much older cousin. And her daughter, Aida Margarita, who was adopted, una hija de crianza.[8] My uncle of affection, Tío José, brought my madrina[9] Tía Amelia and her comadre[10] Tía Pilar. My friends rarely had more than a "Mom and Dad" to introduce.

After the commencement ceremony, my family waited outside in the parking lot while my friends and I signed yearbooks with nicknames which recalled our high school good times: "Beans" and "Pepperoni" and "Alcatraz." We hugged and cried and promised to keep in touch.

Our goodbyes went on too long. I heard my father's voice calling out across the parking lot, "*Hoo-lee-tah!* Vámonos!"[11]

Back home, my tíos and tías and primas,[12] Mami and Papi, and mis hermanas[13] had a party for me with sancocho and a store-bought pudín,[14] inscribed with *Happy Graduation, Julie.* There were many gifts—that was a plus to a large family! I got several wallets and a suitcase with my initials and a graduation charm from my godmother and money from my uncles. The biggest gift was a portable typewriter from my parents for writing my stories and poems.

Someday, the family predicted, my name would be well-known throughout the United States. I laughed to myself, wondering which one I would go by.

---

8. **una hija de crianza** (o͞o′nä ē′hä de krē·än′sä): Spanish for "an adopted daughter." *Crianza* means "upbringing."
9. **madrina** (mä·drē′nä) *n.:* Spanish for "godmother."
10. **comadre** (kô·mä′drä) *n.:* informal Spanish for "close friend." *Comadre* is the name used by the mother and the godmother of a child for each other.
11. **Vámonos!** (vä′mô·nôs): Spanish for "Let's go!"
12. **primas** (prē′mäs) *n.:* Spanish for "female cousins."
13. **mis hermanas** (mēs er·mä′näs): Spanish for "my sisters."
14. **pudín** (po͞o·dēn′) *n.:* Spanish cake.

Names/Nombres

Main Idea Chart   Fill in the following chart with details from "Names/Nombres." Then, review those details and identify the **main idea** of the essay.

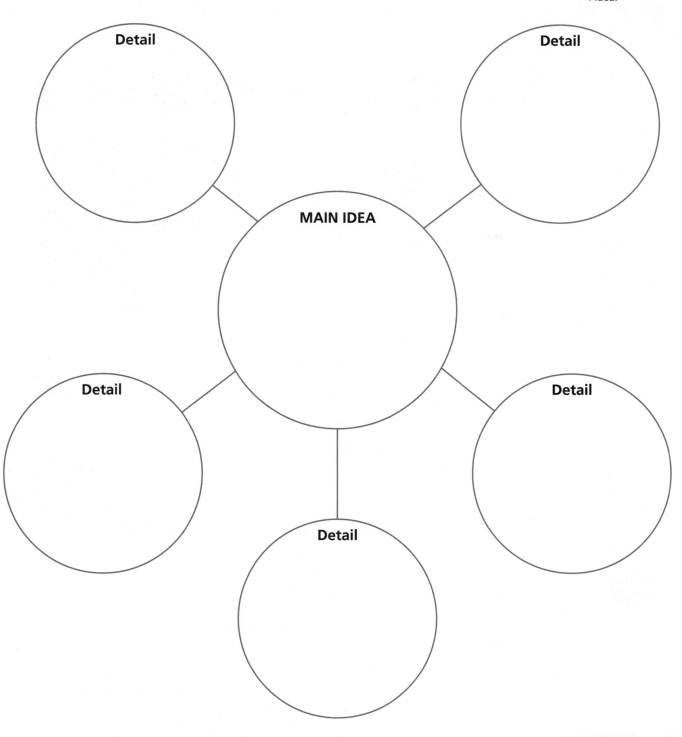

Detail

Detail

MAIN IDEA

Detail

Detail

Detail

Skills Review

Names/Nombres

VOCABULARY AND COMPREHENSION

Word Bank

ethnicity
exotic
heritage
convoluted

A. Clarifying Word Meanings: Using Definitions Read each sentence carefully. Then, within each sentence, locate and underline the definition of the boldface word.

1. Eli's sister wears **exotic** perfumes—those that come from a foreign country.

2. The first chapter of this novel is very **convoluted.** To state it more plainly: The chapter was very complicated and hard to read.

3. Can you describe your cultural **heritage,** your family traditions, for me?

4. When applying for a job, you do not have to reveal your **ethnicity,** or cultural background, unless you want to.

B. Reading Comprehension Answer each question below.

1. Who is the narrator of "Names/Nombres"? _____

_____

2. Where was Julia born? _____

_____

3. Where is Julia's family from? _____

_____

4. Why do Julia's friends ask her to say her name in Spanish? _____

_____

5. Why does Julia's family predict that someday her name will be well-

known throughout the United States? _____

_____

SKILLS FOCUS

Vocabulary Skills
Clarify word meanings by using definitions.

Thanksgiving with the Conners

by Lensey Namioka

LITERARY FOCUS: POINT OF VIEW

When a story's narrator is a character in the story who tells about his or her personal thoughts, feelings, and experiences, we say the story is told from the first-person point of view. In the **first-person point of view,** a narrator uses the pronouns *I, me, my,* and *mine* to refer to himself or herself. The boldface words in the following passage are clues that it's written from a first-person point of view.

> Example: Just as the band turned the corner in front of the judges' stand, one of the baton twirlers tripped. Her baton sailed wildly toward the back of the band, and she crashed headlong into the drum major. **I** didn't know whether to laugh or cry. **I** bit down so hard on **my** saxophone mouthpiece that **my** reed split in two.

READING SKILLS: MAKING INFERENCES

Writers don't usually tell you everything about every character in a story. You have to make educated guesses, or **inferences,** based on your own experiences and on what the writer *does* tell you. Read the following passage, and look at three inferences you could make based on its details.

Yannis rolled his eyes when Deborah asked to go with him to the movie for the third time.		
	Sample Inferences	
Deborah has a crush on Yannis.	Yannis doesn't want Deborah's company.	Deborah drives Yannis crazy.

As you read "Thanksgiving with the Conners," pay attention to the characters' reactions to conversation around the dinner table. Then, make inferences about what the characters are thinking.

SKILLS FOCUS

Literary Skills
Understand first-person point of view.

Reading Skills
Make inferences.

Vocabulary Skills
Clarify word meanings by using context clues.

VOCABULARY DEVELOPMENT

PREVIEW SELECTION VOCABULARY

Take a few minutes to preview these words before you read "Thanksgiving with the Conners."

aggressive (ə·gres′iv) *adj.:* inclined to start fights or quarrels.

> *The dress's huge shoulder pads made even my slender mother look aggressive.*

savory (sā′vər·ē) *adj.:* delicious to taste or smell.

> *Our plates held a savory combination of turkey, stuffing, and cranberry sauce.*

winced (winst) *v.:* drew back, with a facial expression of pain or embarrassment.

> *I winced when Mother asked our hostess how old she was.*

disgracing (dis·grās′iŋ) *v.:* bringing shame or dishonor upon.

> *I was worried that we were disgracing ourselves because we didn't know American customs.*

determination (dē·tʉr′min·ā′shən) *n.:* firmness of purpose.

> *My brother was small compared with the other boys on the baseball team, but he made up for it with sheer determination.*

CLARIFYING WORD MEANINGS: CONTEXT CLUES

You can often figure out what an unfamiliar word means by the context in which it is used. Context clues can be in the form of *definitions, examples, restatements,* and *contrast words.* Here's an example of how context clues can help clarify the meaning of an unfamiliar word. The context clues are in italics.

DEFINITION: **Aggressive** people, *those people who tend to fight a lot,* don't make the best friends.

EXAMPLE: If you *continually argue* with the coach, she might begin to think you're too **aggressive.**

RESTATEMENT: You are too **aggressive.** You *fight too much* with the others in our classroom.

CONTRAST: Our debate team is **aggressive,** but our team captain is so *mild mannered* that he never gets into arguments.

Thanksgiving with the Conners

Lensey Namioka

BEFORE YOU READ

This story is from Lensey Namioka's collection of stories called *Yang the Third and Her Impossible Family.* The story has a first-person narrator, Yingmei, who calls the children in the family by their traditional Chinese family names ("Fourth Brother" and "Eldest Brother"). This story is about the cultural differences that cause conflict when the narrator's family attends their first American Thanksgiving Day dinner.

"The Conners are inviting us for Thanksgiving dinner!" yelled Fourth Brother as he hung up the phone.

The Conners are our neighbors here in Seattle, and Matthew Conner is Fourth Brother's best friend. He takes violin lessons from Father, and he also plays in our family string quartet.

Eldest Brother plays first violin, and Second Sister plays viola. I'm the third sister in the Yang family, and I play cello. Fourth Brother plays baseball. He has a terrible ear, and he was relieved when Matthew took his place as the second violin.

We were all happy about the invitation. For weeks, we had been hearing about the American holiday called Thanksgiving. Since coming to this country, we have tried our best to do everything properly, but when Mother heard

IDENTIFY

Pause at line 11. Who is telling the story? Underline the sentence that tells you something about the narrator. Then, circle the words that reveal that the story is told from the **first-person point of view.** Put a box around the phrase that tells you where the story is set.

_____

_____

_____

_____

_____

_____

"Thanksgiving with the Conners" from *Yang the Third and Her Impossible Family* by Lensey Namioka. Copyright © 1995 by **Lensey Namioka.** All rights reserved. Reproduced by permission of the author.

that preparing a Thanksgiving dinner involved roasting a turkey, she was horrified.

"I can't even roast a pigeon," she cried. "If I tried to wrestle with a turkey, I'd lose!"

We didn't have an oven in China. Almost nobody does. If you want a roast duck or chicken, you buy it already cooked in the store—sometimes chopped into bite-size pieces. When Mother saw the big box under the stove in our Seattle kitchen, she didn't know what it was at first. Even now, months later, she was still nervous about the black cavity and thought of it as a chamber of horrors.

Now we'd learn how real Americans celebrate Thanksgiving. We'd get a delicious meal, like the ones I had seen illustrated in all the papers and magazines.

What excited me most was hearing that Holly Hanson and her mother were invited, too. Holly was in the school orchestra with me. She played in the viola section, so I didn't get a chance to talk to her much. But I really wanted to.

When I was little, we had a tin candy box, and on the lid was the picture of a princess with curly blond hair. Holly Hanson looked just like the princess in that picture. She was in a couple of my classes in school, and she always spoke in a soft, unhurried way. I thought that if the princess on the candy box spoke, she would sound just like that.

At the Conners' I would finally get a chance to get acquainted with Holly. But I was nervous, too, because I wanted so much to have my family make a good impression.

When Thanksgiving Day came, the whole Yang family showed up at the Conners' exactly at two o'clock. We'd thought two was a strange time for a dinner party, but

Matthew explained that since people stuff themselves
50 at Thanksgiving, eating early gives everybody a chance
to digest.

We all tried to look our best for the dinner. Father had
on the dark suit he wore for playing in public. Instead of
her usual cotton slacks and shirt, Mother wore a dress she
had bought at the Goodwill store for three dollars. It was a
very nice dress, but on her slender figure, the huge shoulder
pads made her look like a stranger—an **aggressive** stranger.

Eldest Brother wore a suit, too. Second Sister and I
wore skirts, and Fourth Brother had on his clean blue jeans.
60 I hoped we'd all look presentable when we met Holly and
her mother.

Mrs. Hanson and Holly arrived a few minutes after we
did, and we were introduced. My parents had told us we
should all shake hands with the Hansons. Mrs. Hanson
looked a little startled when six Yang hands were extended
toward her. Although our etiquette book clearly said shaking hands is the polite thing to do, I decided that in
America, children don't usually do it.

Except for that, things seemed to be going pretty well.
70 The dining table looked beautiful, with china plates and tall
wine glasses—even for the young people, who drank juice.
I carefully studied the way the knives, forks, and spoons
were set.

I was delighted when Mrs. Conner seated me next to
Holly, but the only thing I could think to say was "I've seen
you in the orchestra."

It sounded stupid as soon as I'd said it, but Holly just
nodded and murmured something.

The dinner began with Mr. Conner saying some
80 words of thanks for his family's good fortune. It was like
a toast at a Chinese banquet, and I thought he sounded
very dignified.

COMPARE &
CONTRAST

Underline the words in lines
52–57 that describe what the
narrator thinks of her mother's dress. How do you think
her mother thinks she looks?

_____

_____

_____

_____

_____

VOCABULARY

aggressive (ə·gres′iv) adj.:
inclined to start fights or
quarrels.

IDENTIFY

What reasons does the
narrator give for the Yang
children's behavior as they
are introduced (lines 62–68)?
Underline those reasons.

INFER

Pause at line 78. If the
narrator could reveal
Holly's thoughts, what
might those thoughts be?

_____

_____

_____

_____

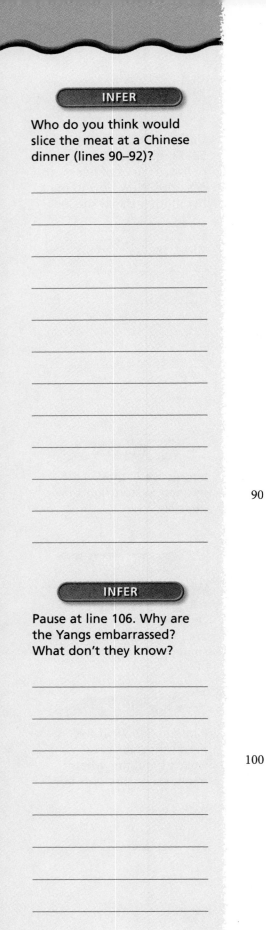

INFER

Who do you think would slice the meat at a Chinese dinner (lines 90–92)?

_____

_____

_____

_____

_____

_____

_____

_____

_____

_____

INFER

Pause at line 106. Why are the Yangs embarrassed? What don't they know?

_____

_____

_____

_____

_____

_____

_____

_____

_____

© Brand X Pictures/Getty Images.

Mrs. Conner carried the whole roast turkey into the dining room on a platter, and we all exclaimed at the size of the turkey. It was the largest bird I had ever seen, dead or alive.

Mr. Conner began sharpening a wicked-looking knife. Then he took up the knife and a big fork, and began to cut thin slices of meat from the bird.

90 We Yangs looked at one another in wonder. Instead of complaining about being made to do the slicing, Mr. Conner looked pleased and proud.

After slicing a pile of turkey meat, Mr. Conner started to scoop from the stomach of the bird. I was horrified. Had Mrs. Conner forgotten to dress the turkey and left all the guts behind?

Chicken is an expensive treat in China. When Mother wanted to boil or stir-fry a chicken, she had to buy the bird live to make sure it was fresh. Killing, plucking, and dress-

100 ing the chicken was a gruesome job, and Mother hated it. The worst part was pulling all the guts out of the stomach. Sometimes, when the bird was a hen, she would even find a cluster of eggs inside.

Watching Mr. Conner scooping away, I was embarrassed for him. I exchanged glances with the rest of my family, and I could see that they were dismayed, too.

To my astonishment—and relief—what Mr. Conner scooped out was not the messy intestines. Mrs. Conner had not forgotten to dress the bird after all. She had stuffed the stomach of the bird with a **savory** mixture of bread and onions!

We gasped with admiration, and Mrs. Conner looked pleased. "I hope you like the stuffing. I'm trying out a new recipe."

Mr. Conner placed some slices of turkey meat on each plate, then added a spoonful of the stuffing mixture. Next he ladled a brown sauce over everything. He passed the first plate to Mother.

"Oh, I couldn't take this," Mother said politely. She passed the plate on to Mrs. Hanson.

Mrs. Hanson was jammed up against Mother's shoulder pad at the crowded table. She passed the plate back to Mother. "Oh, no, it's meant for you, Mrs. Yang."

Mother handed the plate back again. "You're so much older, Mrs. Hanson, so you should be served first."

Mrs. Hanson froze. In the silence, I could hear the sauce going *drip, drip* from Mr. Conner's ladle.

"What makes you think so?" asked Mrs. Hanson stiffly. "Just what makes you think I'm older?"

"Mom, let's skip it," Holly whispered.

I had already learned that in America it isn't considered an honor to be old. Instead of respecting older people, as we do, Americans think it is pitiful to be old. Mrs. Hanson must have thought that Mother was trying to insult her. Would Mother say something else embarrassing?

She didn't disappoint me. "Well, how old are you, then?" Mother asked Mrs. Hanson.

I **winced.** In school, I had once asked a friend how old our teacher was. We do this a lot. When we meet a stranger,

VOCABULARY

savory (sā′vər·ē) *adj.*: delicious to taste or smell.

CONNECT

Pause at line 135. Why is it important that the narrator explain this information to readers?

_____

_____

_____

_____

_____

_____

_____

_____

_____

_____

_____

_____

_____

_____

_____

_____

VOCABULARY

winced (winst) *v.*: drew back, with a facial expression of pain or embarrassment.

DECODING TIP

Circle the word *whuffling* (line 148). *Whuffling* is an example of **onomatopoeia**, a word that sounds like what it is. If you say *whuffling* aloud with a lot of breath and force behind it, you will have an idea of what *whuffling* sounds like.

IDENTIFY

Re-read lines 152–153. What does the narrator reveal here? How does this information make you feel about her?

_____

_____

_____

_____

_____

_____

_____

_____

_____

_____

_____

_____

_____

_____

_____

_____

140 we often ask him how old he is. My friend told me, however, that in America it's rude to ask people's ages. I was really grateful to her for the warning.

After Mother's question, Mrs. Hanson sat completely still. "I am thirty-six," she replied finally, each syllable falling like a chunk of ice.

"Oh, really?" said Mother brightly. "You look much older!"

A whuffling sound came from Matthew and his brother, Eric. Unable to look at the Hansons, I stole a glance at

150 Mr. Conner. His face was bright red, and he seemed to be having trouble breathing. Mrs. Conner was bent over, as if in pain. I looked down at my plate and wished I could disappear.

Somehow, the dinner went on. Mrs. Hanson finally unclenched her jaw and told Mrs. Conner how delicious the cranberry sauce was. I figured she was referring to the red sticky mound of poisonous-looking berries. I put a berry in my mouth and almost gagged at its sour taste. Next to me, Fourth Brother quietly spat his cranberries into

160 his paper napkin. When he caught my eye, he looked guilty. He wadded up the napkin and stuffed it into his pocket. I hoped he wouldn't forget about it later.

The rest of the food was delicious, though. I thought the stuffing tasted even better than the turkey meat. The good food seemed to relax everybody, and people began to chat. Eldest Brother, who liked to do carpentry, was asking Mr. Conner's advice about various kinds of saws. Mrs. Hanson and Mrs. Conner talked about what kind of cake they were planning to make for the bake sale at the next

170 PTA meeting.

I took a deep breath and turned to Holly. "How do you like the piece we're playing for the winter concert? The violas have a pretty good part."

Holly picked at her cranberries. "I may have to pass up the concert. My viola teacher wants me to play in a recital, and I have to spend all my time practicing for that."

Holly spoke in her usual pleasant voice, but she didn't sound enthusiastic about the recital.

"Do you like your viola teacher?" I asked. "My father teaches viola, as well as violin, you know."

Mrs. Hanson turned her head. "Holly takes lessons from the first violist of the Seattle Symphony!"

I flushed. She sounded as if she thought I was drumming up lessons for my father.

Father looked interested. "Does Holly take lessons from Silverman? He's a marvelous musician! It must be wonderful to be accepted as his pupil!"

Mrs. Hanson's expression softened. "Holly works awfully hard. She can be a regular whirlwind at times!"

180

RETELL

The narrator finally gets to chat with Holly (lines 171–189). What happens during their conversation?

© Michael Newman/Photo Edit, Inc.

disgracing (dis·grās′iŋ) *v.*: bringing shame or dishonor upon.

INFER

Pause at line 202. Because the narrator doesn't know what's going on in Holly's mind, we don't know either. What do you guess Holly is feeling?

_____

_____

_____

_____

INTERPRET

Pause at line 209. Why are the characters' cultural backgrounds so important to this story?

_____

_____

_____

_____

CLARIFY

The narrator doesn't know what kinds of records Mrs. Hanson works with. What mistake does she make (lines 218–220)?

_____

_____

_____

190   I stopped worrying. Apparently Mrs. Hanson had got over her anger at being called old, and we Yangs were not **disgracing** ourselves. We all used our knives and forks correctly and waited for permission before helping ourselves from the serving dishes in the middle of the table.

I asked Holly about herself. "Do you have any brothers or sisters?"

"No, there's just Mom and me at home." She added softly, "My parents were divorced three years ago."

I tried to find something sympathetic to say but
200   couldn't think of anything. Holly's expression didn't tell me much. "Do you spend much time with your father?" I finally asked.

"I stay with him during the summer," said Holly. "He has a boat and takes me sailing."

I was impressed. "A boat? Your father must be rich!"

As soon as the words left my mouth, I wished I could take them back. I had forgotten that in America it isn't polite to discuss money. However hard I tried, I just couldn't remember everything.

210   Holly was silent for a moment. Finally she said, "My mom supports the two of us. She works in the records department in a hospital. But Dad pays for my music lessons." She looked curiously at me. "Does your mother work?"

"No, she spends all her time shopping and cooking," I admitted. Suddenly my mother, with her ridiculous shoulder pads, looked dumpy sitting next to the elegant Mrs. Hanson, who worked with records in a hospital. Were they LP records, cassette tapes, or CDs? I wondered. It sounded
220   like a glamorous job.

"I wish my mother had a job," I said wistfully. Mother had been a professional pianist, but in Seattle she hadn't been able to find work.

At least Second Sister and I earned some money baby-sitting, which is something girls don't do in China. If Chinese parents have to go out, they usually try to get the grandparents to look after the children.

"Do you do any baby-sitting?" I asked.

"I do a little," said Holly. Suddenly she smiled. "What I
230 like best is to baby-sit dogs."

"Baby-sit dogs," I repeated slowly. "You mean dog-sit?"

Holly laughed. I could see *this* was something she really enjoyed talking about. "When my neighbors are busy, I take their dogs for walks," she explained. "I just love animals."

"If Holly had her way, our house would be overflowing with pets," said Mrs. Hanson.

"Did you keep pets in China?" Holly asked me.

I shook my head. "We didn't have room."

240 "We could barely squeeze our family into our Shanghai apartment," said Father, "much less have room for pets."

"Until recently, it was actually illegal to keep a dog in many cities," added Mother. "If a dog was heard barking, the police would come to investigate."

Holly looked shocked. "How about cats, then? Are you allowed to keep cats?"

"Cats are allowed," said Father. "They don't take up much room, and they don't create a sanitation problem in the streets. But keeping them is still a luxury most people
250 can't afford."

"Well, it's different here," said Mrs. Hanson. "Holly and I have a cat and six kittens at the moment."

"If you have a house with a yard, you'd have room enough for a cat," Holly said to me. "Do you live in a house?"

I wondered why she sounded so eager as she asked the question. Before I could say anything, Father answered.

INFER

What can you infer about Holly from what you learn in lines 229–252?

_____

_____

_____

_____

_____

_____

_____

_____

_____

_____

_____

_____

_____

_____

_____

_____

_____

INFER

Pause at line 264. Why do *you* think Holly is disappointed?

_____

_____

_____

_____

_____

_____

_____

IDENTIFY

What does Father think of when he hears the word *sprout* (line 268)?

_____

_____

_____

_____

_____

_____

_____

_____

IDENTIFY

In lines 275–280, the story's narrator reveals her name or names. Circle them.

"We're renting half of a house, but it would be quite impossible for us to keep a cat. We have so many instruments and
260   piles of sheet music lying around that any kind of pet would be a disaster."

The excitement faded from Holly's face, and I knew our family had disappointed her in some way. I wondered why.

Mrs. Conner began to clear the dinner plates. Matthew and his brother, Eric, jumped up to help her. Fourth Brother also got up, but Mrs. Conner told him to sit down again. "Two helpers are all I need, Sprout. The kitchen isn't big enough for more than that."

270   "Sprout?" said Father. I knew he loved stir-fried bean sprouts. He looked eagerly around the table and was disappointed when he didn't see any.

I laughed. "Sprout is what everybody calls Fourth Brother, Father."

My American friends call me Mary, the name I picked for myself, since my Chinese name, Yingmei, is too hard for them to remember. In fact I had trouble remembering *American* names when I first came. I still keep a list of new words and phrases for memorizing, and a lot of the entries
280   are names.

My family could never remember my new American name, though. When people mentioned Mary, the Yangs would say, "Who is Mary?" So it was good to see Father puzzled by Sprout for a change.

Mr. Conner nodded. "Yeah, Sprout is a good name for the little guy." He added quickly, "The little guy with the big bat." Mr. Conner was proud of Fourth Brother's success with baseball, because he was the one who had coached him.

290 Mr. Conner was right. Sprouts look small and weedy, but they push up from the earth with a lot of **determination.** Fourth Brother is like that.

After the plates were cleared, Mrs. Conner brought in dessert: ice cream and three different kinds of pies. From the way their eyes were shining, I guessed that Eric and Matthew thought this was the best part of the meal. Personally, I enjoyed the turkey and the stuffing so much that I didn't feel like eating anything more, especially something sweet.

300 Again, the first slice of pie went to Mother. This time she didn't try to pass it to Mrs. Hanson. She had learned her lesson.

Mrs. Hanson looked at the piece of pie served to her. "Oh, I couldn't eat all this. I've already put on two pounds this month, and I can't afford to gain another ounce."

"Of course you can afford it!" Mrs. Conner said heartily. "You're so skinny, you could put on ten pounds and still look terrific."

Mother was staring at Mrs. Hanson and Mrs. Conner
310 during this exchange. We Chinese think that being fat is good. It's a sign of good fortune. Thin people are considered unfortunate and miserable.

But I knew that here, being thin is supposed to be attractive. A lot of the girls in school are worried about their weight, and some of them even go on diets.

I saw Mother open her mouth. Don't say it, Mother, I wanted to shout. Don't say it!

But she did. Radiating good will, Mother said, "Why, you're not skinny at all, Mrs. Hanson. You're actually
320 quite fat!"

VOCABULARY

determination
(dē·tʉr′min·ā′shən) n.:
firmness of purpose.

IDENTIFY

Pause at line 312. Underline the passage that tells what Chinese people think about being fat.

INTERPRET

What does Mother want to express to Mrs. Hanson (lines 318–320)? What does she actually say?

Thanksgiving with the Conners

SKILLS FOCUS

Literary Skills
Analyze first-person point of view.

Narrator Chart   A **first-person narrator** takes part in the story he or she tells. Identify the narrator of "Thanksgiving with the Conners" in the top box. Then, give three details from the story that reveal the narrator's thoughts or observations.

<table>
<tr><td align="center">Narrator</td></tr>
</table>

Narrator's Observation	**Narrator's Observation**	**Narrator's Observation**

Whose Point of View?   Think for a moment about how "Thanksgiving with the Conners" would differ if it were told by another person in the story. Pick one story character, such as Mrs. Conner or Holly, and explain how the story would be different if told by that character.

_____

_____

_____

_____

_____

Skills Review

Thanksgiving with the Conners

VOCABULARY AND COMPREHENSION

A. Clarifying Word Meanings: Context Clues   Circle the context clues that help you figure out the meaning of each boldface word.

1. Mary enjoyed the **savory** mixture called *stuffing*. Long after the meal, she remembered how tasty it had been.

2. Mary **winced** and made a face when Mrs. Yang asked Mrs. Hanson her age.

3. Mother looked so **aggressive** that Mrs. Hanson was sure she was quarrelsome.

4. Soon, everyone realized that Mrs. Yang was not purposely **disgracing** the family. She hated bringing shame on anyone.

5. Mary did not give up; her **determination** to fit in finally won out.

B. Reading Comprehension   Answer each question below.

1. Where do the narrator and her family live now? Where did they live

   before moving to the United States? _____

   _____

2. Why has the Yang family been invited to the Conners' house?

   _____

   _____

3. What do Holly and Yingmei have in common? _____

   _____

4. What two "mistakes" does Mrs. Yang make when she talks to Mrs.

   Hanson about age and weight? What does Mrs. Yang intend to

   convey? What happens instead? _____

   _____

   _____

SKILLS FOCUS

Vocabulary Skills
Clarify word meanings by using context clues.

Worlds of Words: Prose and Poetry

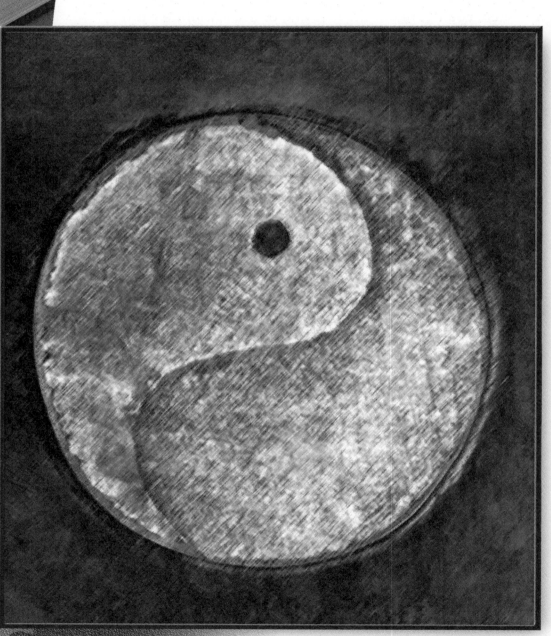

Academic Vocabulary for Collection 5

These are the terms you should know
as you read and analyze the selections in this collection.

———————

Prose Writing that isn't poetry. Prose is generally divided into
fiction—made-up stories—and **nonfiction,** which relates facts
about real people, places, things, and events.

Poetry A kind of rhythmic, compressed language that uses figures
of speech and images that appeal to emotion and imagination.

Short Stories Short works of fiction, which can generally be read in
one sitting. Unlike novels, which may have several main characters and several intertwining plots and conflicts, short stories
typically have one main character who has a basic conflict.

Vignettes Short short stories. Vignettes (vin·yets') are short sketches
that are often no longer than a page. They provide a glimpse
into a character's life or a brief description of something.

Conflict Struggle between opposing forces. In an **external conflict,**
a character struggles against some outside force, such as an
enemy or a hurricane. An **internal conflict** takes place within
a character's heart or mind.

● ● ●

Stanzas Groups of lines in a poem. Stanzas can make reading a poem
easier and can help you see patterns of rhythm and rhyme.

Figures of Speech Language that helps make connections between
seemingly unlike things. The two most common kinds of figures
of speech are **similes** and **metaphors.**

Meter Regular pattern of stressed and unstressed syllables.

Free Verse Poetry that does not have a regular meter, or pattern of
stressed and unstressed syllables.

Alliteration Repetition of consonant sounds in words that are close
together.

Onomatopoeia The use of words with sounds that echo what they
mean. Examples include *whoosh* and *zip.*

This selection also appears in *Elements of Literature.*

Amigo Brothers by Piri Thomas

LITERARY FOCUS: THE SHORT STORY

Most television shows are only a half-hour or an hour long. Because TV shows don't have as much time to develop a story as full-length movies do, their plots and conflicts tend to be less involved or complicated. The same is true of short stories and novels. A **short story** is usually between five and twenty pages long, whereas a novel is usually more than one hundred pages long. Although short stories and novels may have identical plot patterns, such as the one shown below, the action in a short story unfolds much more quickly than it does in most novels.

Short Story Structure
Meet **main characters** → Learn their **problems** → Sort out **complications**
⮑ Move to the story's **climax** → **Resolution**

CONFLICT

Conflict is the struggle or battle that characters in a story face. In "Amigo Brothers," the two main characters face both external and internal conflict. The two best friends must battle each other in a boxing ring, an **external conflict.** Each boy also struggles with this **internal conflict:** How can he do his best in the ring and at the same time avoid hurting his best friend?

READING SKILLS: COMPARISON AND CONTRAST

You compare and contrast things all the time without even thinking about it. When buying sneakers, for example, you may discover that although two pairs both are lace up, nylon, and designed for running (points of comparison), you like the blue pair better than the white pair (point of contrast).

Use the same strategy when you read "Amigo Brothers." Take notes as you discover what makes the two main characters alike and different.

SKILLS FOCUS

Literary Skills
Understand forms of prose: the short story; understand internal and external conflict.

Reading Skills
Understand comparison and contrast.

Vocabulary Skills
Recognize synonyms.

VOCABULARY DEVELOPMENT

PREVIEW SELECTION VOCABULARY

Preview the following words before you begin to read "Amigo Brothers."

bouts (bouts) *n.:* matches; contests.

> *Both boxers had won many bouts.*

pensively (pen'siv·lē) *adv.:* thoughtfully.

> *Felix nodded pensively as he rested.*

torrent (tôr'ənt) *n.:* flood or rush.

> *A torrent of emotion left him close to tears.*

dispelled (di·speld') *v.:* driven away.

> *All doubt was dispelled the moment Tony made up his mind.*

frenzied (fren'zēd) *adj.:* wild.

> *The audience's reaction was as frenzied as the battle in the ring.*

CLARIFYING WORD MEANINGS: CHOOSING SYNONYMS

Synonyms are words that have the same meaning. It's helpful when learning a new word to also learn its synonyms. Each sentence below contains an italicized word or phrase that is a synonym for one of the vocabulary words. The vocabulary word appears in parentheses following its synonym.

- In a ninth-inning rally, the hitters poured out a *flood* (torrent) of line drives on the tired infielders.
- The champion boxer was undefeated in his last twenty *fights* (bouts).
- After winning the relay by six seconds, our swim team *drove away* (dispelled) our coach's fear that we couldn't work as a team.
- A group of *wild* (frenzied) fans ran onto the field after the soccer final.
- Michelle studied the basket *thoughtfully* (pensively) before the last-second free throw.

AMIGO BROTHERS

Piri Thomas

BACKGROUND: Literature and Social Studies
This story is about two friends (*amigos* in Spanish) living on the Lower East Side of New York City. Many boys from the Lower East Side have dreamed of building a better life by winning the New York Golden Gloves, a tournament started in 1927 by Paul Gallico, a newspaper writer. This tournament marks an amateur's entry into the world of big-time boxing.

Notes _____

_____

_____

_____

_____

_____

_____

_____

_____

_____

IDENTIFY

Re-read lines 1–17. Underline the names of the two **main characters**. Circle three details that tell how similar, or alike, they are.

Antonio Cruz and Felix Vargas were both seventeen years old. They were so together in friendship that they felt themselves to be brothers. They had known each other since childhood, growing up on the Lower East Side of Manhattan in the same tenement[1] building on Fifth Street between Avenue A and Avenue B.

Antonio was fair, lean, and lanky, while Felix was dark, short, and husky. Antonio's hair was always falling over his eyes, while Felix wore his black hair in a natural Afro style.

10 Each youngster had a dream of someday becoming lightweight champion of the world. Every chance they had, the boys worked out, sometimes at the Boys' Club on 10th Street and Avenue A and sometimes at the pro's gym on 14th Street. Early morning sunrises would find them running along the East River Drive, wrapped in sweat shirts, short towels around their necks, and handkerchiefs Apache style around their foreheads.

"Amigo Brothers" from *Stories from El Barrio* by **Piri Thomas**. Copyright © 1978 by Piri Thomas. Reproduced by permission of the author.

1. **tenement** *n.* used as *adj.*: apartment. Tenement buildings are often cheaply built and poorly maintained.

While some youngsters were into street negatives, Antonio and Felix slept, ate, rapped, and dreamt positive. Between them, they had a collection of *Fight* magazines second to none, plus a scrapbook filled with torn tickets to every boxing match they had ever attended, and some clippings of their own. If asked a question about any given fighter, they would immediately zip out from their memory banks divisions, weights, records of fights, knockouts, technical knockouts, and draws or losses.

Each had fought many **bouts** representing their community and had won two gold-plated medals plus a silver and bronze medallion. The difference was in their style. Antonio's lean form and long reach made him the better boxer, while Felix's short and muscular frame made him the better slugger. Whenever they had met in the ring for sparring sessions,[2] it had always been hot and heavy.

Now, after a series of elimination **bouts,** they had been informed that they were to meet each other in the division finals that were scheduled for the seventh of August, two weeks away—the winner to represent the Boys' Club in the Golden Gloves Championship Tournament.

The two boys continued to run together along the East River Drive. But even when joking with each other, they both sensed a wall rising between them.

One morning less than a week before their bout, they met as usual for their daily workout. They fooled around with a few jabs at the air, slapped skin, and then took off, running lightly along the dirty East River's edge.

Antonio glanced at Felix, who kept his eyes purposely straight ahead, pausing from time to time to do some fancy leg work while throwing one-twos followed by uppercuts to an imaginary jaw. Antonio then beat the air with a barrage

2. **sparring sessions:** practice matches in which boxers use light punches.

INTERPRET

Underline the details that describe each youngster's fighting style (lines 27–33). What does the author mean when he says Antonio is "the better boxer," while Felix is "the better slugger"?

_____

_____

_____

_____

_____

_____

VOCABULARY

bouts (bouts) *n.:* matches; contests.

INTERPRET

The two boys "sensed a wall rising between them" (lines 40–41). What is happening to their friendship? What is the wall?

_____

_____

_____

_____

_____

WORD STUDY

What might the word *ace-boon* in lines 56–57 mean? Use context clues to help you.

_____

_____

_____

_____

_____

_____

_____

_____

_____

_____

PREDICT

Pause at line 74. How do you think Antonio and Felix will solve the problem they have about fighting each other?

_____

_____

_____

_____

_____

_____

_____

_____

_____

_____

50 of body blows and short devastating lefts with an overhead jaw-breaking right.

After a mile or so, Felix puffed and said, "Let's stop a while, bro. I think we both got something to say to each other."

Antonio nodded. It was not natural to be acting as though nothing unusual was happening when two ace-boon buddies were going to be blasting each other within a few short days.

They rested their elbows on the railing separating 60 them from the river. Antonio wiped his face with his short towel. The sunrise was now creating day.

Felix leaned heavily on the river's railing and stared across to the shores of Brooklyn. Finally, he broke the silence.

"Man. I don't know how to come out with it."

Antonio helped. "It's about our fight, right?"

"Yeah, right." Felix's eyes squinted at the rising orange sun.

"I've been thinking about it too, panin.³ In fact, since we found out it was going to be me and you, I've been awake 70 at night, pulling punches on you, trying not to hurt you."

"Same here. It ain't natural not to think about the fight. I mean, we both are cheverote⁴ fighters and we both want to win. But only one of us can win. There ain't no draws in the eliminations."

Felix tapped Antonio gently on the shoulder. "I don't mean to sound like I'm bragging, bro. But I wanna win, fair and square."

Antonio nodded quietly. "Yeah. We both know that in the ring the better man wins. Friend or no friend, brother 80 or no . . ."

---

3. **panin** (pä·nēn′) *n.:* Puerto Rican Spanish slang for "pal" or "buddy."
4. **cheverote** (che′ve·rô′tä) *adj.:* Puerto Rican Spanish slang for "the greatest."

© Royalty-Free/CORBIS.

RETELL

Re-read lines 75–91. Then, retell what the friends decide about how they will fight and how they will prepare for the fight.

Felix finished it for him. "Brother. Tony, let's promise something right here. OK?"

"If it's fair, hermano,[5] I'm for it." Antonio admired the courage of a tugboat pulling a barge five times its welterweight size.

"It's fair, Tony. When we get into the ring, it's gotta be like we never met. We gotta be like two heavy strangers that want the same thing and only one can have it. You understand, don't cha?"

90   "Sí, I know." Tony smiled. "No pulling punches. We go all the way."

"Yeah, that's right. Listen, Tony. Don't you think it's a good idea if we don't see each other until the day of the fight? I'm going to stay with my Aunt Lucy in the Bronx. I can use Gleason's Gym for working out. My manager says he got some sparring partners with more or less your style."

---

5. **hermano** (er·mä′nô) *n.:* Spanish for "brother."

VOCABULARY

pensively (pen′siv·lē) *adv.:* thoughtfully.

INTERPRET

Pause at line 108. **Conflict** is a struggle between opposing characters or forces. In this story, the fight is an example of **external conflict**. One friend is supposed to knock the other one out. The friends also struggle with **internal conflict,** a fight that takes place inside a character's mind. What internal conflict do they have?

_____

_____

_____

_____

_____

_____

INFER

The night before the fight, why does Tony try not to think of Felix (lines 120–127)?

_____

_____

_____

_____

_____

_____

_____

_____

Tony scratched his nose **pensively.** "Yeah, it would be better for our heads." He held out his hand, palm upward. "Deal?"

100 "Deal." Felix lightly slapped open skin.

"Ready for some more running?" Tony asked lamely.

"Naw, bro. Let's cut it here. You go on. I kinda like to get things together in my head."

"You ain't worried, are you?" Tony asked.

"No way, man." Felix laughed out loud. "I got too much smarts for that. I just think it's cooler if we split right here. After the fight, we can get it together again like nothing ever happened."

The amigo brothers were not ashamed to hug each
110 other tightly.

"Guess you're right. Watch yourself, Felix. I hear there's some pretty heavy dudes up in the Bronx. Suavecito,[6] OK?"

"OK. You watch yourself too, sabe?"[7]

Tony jogged away. Felix watched his friend disappear from view, throwing rights and lefts. Both fighters had a lot of psyching up to do before the big fight.

The days in training passed much too slowly. Although they kept out of each other's way, they were aware of each other's progress via the ghetto grapevine.

120 The evening before the big fight, Tony made his way to the roof of his tenement. In the quiet early dark, he peered over the ledge. Six stories below, the lights of the city blinked and the sounds of cars mingled with the curses and the laughter of children in the street. He tried not to think of Felix, feeling he had succeeded in psyching his mind. But only in the ring would he really know. To spare Felix hurt, he would have to knock him out, early and quick.

---

6. **suavecito** (swä′vā·sē′tô) *adj.:* Puerto Rican Spanish slang for "cool."
7. **sabe** (sä′bä) *v.:* Spanish for "you know."

Up in the South Bronx, Felix decided to take in a movie in an effort to keep Antonio's face away from his

130 fists. The flick was *The Champion* with Kirk Douglas, the third time Felix was seeing it.

The champion was getting beaten, his face being pounded into raw, wet hamburger. His eyes were cut, jagged, bleeding, one eye swollen, the other almost shut. He was saved only by the sound of the bell.

Felix became the champ and Tony the challenger.

The movie audience was going out of its head, roaring in blood lust at the butchery going on. The champ hunched his shoulders, grunting and sniffing red blood back into his

140 broken nose. The challenger, confident that he had the championship in the bag, threw a left. The champ countered with a dynamite right that exploded into the challenger's brains.

Felix's right arm felt the shock. Antonio's face, superimposed on the screen, was shattered and split apart by the awesome force of the killer blow. Felix saw himself in the ring, blasting Antonio against the ropes. The champ had to be forcibly restrained. The challenger was allowed to crumble slowly to the canvas, a broken bloody mess.

150 When Felix finally left the theater, he had figured out how to psych himself for tomorrow's fight. It was Felix the Champion vs. Antonio the Challenger.

He walked up some dark streets, deserted except for small pockets of wary-looking kids wearing gang colors. Despite the fact that he was Puerto Rican like them, they eyed him as a stranger to their turf. Felix did a fast shuffle, bobbing and weaving, while letting loose a **torrent** of blows that would demolish whatever got in its way. It seemed to impress the brothers, who went about their own business.

CLARIFY

Pause at line 152. How does watching the movie help Felix prepare for the fight?

VOCABULARY

torrent (tôr′ənt) *n.:* flood or rush.

INTERPRET

How would you describe
Antonio's **conflict** in lines
166–177? What does he fear
will happen to his friendship
with Felix?

_____

_____

_____

_____

_____

_____

_____

_____

PREDICT

Pause at line 187. Who do
you think will win the fight?
Will Antonio and Felix still be
friends after the fight? Tell
what you think will happen.

_____

_____

_____

_____

_____

_____

_____

_____

_____

160   Finding no takers, Felix decided to split to his aunt's.
Walking the streets had not relaxed him; neither had the
fight flick. All it had done was to stir him up. He let himself
quietly into his Aunt Lucy's apartment and went straight to
bed, falling into a fitful sleep with sounds of the gong for
Round One.

Antonio was passing some heavy time on his rooftop.
How would the fight tomorrow affect his relationship with
Felix? After all, fighting was like any other profession.
Friendship had nothing to do with it. A gnawing doubt crept
170   in. He cut negative thinking real quick by doing some speedy
fancy dance steps, bobbing and weaving like mercury. The
night air was blurred with perpetual motions of left hooks
and right crosses. Felix, his amigo brother, was not going to
be Felix at all in the ring. Just an opponent with another face.
Antonio went to sleep, hearing the opening bell for the first
round. Like his friend in the South Bronx, he prayed for
victory via a quick clean knockout in the first round.

Large posters plastered all over the walls of local shops
announced the fight between Antonio Cruz and Felix
180   Vargas as the main bout.

The fight had created great interest in the neighbor-
hood. Antonio and Felix were well liked and respected. Each
had his own loyal following. Betting fever was high and
ranged from a bottle of Coke to cold hard cash on the line.

Antonio's fans bet with unbridled faith in his boxing
skills. On the other side, Felix's admirers bet on his
dynamite-packed fists.

Felix had returned to his apartment early in the morning of August 7th and stayed there, hoping to avoid seeing
190   Antonio. He turned the radio on to salsa[8] music sounds and
then tried to read while waiting for word from his manager.

---

8. **salsa** (säl′sə) *n.* used as *adj.:* Latin American dance music, usually
played at fast tempos.

The fight was scheduled to take place in Tompkins Square Park. It had been decided that the gymnasium of the Boys' Club was not large enough to hold all the people who were sure to attend. In Tompkins Square Park, everyone who wanted could view the fight, whether from ringside or window fire escapes or tenement rooftops.

The morning of the fight Tompkins Square was a beehive of activity with numerous workers setting up the
200 ring, the seats, and the guest speakers' stand. The scheduled bouts began shortly after noon and the park had begun filling up even earlier.

The local junior high school across from Tompkins Square Park served as the dressing room for all the fighters. Each was given a separate classroom with desk tops, covered with mats, serving as resting tables. Antonio thought he caught a glimpse of Felix waving to him from a room at the far end of the corridor. He waved back just in case it had been him.

210 The fighters changed from their street clothes into fighting gear. Antonio wore white trunks, black socks, and black shoes. Felix wore sky-blue trunks, red socks, and white boxing shoes. They had dressing gowns to match their fighting trunks with their names neatly stitched on the back.

The loudspeakers blared into the open windows of the school. There were speeches by dignitaries, community leaders, and great boxers of yesteryear. Some were well prepared; some improvised on the spot. They all carried the same message of great pleasure and honor at being part of
220 such a historic event. This great day was in the tradition of champions emerging from the streets of the Lower East Side.

Interwoven with the speeches were the sounds of the other boxing events. After the sixth bout, Felix was much

IDENTIFY

Circle the details in lines 192–216 that help to build **suspense**.

DECODING TIP

Yesteryear (line 217) is a term that is not in common use today. Draw a line between "yester" and "year." What might that word mean?

© S. Meltzer/PhotoLink/Getty Images.

relieved when his trainer, Charlie, said, "Time change. Quick knockout. This is it. We're on."

Waiting time was over. Felix was escorted from the classroom by a dozen fans in white T-shirts with the word FELIX across their fronts.

Antonio was escorted down a different stairwell and
230 guided through a roped-off path.

As the two climbed into the ring, the crowd exploded with a roar. Antonio and Felix both bowed gracefully and then raised their arms in acknowledgment.

Antonio tried to be cool, but even as the roar was in its first birth, he turned slowly to meet Felix's eyes looking directly into his. Felix nodded his head and Antonio responded. And both as one, just as quickly, turned away to face his own corner.

Bong—bong—bong. The roar turned to stillness.

"Ladies and Gentlemen, Señores y Señoras."

The announcer spoke slowly, pleased at his bilingual efforts.

"Now the moment we have all been waiting for—the main event between two fine young Puerto Rican fighters, products of our Lower East Side."

"Loisaida,"[9] called out a member of the audience.

"In this corner, weighing 134 pounds, Felix Vargas. And in this corner, weighing 133 pounds, Antonio Cruz. The winner will represent the Boys' Club in the tournament of champions, the Golden Gloves. There will be no draw. May the best man win."

The cheering of the crowd shook the window panes of the old buildings surrounding Tompkins Square Park. At the center of the ring, the referee was giving instructions to the youngsters.

"Keep your punches up. No low blows. No punching on the back of the head. Keep your heads up. Understand? Let's have a clean fight. Now shake hands and come out fighting."

Both youngsters touched gloves and nodded. They turned and danced quickly to their corners. Their head towels and dressing gowns were lifted neatly from their shoulders by their trainers' nimble fingers. Antonio crossed himself. Felix did the same.

BONG! BONG! ROUND ONE. Felix and Antonio turned and faced each other squarely in a fighting pose. Felix wasted no time. He came in fast, head low, half-hunched toward his right shoulder, and lashed out with a straight left. He missed a right cross as Antonio slipped the punch and countered with one-two-three lefts that snapped Felix's head back, sending a mild shock coursing through

240

250

260

270

9. **Loisaida** (loi·sī′dä) *n.:* Puerto Rican English dialect for "Lower East Side."

Notes _____

_____

_____

_____

_____

_____

_____

_____

_____

_____

_____

_____

_____

_____

FLUENCY

Re-read the boxed passage silently. Re-read it again, aloud. Pretend you are the announcer, and use a tone of voice that will get the attention of the crowd and help build suspense.

VISUALIZE

Re-read the description of the first round in lines 264–286. Notice the details that help you see, hear, and even feel what's happening in the ring. Circle five of the details that help you picture the fight.

COMPARE & CONTRAST

Highlight or color-mark Antonio's actions in lines 264–286. Use a different color to highlight Felix's actions. In what way are the fighters the same? In what way are they different?

_____

_____

_____

_____

_____

_____

VOCABULARY

dispelled (di·speld') _v._: driven away.

PREDICT

Pause at line 299. What do you think will happen in round two?

_____

_____

_____

_____

_____

_____

_____

_____

him. If Felix had any small doubt about their friendship affecting their fight, it was being neatly **dispelled.**

Antonio danced, a joy to behold. His left hand was like a piston pumping jabs one right after another with seeming ease. Felix bobbed and weaved and never stopped boring in. He knew that at long range he was at a disadvantage. Antonio had too much reach on him. Only by coming in close could Felix hope to achieve the dreamed-of knockout.

Antonio knew the dynamite that was stored in his
280 amigo brother's fist. He ducked a short right and missed a left hook. Felix trapped him against the ropes just long enough to pour some punishing rights and lefts to Antonio's hard midsection. Antonio slipped away from Felix, crashing two lefts to his head, which set Felix's right ear to ringing.

Bong! Both amigos froze a punch well on its way, sending up a roar of approval for good sportsmanship.

Felix walked briskly back to his corner. His right ear had not stopped ringing. Antonio gracefully danced his way toward his stool none the worse, except for glowing glove
290 burns showing angry red against the whiteness of his midribs.

"Watch that right, Tony." His trainer talked into his ear. "Remember Felix always goes to the body. He'll want you to drop your hands for his overhand left or right. Got it?"

Antonio nodded, spraying water out between his teeth. He felt better as his sore midsection was being firmly rubbed.

Felix's corner was also busy.

"You gotta get in there, fella." Felix's trainer poured water over his curly Afro locks. "Get in there or he's gonna chop you up from way back."

300 _Bong! Bong!_ Round two. Felix was off his stool and rushed Antonio like a bull, sending a hard right to his head. Beads of water exploded from Antonio's long hair.

© Karl Weatherly/CORBIS.

IDENTIFY

Circle five details in lines 310–314 that use boxing terms to help you picture the fast action.

Antonio, hurt, sent back a blurring barrage of lefts and rights that only meant pain to Felix, who returned with a short left to the head followed by a looping right to the body. Antonio countered with his own flurry, forcing Felix to give ground. But not for long.

Felix bobbed and weaved, bobbed and weaved, occasionally punching his two gloves together.

310   Antonio waited for the rush that was sure to come. Felix closed in and feinted with his left shoulder and threw a right instead. Lights suddenly exploded inside Felix's head as Antonio slipped the blow and hit him with a pistonlike left, catching him flush on the point of his chin.

Bedlam broke loose as Felix's legs momentarily buckled. He fought off a series of rights and lefts and came back with a strong right that taught Antonio respect.

Antonio danced in carefully. He knew Felix had the habit of playing possum when hurt, to sucker an opponent 320 within reach of the powerful bombs he carried in each fist.

WORD STUDY

The author states that Felix had the habit of "playing possum when hurt" (lines 318–319). Possums (short for opossums) are animals that pretend to be asleep, ill, or dead when in danger. Why might Felix choose to "play possum" when boxing?

Amigo Brothers   **169**

IDENTIFY

Underline the details in lines 328–343 that tell you that Antonio and Felix are no longer thinking about their friendship.

VOCABULARY

frenzied (fren′zēd) *adj.*: wild.

RETELL

Pause at line 355. Retell what has happened in the second round.

_____

_____

_____

_____

_____

_____

_____

_____

_____

_____

_____

_____

_____

_____

_____

_____

A right to the head slowed Antonio's pretty dancing. He answered with his own left at Felix's right eye that began puffing up within three seconds.

Antonio, a bit too eager, moved in too close, and Felix had him entangled into a rip-roaring, punching toe-to-toe slugfest that brought the whole Tompkins Square Park screaming to its feet.

Rights to the body. Lefts to the head. Neither fighter was giving an inch. Suddenly a short right caught Antonio

330 squarely on the chin. His long legs turned to jelly and his arms flailed out desperately. Felix, grunting like a bull, threw wild punches from every direction. Antonio, groggy, bobbed and weaved, evading most of the blows. Suddenly his head cleared. His left flashed out hard and straight, catching Felix on the bridge of his nose.

Felix lashed back with a haymaker, right off the ghetto streets. At the same instant, his eye caught another left hook from Antonio. Felix swung out, trying to clear the pain. Only the **frenzied** screaming of those along ringside

340 let him know that he had dropped Antonio. Fighting off the growing haze, Antonio struggled to his feet, got up, ducked, and threw a smashing right that dropped Felix flat on his back.

Felix got up as fast as he could in his own corner, groggy but still game. He didn't even hear the count. In a fog, he heard the roaring of the crowd, who seemed to have gone insane. His head cleared to hear the bell sound at the end of the round. He was glad. His trainer sat him down on the stool.

350 In his corner, Antonio was doing what all fighters do when they are hurt. They sit and smile at everyone.

The referee signaled the ring doctor to check the fighters out. He did so and then gave his OK. The cold-water sponges brought clarity to both amigo brothers. They were rubbed until their circulation ran free.

Bong! Round three—the final round. Up to now it had been tic-tac-toe, pretty much even. But everyone knew there could be no draw and that this round would decide the winner.

360   This time, to Felix's surprise, it was Antonio who came out fast, charging across the ring. Felix braced himself but couldn't ward off the barrage of punches. Antonio drove Felix hard against the ropes.

The crowd ate it up. Thus far the two had fought with mucho corazón.[10] Felix tapped his gloves and commenced his attack anew. Antonio, throwing boxer's caution to the winds, jumped in to meet him.

Both pounded away. Neither gave an inch and neither fell to the canvas. Felix's left eye was tightly closed. Claret-red 370 blood poured from Antonio's nose. They fought toe-to-toe.

The sounds of their blows were loud in contrast to the silence of a crowd gone completely mute. The referee was stunned by their savagery.

Bong! Bong! Bong! The bell sounded over and over again. Felix and Antonio were past hearing. Their blows continued to pound on each other like hailstones.

Finally the referee and the two trainers pried Felix and Antonio apart. Cold water was poured over them to bring them back to their senses.

380   They looked around and then rushed toward each other. A cry of alarm surged through Tompkins Square Park. Was this a fight to the death instead of a boxing match?

The fear soon gave way to wave upon wave of cheering as the two amigos embraced.

---

10. **mucho corazón** (mōō′chô kô′rä·sôn′): Spanish for "a lot of heart."

IDENTIFY

Re-read lines 356–384. Underline details that build suspense right up to the **climax** of the story. Circle the action that resolves the **internal conflict,** when you find out whether Antonio and Felix can still be friends.

RETELL

Retell what happens in the final round of the fight.

_____

_____

_____

_____

_____

_____

_____

_____

_____

INTERPRET

The last sentence of the story refers to both fighters as "champions." In what way are they both champions?

_____

_____

_____

_____

_____

_____

_____

_____

_____

_____

_____

No matter what the decision, they knew they would always be champions to each other.

BONG! BONG! BONG! "Ladies and Gentlemen. Señores and Señoras. The winner and representative to the Golden Gloves Tournament of Champions is . . ."

390   The announcer turned to point to the winner and found himself alone. Arm in arm the champions had already left the ring.

© Royalty-Free/CORBIS.

Amigo Brothers

Venn Diagram   Piri Thomas begins his story by contrasting the two best friends: "Antonio was fair, lean, and lanky, while Felix was dark, short, and husky." A **comparison** points out similarities between things; a **contrast** points out differences. Go back over the story, and use a Venn diagram to help you identify the ways in which Felix and Antonio are alike and different. Write their likenesses in the part where the circles overlap.

SKILLS FOCUS

Reading Skills
Understand comparison and contrast.

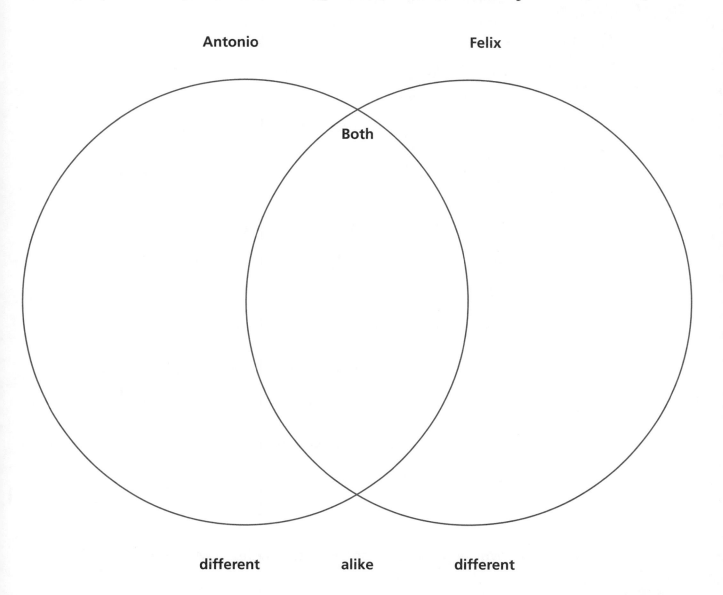

Antonio   Felix

Both

different   alike   different

Skills Review

Amigo Brothers

VOCABULARY AND COMPREHENSION

A. Clarifying Word Meanings: Choosing Synonyms   Choose the word or phrase that is the best synonym for each Word Bank word. Write the letter of the synonym in the correct blank.

_____ **1.** torrent

_____ **2.** pensively

_____ **3.** bouts

_____ **4.** frenzied

_____ **5.** dispelled

a. driven away

b. flood

c. thoughtfully

d. wild

e. contests

B. Reading Comprehension   Answer each question below.

1. Where do Antonio and Felix live? How long have they known each other? _____

_____

2. What dream do Antonio and Felix share? _____

_____

3. Why do Antonio and Felix stop training together? What agreement do they make? _____

_____

4. Why don't Antonio and Felix stop fighting when the final bell sounds?

_____

5. Does the fight end the friendship between Antonio and Felix? Explain. _____

_____

SKILLS FOCUS

Vocabulary Skills
Recognize synonyms.

This selection also appears in *Elements of Literature.*

I'm Nobody! by Emily Dickinson

LITERARY FOCUS: FIGURES OF SPEECH

Have you ever thought of a cloud as lonely? William Wordsworth compared a lonely afternoon stroll to a drifting cloud in his well-known poem "I Wandered Lonely As a Cloud." Comparisons of things that seem very different are called **figures of speech.** Many poets, including Emily Dickinson, use imaginative comparisons to help us think about everyday items or events in a new way.

Two common figures of speech are similes and metaphors. **Similes** compare unlike things by using words such as *like* or *as.* The comparison in the title of Wordsworth's poem is a simile because it uses the word *as.* **Metaphors** compare unlike things without using a specific word of comparison. The chart below provides a few examples of similes and metaphors.

Similes	Metaphors
The track star ran faster *than* a speeding bullet.	The track star was a bullet, speeding past the other racers.
Our neighbor's St. Bernard is *as* big *as* an elephant.	Our neighbor's St. Bernard is an elephant.
The idea rumbled through my mind *like* a freight train.	The idea was a freight train rumbling through my head.

READING SKILLS: PUNCTUATION CLUES

When you read poetry, it is important to pay attention to punctuation. Line endings in poetry don't necessarily signal the ends of phrases or sentences. Keep the following tips in mind as you read "I'm Nobody!"

- Stop briefly at semicolons and after periods, question marks, and exclamation points.
- Pause at commas.
- Look for sudden shifts in thought after dashes.
- Do not come to a full stop if a line does not end with punctuation. Pause very briefly, and continue to the end of the sentence.

SKILLS FOCUS

Literary Skills
Understand figures of speech, such as simile and metaphor.

Reading Skills
Use punctuation clues.

I'm Nobody!

Emily Dickinson

I'm Nobody! Who are you?
Are you Nobody too?
Then there's a pair of us!
Don't tell! they'd banish us, you know!

5   How dreary to be Somebody!
How public—like a Frog—
To tell your name the livelong June
To an admiring Bog!

© Christie's Images/CORBIS.

INTERPRET

Who is the "they" referred to in line 4?

_____

_____

IDENTIFY

Locate and circle the **simile** in the second stanza of the poem.

IDENTIFY

Whom is the speaker referring to as an "admiring Bog" (line 8)?

_____

_____

INTERPRET

Re-read the poem until you're confident you understand its meaning. What idea is the poem's speaker conveying?

_____

_____

FLUENCY

Read the poem aloud several times. Use the punctuation clues to guide your reading.

I'm Nobody!

Punctuation Clues   Poetry often comes to life when it is read aloud. In the chart below briefly describe how you would read each line of "I'm Nobody!" You might want to review the tips on reading punctuation clues on page 175.

SKILLS FOCUS

Reading Skills
Use punctuation clues.

How to Read "I'm Nobody!"	
Line 1	
Line 2	
Line 3	
Line 4	
Line 5	
Line 6	
Line 7	
Line 8	

Skills Review

I'm Nobody!

COMPREHENSION

Reading Comprehension   Answer each question below.

1. Who does the speaker claim to be?

   _____

   _____

   _____

2. Whom is the speaker addressing?

   _____

   _____

   _____

3. What does the speaker think it would be like to be "Somebody"?

   _____

   _____

   _____

4. To what does the speaker compare "public" people in the second stanza? Is that comparison an example of a simile or a metaphor?

   _____

   _____

   _____

5. How do you think the speaker feels about fame? Do you agree? Explain.

   _____

   _____

   _____

Before You Read

POEM

This selection also appears in *Elements of Literature*.

Sarah Cynthia Sylvia Stout Would Not Take the Garbage Out

by Shel Silverstein

LITERARY FOCUS: HUMOROUS POEMS

Poems can be serious, thoughtful, angry, or even funny. A **humorous poem,** though funny, can also make a serious point. One way humorous poems can make a point is through exaggeration, describing something as bigger, smaller, better, or worse than it really is. It won't take you long to notice the exaggeration in "Sarah Cynthia Sylvia Stout Would Not Take the Garbage Out."

RHYTHM

Something else you'll notice about this poem—probably as soon as you read the title—is its rhythm. If you've ever listened to rap music, you know how important rhythm can be. **Rhythm** is the repetition of stressed and unstressed syllables or the repetition of certain other sound patterns. When the stressed and unstressed syllables are arranged in a regular pattern, the pattern is called **meter.** Can you imagine a rap artist stressing the wrong syllables? You probably wouldn't listen very long.

READING SKILLS: READING ALOUD

Many poems must be read aloud to have their full effect. When you read aloud, notice how the rhythm of the words adds color and meaning to the poem. To practice reading for rhythm, read the poem title below. Repeat the title several times, and notice the rhythm created by slightly stressing the syllables in capital letters.

> SARah CYNthia SYLvia STOUT
> WOULD not TAKE the GARbage OUT

SKILLS FOCUS

Literary Skills
Understand humorous poems and exaggeration; understand rhythm and meter.

Reading Skills
Read aloud.

Sarah Cynthia Sylvia Stout Would Not Take the Garbage Out

Shel Silverstein

IDENTIFY

In lines 1–6 circle the **alliteration**—repetition of the same consonant sound. What effect does the use of alliteration have on you, the reader?

_____

_____

_____

_____

_____

_____

_____

IDENTIFY

Underline the adjectives in lines 16–32 that describe the garbage. What effect do these words have on you?

_____

_____

_____

_____

_____

_____

Sarah Cynthia Sylvia Stout
Would not take the garbage out!
She'd scour the pots and scrape the pans,
Candy the yams and spice the hams,
5 And though her daddy would scream and shout,
She simply would not take the garbage out.
And so it piled up to the ceilings:
Coffee grounds, potato peelings,
Brown bananas, rotten peas,
10 Chunks of sour cottage cheese.
It filled the can, it covered the floor,
It cracked the window and blocked the door
With bacon rinds and chicken bones,
Drippy ends of ice cream cones,
15 Prune pits, peach pits, orange peel,
Gloppy glumps of cold oatmeal,
Pizza crusts and withered greens,
Soggy beans and tangerines,
Crusts of black burned butter toast,
20 Gristly bits of beefy roasts . . .
The garbage rolled on down the hall,
It raised the roof, it broke the wall . . .

Greasy napkins, cookie crumbs,
Globs of gooey bubble gum,
25 Cellophane from green baloney,
Rubbery blubbery macaroni,
Peanut butter, caked and dry,
Curdled milk and crusts of pie,
Moldy melons, dried-up mustard,
30 Eggshells mixed with lemon custard,
Cold french fries and rancid meat,
Yellow lumps of Cream of Wheat.
At last the garbage reached so high
That finally it touched the sky.
35 And all the neighbors moved away,
And none of her friends would come to play.
And finally Sarah Cynthia Stout said,
"OK, I'll take the garbage out!"
But then, of course, it was too late . . .
40 The garbage reached across the state,
From New York to the Golden Gate.
And there, in the garbage she did hate,
Poor Sarah met an awful fate,
That I cannot right now relate
45 Because the hour is much too late.
But children, remember Sarah Stout
And always take the garbage out!

INFER

What do you think happened to Sarah Cynthia Sylvia Stout (line 43)?

_____
_____
_____
_____
_____
_____
_____
_____
_____

INTERPRET

Re-read the last two lines of the poem. What is the poem's speaker doing?

_____
_____
_____
_____
_____
_____
_____
_____
_____

Sarah Cynthia Sylvia Stout
Would Not Take the Garbage Out

Rhythm Chart   Read lines 23–32 of Shel Silverstein's poem, below. Circle the syllables you think should be stressed when the poem is read aloud. Then, take turns reading this passage aloud with a partner. As you read and listen, pay attention to the rhythm created by stressing the circled syllables.

. . . Greasy napkins, cookie crumbs,

Globs of gooey bubble gum,

Cellophane from green baloney,

Rubbery blubbery macaroni,

Peanut butter, caked and dry,

Curdled milk and crusts of pie,

Moldy melons, dried-up mustard,

Eggshells mixed with lemon custard,

Cold french fries and rancid meat,

Yellow lumps of Cream of Wheat.

from "Sarah Cynthia Sylvia Stout

Would Not Take the Garbage Out"

**SKILLS
FOCUS**

Literary Skills
Analyze rhythm
and meter.

Reading Skills
Read aloud.

Skills Review

Sarah Cynthia Sylvia Stout Would Not Take the Garbage Out

COMPREHENSION

Reading Comprehension   Answer each question below.

1. What work does the poem say Sarah *would* do?

_____

_____

_____

2. How does Sarah's daddy try to persuade her to take the garbage out?

_____

_____

_____

3. How do Sarah's friends and neighbors react?

_____

_____

_____

4. What do you think happens to Sarah toward the end of the poem?

_____

_____

_____

5. What "lesson" does the speaker want you to take from the poem?

_____

_____

_____

from **The House on Mango Street**

by Sandra Cisneros

LITERARY FOCUS: PROSE—VIGNETTES

If a short story can be compared to a half-hour TV show, a vignette can be compared to a snapshot with a camera. A **vignette** (vin·yet′) is a literary sketch or description that is often no longer than a page. You can think of a vignette as a short short story, but vignettes usually don't have a plot.

The following excerpt from *The House on Mango Street* is composed of three vignettes.

READING SKILLS: MAKING INFERENCES

Writers don't tell you everything about a person, place, or thing. That would spoil part of the fun of reading. Instead, you are invited to make educated guesses, or **inferences,** based on what the writer tells you and on your own experience. As you read the selections from *The House on Mango Street,* record your inferences in a chart like this one:

Inferences Chart	
Detail(s):	Inference:
Detail(s):	Inference:
Detail(s):	Inference:

SKILLS FOCUS

Literary Skills
Understand forms of prose.

Reading Skills
Make inferences.

Vocabulary Skills
Clarify word meanings by using word roots and affixes.

VOCABULARY DEVELOPMENT

PREVIEW SELECTION VOCABULARY

Get to know these words before you begin to read the excerpts from *The House on Mango Street.*

appreciate (ə·prē′shē·āt′) *v.:* think well of; enjoy.

I love the sound of wind blowing through our trees, but my sister doesn't appreciate it.

ferocious (fə·rō′shəs) *adj.:* very great. *Ferocious* can also mean "fierce" or "savage."

The trees look fragile, but they have a ferocious will to survive.

despite (di·spīt′) *prep.:* in defiance of.

They look out of place so close to the street; they have grown despite their surroundings.

content (kən·tent′) *adj.:* happy enough with what one has; satisfied.

Our lonely trees seem content to stand guard over our house.

USING AFFIXES

Many English words are built from Latin or Greek words or contain word parts that come from those languages. Knowing the meanings of various word parts will help you figure out the meanings of unfamiliar words. The vocabulary word *content,* for example, is built from the Latin *con–,* meaning "with" or "together," and *tener,* meaning "to have" or "to hold." A person who has got hold of what he or she wants is content. Here are some other affixes that you should know.

Word Part	Meaning	Example
tri–	having three	*tri*colored: having three colors
in–	not; without	*in*effective: not effective
anti–	against; opposite	*anti*social: against society

Sandra Cisneros

IDENTIFY

Who are the "only ones" (line 1) who understand the narrator? Underline the two traits the "only ones" have in common with the narrator.

_____

_____

_____

VOCABULARY

appreciate (ə·prē′shē·āt′) *v.:* think well of; enjoy.

ferocious (fə·rō′shəs) *adj.:* very great. *Ferocious* can also mean "fierce" or "savage."

despite (di·spīt′) *prep.:* in defiance of.

INFER

In the last paragraph, circle the three words that tell you how the narrator sometimes feels. How do the trees help her?

_____

_____

_____

Four Skinny Trees

They are the only ones who understand me. I am the only one who understands them. Four skinny trees with skinny necks and pointy elbows like mine. Four who do not belong here but are here. Four raggedy excuses planted by the city. From our room we can hear them, but Nenny just sleeps and doesn't **appreciate** these things.

Their strength is secret. They send **ferocious** roots beneath the ground. They grow up and they grow down and grab the earth between their hairy toes and bite the sky
10 with violent teeth and never quit their anger. This is how they keep.

Let one forget his reason for being, they'd all droop like tulips in a glass, each with their arms around the other. Keep, keep, keep, trees say when I sleep. They teach.

When I am too sad and too skinny to keep keeping, when I am a tiny thing against so many bricks, then it is I look at trees. When there is nothing left to look at on this street. Four who grew **despite** concrete. Four who reach and do not forget to reach. Four whose only reason is to be
20 and be.

Bums in the Attic

I want a house on a hill like the ones with the gardens where Papa works. We go on Sundays, Papa's day off. I used to go. I don't anymore. You don't like to go out with us, Papa says. Getting too old? Getting too stuck-up, says Nenny. I don't tell them I am ashamed—all of us staring out the window like the hungry. I am tired of looking at what we can't have. When we win the lottery . . . Mama begins, and then I stop listening.

10 People who live on hills sleep so close to the stars they forget those of us who live too much on earth. They don't look down at all except to be **content** to live on hills. They have nothing to do with last week's garbage or fear of rats. Night comes. Nothing wakes them but the wind.

One day I'll own my own house, but I won't forget who I am or where I came from. Passing bums will ask, Can I come in? I'll offer them the attic, ask them to stay, because I know how it is to be without a house.

Some days after dinner, guests and I will sit in front of a fire. Floorboards will squeak upstairs. The attic grumble.

20 Rats? they'll ask.

Bums, I'll say, and I'll be happy.

FLUENCY

Read the boxed passage in "Bums in the Attic" to yourself. Put quotation marks around the words that each character says. Then, read the boxed passage aloud. Change your tone of voice to make it clear that three different characters speak.

VOCABULARY

content (kən·tent') adj.: happy enough with what one has; satisfied.

Content is made up of the Latin prefix *con–,* meaning "with" or "together," and the Latin word *tener,* meaning "have" or "hold."

If you put the accent on the first syllable (kän'tent'), what does the word mean?

_____

_____

_____

INFER

Is the story's narrator generous? Explain. Box the text that helps you make your inference.

_____

_____

_____

_____

_____

_____

A House of My Own

INFER

Circle the words that tell what kind of place the speaker does *not* want to live in. What inference can you make about why she wants a house of her own?

Not a flat. Not an apartment in back. Not a man's house. Not a daddy's. A house all my own. With my porch and my pillow, my pretty purple petunias. My books and my stories. My two shoes waiting beside the bed. Nobody to shake a stick at. Nobody's garbage to pick up after.

Only a house quiet as snow, a space for myself to go, clean as paper before the poem.

© Royalty-Free/CORBIS.

from The House on Mango Street

Inferences Chart   An **inference** is an educated guess that is based on what you observe and your past experience. Based on details in the three selections from *The House on Mango Street* and on your own experience, make inferences about the story in the chart below. Give at least one detail from the text to support each inference.

Reading Skills
Make inferences.

The speaker	The speaker's childhood house	The speaker's ideas about life
My inference . . .	My inference . . .	My inference . . .
Supporting detail(s):	Supporting detail(s):	Supporting detail(s):

Skills Review

from The House on Mango Street

VOCABULARY AND COMPREHENSION

A. Using Affixes   Write words from the Word Bank to complete the paragraph below. Then, re-read the paragraph and circle words that have the affixes *un–*, *con–*, and *anti–*.

Manuela decided to visit Bolivia (1) _____ the unceasing protests of her best friend, who wanted her to visit Italy with her family. Manuela didn't want to make her friend angry. But she had had a very strong, almost (2) _____ desire to see the land of her ancestors. She didn't mean to be antisocial; she simply wanted to learn to (3) _____ the culture of the Bolivian people. After a few happy weeks in Bolivia, Manuela was (4) _____, happy to have experienced life in the land of her past.

B. Reading Comprehension   Answer each question below.

1. How does the speaker describe her appearance in "Four Skinny Trees"?

_____

_____

2. What is "secret" about the trees? Why is it secret? _____

_____

3. In "Bums in the Attic," why doesn't the speaker go out with her family on Sundays? _____

_____

4. What does the speaker in these excerpts want most of all? _____

_____

SKILLS FOCUS

Vocabulary Skills
Clarify word meanings by using word roots and affixes.

Bats by Randall Jarrell

LITERARY FOCUS: POETRY—RHYTHM AND RHYME

Do you ever find yourself moving to the beat of a great song? Most songs have a regular, repeating **rhythm,** and so do many poems. Poetry that has a regular pattern of stressed and unstressed syllables is written in **meter.** "Bats" is written in meter. Poetry that doesn't have a regular pattern of stressed and unstressed syllables is called **free verse.** Free-verse poetry sounds more like ordinary speech.

Another thing many poems share with popular songs is rhyme. **Rhyme** is the repetition of accented vowel sounds and all sounds following them in words close together: *writing* rhymes with *fighting; pale* rhymes with *hail; mister* rhymes with *sister.* Nursery rhymes are great examples of rhythm and rhyme. In the example here, the stressed syllables are in capital letters, and the rhymes are underlined:

> LITtle Miss MUFfet
> SAT on a TUFfet,
> EATing her CURDS and WHEY.
> aLONG came a SPIder,
> Who SAT down beSIDE her,
> And FRIGHTened Miss MUFfet aWAY.

READING SKILLS: READING ALOUD

Reading aloud a rhythmic poem such as "Bats" will help you understand and appreciate it more fully. Here are a few tips to get you started.

- Pay attention to punctuation. Stop briefly at semicolons and ends of sentences.
- Think about how fast you would read and where you would speed up and slow down.
- Think about how loudly or softly you would read different sections of the poem.
- Think about where you would raise or lower the pitch of your voice.

SKILLS
FOCUS

Literary Skills
Understand poetry; understand rhythm and rhyme.

Reading Skills
Read aloud.

BATS

Randall Jarrell

IDENTIFY

This poem is written in **meter.** Underline the words or syllables in lines 1–5 that should be stressed.

IDENTIFY

Locate and circle the **rhyming** words in lines 9–20.

FLUENCY

Read aloud lines 9–20 several times. Pay close attention to punctuation and words that rhyme, and read the lines as smoothly as possible.

INTERPRET

How does the bat "live by hearing" (lines 10–16)?

_____

_____

_____

_____

_____

_____

_____

_____

_____

A bat is born
Naked and blind and pale.
His mother makes a pocket of her tail
And catches him. He clings to her long fur
5   By his thumbs and toes and teeth.
And then the mother dances through the night
Doubling and looping, soaring, somersaulting—
Her baby hangs on underneath.

All night, in happiness, she hunts and flies.
10   Her high sharp cries
Like shining needlepoints of sound
Go out into the night and, echoing back,
Tell her what they have touched.
She hears how far it is, how big it is,
15   Which way it's going:
She lives by hearing.
The mother eats the moths and gnats she catches
In full flight; in full flight
The mother drinks the water of the pond
20   She skims across. Her baby hangs on tight.

Her baby drinks the milk she makes him
In moonlight or starlight, in mid-air.
Their single shadow, printed on the moon
Or fluttering across the stars,
25   Whirls on all night; at daybreak

The tired mother flaps home to her rafter.

The others all are there.

They hang themselves up by their toes,

They wrap themselves in their brown wings.

30 Bunched upside-down, they sleep in air.

Their sharp ears, their sharp teeth, their quick sharp faces

Are dull and slow and mild.

All the bright day, as the mother sleeps,

She folds her wings about her sleeping child.

Bats

SKILLS FOCUS

Literary Skills
Analyze poetry;
analyze rhythm
and rhyme.

Rhyme List   In the chart below, list as many rhyming words as you can find in "Bats." (It helps to read aloud when you're finding rhymes.) Record the line numbers in the left-hand column and the rhyming words in the right-hand column. An example is provided for you.

Lines	Rhymes
2 and 3	pale *and* tail
____ and ____	
____ and ____	
____ and ____	
____ and ____	
____ and ____	

Skills Review

Bats

COMPREHENSION

Reading Comprehension   Answer each question below.

1. Where is the baby bat while its mother hunts for food at night?

   _____

   _____

   _____

2. How does the bat sense its surroundings?

   _____

   _____

   _____

3. How do bats sleep? When do they sleep?

   _____

   _____

   _____

4. How does the mother bat protect her baby while sleeping?

   _____

   _____

   _____

5. In what way does the mother bat act like a human mother?

   _____

   _____

   _____

Collection 6

Our Literary Heritage: Greek Myths and World Folk Tales

Academic Vocabulary for Collection 6

These are the terms you should know
as you read and analyze the stories in this collection.

———

Myths Stories that represent the deepest wishes and fears of
humans. Myths are used for these purposes:
- to explain the creation of the world
- to explain natural phenomena or occurrences
- to give story form to ancient religious practices
- to teach moral lessons
- to explain history
- to express the deepest fears and hopes of the human race

Origin Myths Stories that explain how things came to be. The origins
of fire, lightning, and death, for example, are explained in some
origin myths.

Folk Tales Stories passed on by word of mouth, often over many
centuries.

Escape Story Type of folk tale created by African Americans who
were enslaved. This type of folk tale centers on escaping from
bondage to freedom.

Motifs Common features of folk tales. Magic, fairy godmothers, and
acts of heroism are examples of motifs.

MYTH

The Origin of the Seasons

retold by Olivia Coolidge

LITERARY FOCUS: ORIGIN MYTHS

People have an unquenchable thirst for knowledge. Think, for example, of a typical two-year-old child: "Why is the sky blue?" "Who made the ocean, and why is it so salty?" "Why is thunder so loud?"

In ancient times, curious people turned to mythmakers for answers to their questions about the world and how it came to be. The ancients believed that the mythmakers had a direct connection to the gods, the source of all knowledge. Through the telling of **origin myths,** people answered their questions about the natural world.

As you read "Origin of the Seasons," look for details that explain how the seasons came to be.

READING SKILLS: UNDERSTANDING CAUSE AND EFFECT

Origin myths explain how something came to be. Like most explanations, origin myths present a series of causes and effects. Here's an example of a typical cause-and-effect sequence:

Cause→	Effect→	Cause→	Effect
A human requests help from a god.	The god agrees to help.	The human forgets to thank the god.	The god reacts angrily, causing hardship for humanity.

As you read "The Origin of the Seasons," look for cause-and-effect relationships.

SKILLS FOCUS

Literary Skills
Understand origin myths.

Reading Skills
Understand cause and effect.

The ORIGIN of the SEASONS

retold by Olivia Coolidge

Demeter, the great earth mother, was goddess of the harvest. Tall and majestic was her appearance, and her hair was the color of ripe wheat. It was she who filled the ears with grain. In her honor white-robed women brought golden garlands of wheat as first fruits to the altar. Reaping, threshing, winnowing,[1] and the long tables set in the shade for the harvesters' refreshment—all these were hers. Songs and feasting did her honor as the hard-working farmer gathered his abundant fruit. All the laws which the farmer knew came

10 from her: the time for plowing, what land would best bear crops, which was fit for grapes, and which to leave for pasture. She was a goddess whom men called the great mother because of her generosity in giving. Her own special daughter in the family of the gods was named Persephone.

Persephone was the spring maiden, young and full of joy. Sicily was her home, for it is a land where the spring is long and lovely, and where spring flowers are abundant.

---

1. reaping: cutting and gathering the grain; **threshing** and **winnowing:** two ways of separating the grain from the husks.

From "The Origin of the Seasons" from *Greek Myths* by Olivia Coolidge. Copyright 1949 and renewed © 1977 by Olivia E. Coolidge. All rights reserved. Reproduced by permission of **Houghton Mifflin Company.**

WORD STUDY

Many Greek names are pronounced in ways that are surprising to English speakers. For example: Demeter (di·mēt′ər) and Persephone (pər·sef′ə·nē).

IDENTIFY

Pause at line 14. Circle the names of the goddesses you are introduced to in this passage. What is their relationship?

_____

_____

IDENTIFY CAUSE & EFFECT

Re-read lines 1–14. Underline the details that tell you why Demeter is adored by humans.

INFER

Re-read the sentences in lines 18–25. What does this myth-maker imply is the cause of thunder?

_____

_____

_____

_____

_____

_____

_____

_____

_____

_____

_____

_____

_____

_____

_____

_____

FLUENCY

Read the boxed passage silently, and take note of the sequence of events. Then, read the passage aloud several times. Each time you read, strive to improve the smoothness of your delivery as well as your interpretation of the scene.

Here Persephone played with her maidens from day to day till the rocks and valleys rang with the sound of laughter,
20 and gloomy Hades heard it as he sat on his throne in the dark land of the dead. Even his heart of stone was touched by her young beauty, so that he arose in his awful majesty and came up to Olympus to ask Zeus if he might have Persephone to wife. Zeus bowed his head in agreement, and mighty Olympus thundered as he promised.

Thus it came about that as Persephone was gathering flowers with her maidens in the vale of Enna, a marvelous thing happened. Enna was a beautiful valley in whose meadows all the most lovely flowers of the year grew at the
30 same season. There were wild roses, purple crocuses, sweet-scented violets, tall iris, rich narcissus,[2] and white lilies. All these the girl was gathering, yet fair as they were, Persephone herself was fairer far.

As the maidens went picking and calling to one another across the blossoming meadow, it happened that Persephone strayed apart from the rest. Then, as she looked a little ahead in the meadow, she suddenly beheld the marvelous thing. It was a flower so beautiful that none like it had ever been known. It seemed a kind of narcissus, purple
40 and white, but from a single root there sprang a hundred blossoms, and at the sweet scent of it the very heavens and earth appeared to smile for joy. Without calling to the others, Persephone sprang forward to be the first to pick the precious bloom. As she stretched out her hand, the earth opened in front of her, and she found herself caught in a stranger's arms. Persephone shrieked aloud and struggled, while the armful of flowers cascaded down to earth.

However, the dark-eyed Hades was far stronger than she.

---

2. **narcissus** (när·sis′əs): family of lilies including daffodils and jonquils. "Echo and Narcissus" (page 104) gives the ancient Greeks' explanation of how this flower came to be.

He swept her into his golden chariot, took the reins of his
50 coal-black horses, and was gone amid the rumbling sound
of the closing earth before the other girls in the valley could
even come in sight of the spot. When they did get there,
nobody was visible. Only the roses and lilies of Persephone
lay scattered in wild confusion over the grassy turf.

Bitter was the grief of Demeter when she heard the
news of her daughter's mysterious fate. Veiling herself with
a dark cloud, she sped, swift as a wild bird, over land and
ocean for nine days, searching everywhere and asking all
she met if they had seen her daughter. Neither gods nor
60 men had seen her. Even the birds could give no tidings, and
Demeter in despair turned to Phoebus Apollo, who sees all
things from his chariot in the heavens.

"Yes, I have seen your daughter," said the god at last.
"Hades has taken her with the consent of Zeus, that she
may dwell in the land of mist and gloom as his queen. The
girl struggled and was unwilling, but Hades is far stronger
than she."

When she heard this, Demeter fell into deep despair,
for she knew she could never rescue Persephone if Zeus
70 and Hades had agreed. She did not care any more to enter
the palace of Olympus, where the gods live in joy and feasting and where Apollo plays the lyre while the Muses sing.
She took on her the form of an old woman, worn but stately, and wandered about the earth, where there is much sorrow to be seen. At first she kept away from the homes of
people, since the sight of little children and happy mothers
gave her pain. One day, however, as she sat by the side of a
well to rest her weary feet, four girls came down to draw
water. They were kind hearted and charming as they talked
80 with her and concerned themselves about the fate of the
homeless stranger-woman who was sitting at their gates. To

RETELL

Retell the story of
Persephone's disappearance
(lines 34–54).

_____

_____

_____

_____

_____

_____

_____

_____

_____

_____

_____

_____

_____

_____

IDENTIFY
CAUSE & EFFECT

The disappearance of her
beloved daughter caused
Demeter extreme grief. Read
lines 68–77, and underline
details that explain the
effects that resulted from her
sorrow and loss.

La Primavera: Flora (detail) (1477)
by Sandro Botticelli.

account for herself, Demeter told them that she was a
woman of good family from Crete, across the sea, who had
been captured by pirates and was to have been sold for a
slave. She had escaped as they landed once to cook a meal
on shore, and now she was wandering to find work.

    The four girls listened to this story, much impressed by
the stately manner of the strange woman. At last they said
that their mother, Metaneira,[3] was looking for a nurse for
90   their new-born brother, Demophoon.[4] Perhaps the stranger
would come and talk with her. Demeter agreed, feeling a
great longing to hold a baby once more, even if it were not
her own. She went therefore to Metaneira, who was much
struck with the quiet dignity of the goddess and glad to
give her charge of her little son. For a while thereafter

---

3. **Metaneira** (met′ə·nē′rə).
4. **Demophoon** (de·mäf′ō·än′).

Demeter was nurse to Demophoon, and his smiles and babble consoled her in some part for her own darling daughter. She began to make plans for Demophoon: He should be a great hero; he should become an immortal, 100 so that when he grew up she could keep him with her.

Presently the whole household was amazed at how beautiful Demophoon was growing, the more so as they never saw the nurse feed him anything. Secretly Demeter would anoint him with ambrosia,[5] like the gods, and from her breath, as he lay in her lap, he would draw his nourishment. When the night came, she would linger by the great fireside in the hall, rocking the child in her arms while the embers burned low and the people went off to sleep. Then, when all was still, she would stoop quickly down and put 110 the baby into the fire itself. All night long the child would sleep in the red-hot ashes, while his earthly flesh and blood changed slowly into the substance of the immortals. In the morning when people came, the ashes were cold and dead, and by the hearth sat the stranger-woman, gently rocking and singing to the child.

Presently Metaneira became suspicious of the strangeness of it all. What did she know of this nurse but the story she had heard from her daughters? Perhaps the woman was a witch of some sort who wished to steal or transform the 120 boy. In any case it was wise to be careful. One night, therefore, when she went up to her chamber, she set the door ajar and stood there in the crack silently watching the nurse at the fireside crooning over the child. The hall was very dark, so that it was hard to see clearly, but in a little while the mother beheld the dim figure bend forward. A log broke in the fireplace, a little flame shot up, and there clear in the light lay the baby on top of the fire.

---

5. ambrosia (am·brō′zhə): food of the gods.

DECODING TIP

An immortal (line 99) is a being that has everlasting life. The prefix im– means "not," and the word mortal means "a being that must eventually die."

PREDICT

Pause at line 100. Do you think Demeter's plan will come to pass? Explain.

_____

_____

_____

_____

_____

_____

_____

_____

_____

_____

_____

IDENTIFY

Re-read lines 101–115. Underline the details that explain what Demeter does to transform Demophoon into an immortal.

IDENTIFY
CAUSE & EFFECT

Pause at line 138. What causes Metaneira to become suspicious of Demeter? What is the effect of Metaneira's suspicion?

_____

_____

_____

_____

_____

_____

_____

_____

_____

_____

_____

WORD STUDY

The word *vain* is used twice in the second paragraph on this page. *Vain* comes from the Latin *vanus,* meaning "empty." Something done *in vain* means that the effort is useless or futile; it will come to nothing.

IDENTIFY
CAUSE & EFFECT

Re-read lines 139–152, and underline the details that explain the effect of Demeter's neglect of her duties as harvest goddess.

Metaneira screamed loudly and lost no time in rushing forward, but it was Demeter who snatched up the baby. "Fool that you are," she said indignantly to Metaneira, "I would have made your son immortal, but that is now impossible. He shall be a great hero, but in the end he will have to die. I, the goddess Demeter, promise it." With that old age fell from her and she grew in stature. Golden hair spread down over her shoulders so that the great hall was filled with light. She turned and went out of the doorway, leaving the baby on the ground and Metaneira too amazed and frightened even to take him up.

All the while that Demeter had been wandering, she had given no thought to her duties as the harvest goddess. Instead she was almost glad that others should suffer because she was suffering. In vain the oxen spent their strength in dragging the heavy plowshare[6] through the soil. In vain did the sower with his bag of grain throw out the even handfuls of white barley in a wide arc as he strode. The greedy birds had a feast off the seed corn that season; or if it started to sprout, sun baked it and rains washed it away. Nothing would grow. As the gods looked down, they saw threatening the earth a famine such as never had been known. Even the offerings to the gods were neglected by despairing men who could no longer spare anything from their dwindling stores.

At last Zeus sent Iris, the rainbow, to seek out Demeter and appeal to her to save mankind. Dazzling Iris swept down from Olympus swift as a ray of light and found Demeter sitting in her temple, the dark cloak still around her and her head bowed on her hand. Though Iris urged her with the messages of Zeus and offered beautiful gifts or whatever powers among the gods she chose, Demeter

---

6. **plowshare:** cutting blade of a plow.

160 would not lift her head or listen. All she said was that she would neither set foot on Olympus nor let fruit grow on the earth until Persephone was restored to her from the kingdom of the dead.

At last Zeus saw that he must send Hermes of the golden sandals to bring back Persephone to the light. The messenger found dark-haired Hades sitting upon his throne with Persephone, pale and sad, beside him. She had neither eaten nor drunk since she had been in the land of the dead. She sprang up with joy at the message of Hermes, 170 while the dark king looked gloomier than ever, for he really loved his queen. Though he could not disobey the command of Zeus, he was crafty, and he pressed Persephone to eat or drink with him as they parted. Now, with joy in her heart, she should not refuse all food. Persephone was eager

CLARIFY

Pause at line 163. Under what conditions will Demeter agree to resume her duties as harvest goddess?

_____

_____

_____

_____

_____

_____

_____

_____

_____

INFER

Re-read lines 167–171. Has Persephone come to accept her fate as wife of Hades? Explain.

_____

_____

_____

_____

_____

_____

_____

_____

Uffizi Gallery, Florence, Italy. © Erich Lessing/Art Resource, NY.

La Primavera: Flora (detail) (1477) by Sandro Botticelli.

PREDICT

Pause at line 179. Why is Hades so eager for Persephone to eat? What might happen to her?

_____

_____

_____

_____

_____

_____

_____

_____

IDENTIFY CAUSE & EFFECT

Pause at line 195. What effect did Persephone's eating seven pomegranate seeds have on the earth? Underline those details.

IDENTIFY

What natural occurrence does this origin myth explain? Hint: Think about the story's title.

_____

_____

_____

_____

_____

_____

to be gone, but since the king entreated her, she took a pomegranate[7] from him to avoid argument and delay. Giving in to his pleading, she ate seven of the seeds. Then Hermes took her with him, and she came out into the upper air.

180   When Demeter saw Hermes with her daughter, she started up, and Persephone too rushed forward with a glad cry and flung her arms about her mother's neck. For a long time the two caressed each other, but at last Demeter began to question the girl. "Did you eat or drink anything with Hades?" she asked her daughter anxiously, and the girl replied:

"Nothing until Hermes released me. Then in my joy I took a pomegranate and ate seven of its seeds."

"Alas," said the goddess in dismay, "my daughter, what

190   have you done? The Fates have said that if you ate anything in the land of shadow, you must return to Hades and rule with him as his queen. However, you ate not the whole pomegranate, but only seven of the seeds. For seven months of the year, therefore, you must dwell in the under-world, and the remaining five you may live with me."

Thus the Fates had decreed, and even Zeus could not alter their law. For seven months of every year, Persephone is lost to Demeter and rules pale and sad over the dead. At this time Demeter mourns, trees shed their leaves, cold comes,

200   and the earth lies still and dead. But when, in the eighth month, Persephone returns, her mother is glad and the earth rejoices. The wheat springs up, bright, fresh, and green in the plowland. Flowers unfold, birds sing, and young animals are born. Everywhere the heavens smile for joy or weep sudden showers of gladness upon the springing earth.

---

7. **pomegranate** (päm′ə·gran′it): round, red fruit containing many seeds that can be eaten.

The Origin of the Seasons

Cause-and-Effect Chart   Through a series of causes and effects, **origin myths** explain how things came to be in our world. Fill in the chart below with the major causes and effects from "The Origin of the Seasons." Add more boxes if you need them.

Literary Skills
Analyze an
origin myth.

Reading Skills
Analyze cause
and effect.

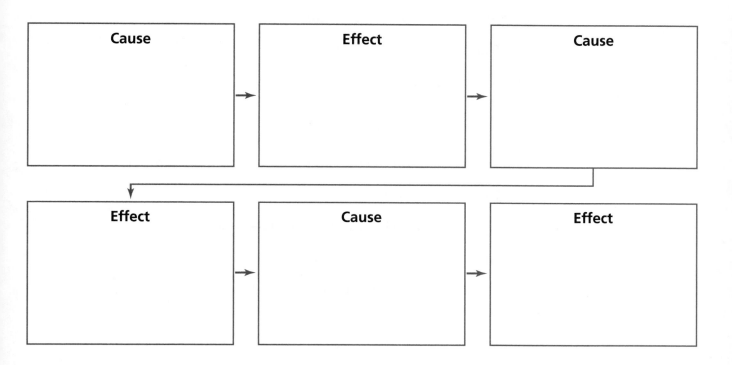

Origin Myths   What aspect of the natural world does this myth explain? Do you find it a convincing explanation? Why or why not?

_____

_____

_____

_____

_____

The Origin of the Seasons

COMPREHENSION

A. Reading Comprehension Check True or False in response to the following statements about the story.

1. Demeter and Persephone are sisters.

   _____ True   _____ False

2. When Hades takes Persephone to be his wife, Zeus becomes very angry.

   _____ True   _____ False

3. The goddess Demeter becomes a nursemaid to a human boy.

   _____ True   _____ False

4. The crops on earth fail because of Demeter's neglect.

   _____ True   _____ False

5. When Persephone defies Zeus, she is condemned to spend her life as Hades' wife.

   _____ True   _____ False

B. Understanding Cause and Effect Describe the effect of each event.

1. Gloomy Hades falls in love with beautiful young Persephone.

   Effect: _____

2. Unhappy about the loss of Persephone, Demeter gives no thought to her duties as the harvest goddess.

   Effect: _____

3. While in the land of the dead, Persephone eats seven seeds from a piece of fruit.

   Effect: _____

SKILLS FOCUS

Reading Skills
Understand
cause and effect.

Oni and the Great Bird

retold by Abayomi Fuja

◆ This selection also appears in *Elements of Literature.*

LITERARY FOCUS: MOTIFS IN FOLK TALES

A **motif** (mō·tēf') is a feature that is repeated in stories throughout the world. Think for a moment about stories you heard during your childhood. Chances are that quite a few of those stories involved magic, villains, and quests to save a kingdom from destruction. Among the most popular motifs in folk tales is the **superhero.** Read on, and meet the superhero featured in the Yoruban folk tale "Oni and the Great Bird."

READING SKILLS: SUMMARIZING

When you **summarize** a text, you extract only the most important ideas or events. A summary is different from a paraphrase, in which all the ideas in a text are restated. Summarizing is a useful tool. By summarizing, you identify the heart of a text and clarify who's who and what's what.

You'll be asked to summarize "Oni and the Great Bird" after you read it. You may want to take notes on a chart like this one to prepare for that summary.

Notes for Summary	
Main Characters	
Conflict(s)	
Main Events	
Story's Ending	

SKILLS FOCUS

Literary Skills
Understand motifs.

Reading Skills
Summarize.

Vocabulary Skills
Clarify meanings by using contrast.

VOCABULARY DEVELOPMENT

PREVIEW SELECTION VOCABULARY

Get to know the following words before you begin "Oni and the Great Bird."

implored (im·plôrd′) *v.:* asked or begged.

> *The old man implored Oni to do nothing dangerous.*

commenced (kə·menst′) *v.:* began.

> *Oni commenced to sing only when the eagle flew near.*

invincible (in·vin′sə·bəl) *adj.:* unbeatable.

> *No one could beat invincible Oni.*

hovered (huv′ərd) *v.:* hung in the air.

> *The great bird flew in and hovered above them.*

impostor (im·päs′tər) *n.:* person who pretends to be someone or something that he or she is not.

> *The hunter who claimed to have done Oni's deeds was an impostor.*

CLARIFYING WORD MEANINGS: CONTRAST

When trying to figure out the meaning of an unfamiliar word, you might try a couple of strategies. Looking for a familiar word or word part within the unfamiliar word and looking for a restatement of the word are good strategies. Here's another good strategy: As you read "Oni and the Great Bird," look at the context to see if the writer gives a clue by telling what the word is *not.*

In these examples, the italicized passages provide context clues for the boldface words.

- Kuki, *never one to give up,* was **relentless** in her pursuit of the Junior Miss title.
- **Vibrant** colors, *not pale pastel colors,* were chosen for the baby's room.
- *Unlike the new cars* on the lot, the **jalopy** was ignored by the customers.

Oní and the Great Bírd

Yoruban, retold by Abayomi Fuja

© Royalty-Free/CORBIS.

There was once a strange boy called Oni who was born wearing a pair of boots. As Oni grew, the boots grew also. When he was a boy of eighteen years of age, war broke out between his people and another village. It was during the battle that Oní made a second discovery about himself, which separated him from his fellow men and made him different. The enemy arrows did not seem to harm him. Many pierced his body, which in the ordinary course of events should have slain him. The other young men noticed 10 this too. They already regarded Oni as strange because of his wonderful boots, but when they discovered that he could not be killed, they were afraid to have him near them. When he returned from the war, several people tried to kill him in various ways but without any success. Finding

---

IDENTIFY

Re-read lines 1–14. Underline the details that describe the way Oni differs from the other boys.

INFER

Pause at line 14. Why do you think Oni is able to escape death?

_____

_____

_____

_____

_____

_____

IDENTIFY

Pause at line 18. Why did the people of the village banish Oni?

_____

_____

_____

_____

_____

_____

_____

_____

PREDICT

Pause at line 38. Why are the people in such a hurry? What do you think the bells might be signaling?

_____

_____

_____

_____

_____

_____

_____

_____

_____

_____

_____

this did not work, it was decided to find an excuse to banish him. He was accused of setting a house on fire in the village, and although Oni had nothing to do with the fire, he was found guilty and banished.

Oni wandered alone on foot for a long time. One afternoon he came to the banks of a great river, and finding an empty canoe and feeling tired of walking, he got into the boat and made his way downstream. Towards evening, when it was growing dark, Oni reached a town and decided to pull into the bank and spend the night there. There were the sounds of many bells being rung and people seemed to be in a hurry. Oni tied up the canoe and climbed the bank, and as he did so, he met an old man. "Good evening, my friend. My name is Oni. I am a stranger to your town and have nowhere to spend the night. Will you take me to your house?" Oni asked the old man.

"Yes, certainly, come along with me, but we must go quickly because the bells are ringing and it is growing dusk," replied the old man.

"What is the name of your town and why do your people ring bells on the approach of darkness?" asked Oni.

"People call this place Ajo, but hurry up, we must get indoors. I will explain the bells to you when we are inside," replied the old man.

When they reached the old man's house, they found his people waiting anxiously for him at the door. The bells had now stopped ringing and they were hurried inside and the door was securely fastened.

"Now," said the old man, "sit down and eat with us and I will explain. For many years now we, the people of Ajo, have been troubled by the nightly arrival of a giant eagle. We call it Anodo. It always appears on the approach of darkness and stays until the approach of dawn. Anybody who is unfortunate enough to be out of doors at the time of its appearance is sure to be killed by it. You were very

50 fortunate, young man, to reach Ajo before darkness. Our king has ordered the ringing of bells to warn the people to return to their homes and lock the doors. None of us knows where the eagle comes from or where it goes when it leaves us at dawn. It is a terrible curse, and in the past it has killed many of our people."

The old man had hardly finished speaking when Oni heard the sound of great wings flapping over the house. It sounded like a great wind, and the windows and doors shook in their frames.

60 "It must be a very great bird," remarked Oni. After Oni had fed, the old man gave him a mat and a cloth and he lay down to sleep in the corner of the room. Sleep would not come to Oni, however, for he heard the constant noise of the great eagle's wings as it flew to and fro over Ajo.

When morning had come and the eagle had departed, Oni thanked the old man for his kindness and set out to find the king of Ajo and to ask for an audience.[1] It was granted.

"My name is Oni and I am a stranger to your town. I have come to offer my services in helping to rid this town

70 of the eagle Anodo," said Oni.

"And what makes you think you will succeed where so many others have tried and failed?" asked the king.

"I have certain powers and juju,"[2] said Oni.

"So had the others. One by one all my hunters have tried and have been killed or carried off by Anodo. Strangers have come from time to time to offer their services, but they too have perished. It is some time now since anybody has tried to kill Anodo, and I have issued orders to my

---

1. **audience** *n.:* here, formal interview with a person of high rank.
2. **juju** *n.:* magic charms used by some West African tribes; the magic of such charms.

CONNECT

In lines 43–55, the old man tells about Anodo, the fierce bird that is terrorizing the village. What other stories do you know that feature the **motif** of terrible beasts?

_____

_____

_____

_____

_____

_____

_____

WORD STUDY

The word *great* (line 60) has several meanings. In this context, it means "huge" or "enormous."

PREDICT

Pause at line 67. What is Oni going to ask the king?

_____

_____

_____

_____

_____

_____

Re-read lines 87–92.

Pause at line 106.

VOCABULARY

implored (im·plôrd′) v.: asked or begged.

commenced (kə·menst′) v.: began.

invincible (in·vin′sə·bəl) adj.: unbeatable.

hovered (huv′ərd) v.: hung in the air.

COMPARE & CONTRAST

Re-read lines 87–92. Describe the different attitudes Oni and the old man's family have about Anodo.

_____

_____

_____

_____

_____

INTERPRET

Pause at line 106. Why does Oni sing a song when Anodo flies over the old man's house?

_____

_____

_____

_____

_____

_____

remaining hunters not to try, as enough of them have been

80 killed already," said the king.

"Have you ever offered a reward to anybody who could succeed in killing the bird?" asked Oni.

"Indeed, yes. The man who succeeds will have half my kingdom. I made that offer long ago," replied the king.

"Then I will try tonight," answered Oni, and he paid his respects to the king and departed.

Oni returned to the old man's house and told him what had happened and of his intention to challenge Anodo. The old man was very frightened and **implored** him to give up

90 the idea, for he would only perish and perhaps all those in the house too. But Oni was not frightened. He took his bow and arrows and knives and examined them carefully.

It seemed ages to Oni before he heard the bells ringing. Never had he known a longer day in his life. The old man was uneasy and his people were almost hostile towards Oni. When they heard the bells ringing at last, they lost no time in fastening the doors and windows and ordered Oni to lie down on his mat and keep quiet.

Presently they heard the noise of a great wind, which

100 heralded the approach of Anodo. Soon the great wings were above the house. Oni waited till the great bird was overhead and then he **commenced** to sing:

> Tonight Oni will be at war with Anodo,
> The eagle whose talons are sharper than knives,
> For now the knives of nature and man will meet.
> Oni is **invincible;** his knife is sharp.

Anodo heard the challenge as he **hovered** over the house, and circling slowly round, he came back and sang:

© Paul Almasy/CORBIS.

A decorated silo supports the thatched roof of a home in Toro, Nigeria.

FLUENCY

Read the boxed passage aloud several times. Use punctuation clues to guide your reading. As you read this chant, or song, use a threatening tone, as fits the story.

IDENTIFY

Pause at line 116. Banishment is a common **motif** in folk tales. This is the second time in the story that Oni has been thrown out of a place. Why was he banished from the old man's house?

_____

_____

_____

_____

_____

_____

_____

_____

_____

_____

_____

_____

_____

_____

_____

_____

_____

_____

> Ah, fortune, I have found a victim tonight,
>
> 110   I have lived many months without a kill,
>
> Will the singer come out and feel the sharpness
>
> Of my talons and of my beak? It will take me
>
> A moment to tear him to pieces. Come out.

All the people in the house were terrified. They seized Oni and threw him out of the house, fearing the vengeance of Anodo on them all.

As they threw Oni out into the road, Anodo swooped down and, seizing him in his talons, drew him upwards. Oni slashed the eagle in the chest with his knife and the 120 eagle dropped him with a scream. Oni fell to the ground, dazed. He picked himself up as the huge bird descended once again. He had time to use his bow and discharge an arrow into Anodo before the wounded bird beat him to the ground with his great wings and pecked him severely. Again Oni's knife tore at the eagle, and he buried it twice in

SUMMARIZE

Take a moment to summarize the events of the battle (lines 117–141).

_____

_____

_____

_____

_____

_____

_____

_____

_____

_____

PREDICT

Following the battle, Oni loses one of his boots (lines 144–148). In what way might he be affected? Will he get his boot back?

_____

_____

_____

_____

_____

_____

_____

_____

_____

_____

Anodo. Slowly the eagle beat his great wings and rose slowly into the air; then he hovered for a last terrible dive on Oni. Oni watched him and, putting an arrow in his bow, took aim. The great bird hovered; then with a terrible noise he tore down on the boy, gathering speed as he came. There was a great roar of wind as he came down. Oni discharged a second arrow, then another and another in quick succession, but still the bird came on. A moment later it had hit Oni and knocked him over. The boy rolled over, a thousand lights dancing before his eyes; then all went blank, and he felt himself sinking down and down into a bottomless pit. He was knocked unconscious and had not seen that the great bird was already dead before it struck him. Its great wings swept the boy to one side, and it plunged on into a cotton tree, which snapped like a twig and came crashing down to bury the eagle and Oni under a mass of leaves.

When Oni recovered, he felt very weak, and it was all he could do to free himself from the great wing of the dead Anodo and the cotton tree leaves. As he struggled, one of his magic boots came off and remained stuck beneath the dead bird. He was very weak and with great difficulty staggered along till he reached the edge of the river; then Oni fainted again.

Early next morning the people came out to see the dead Anodo lying in the broken cotton tree. There was great rejoicing and drumming and the king soon appeared with his chiefs to view the wonderful sight. "Who is the great man who killed Anodo?" he asked. One of his hunters stepped forward and, prostrating[3] himself on the ground, claimed that he was responsible for the deed.

---

3. **prostrating** (präs'trāt'iŋ) v. used as *adj.*: throwing oneself on the ground to show humility and submission, a traditional gesture of respect toward rulers in many cultures.

"Then you will be rewarded generously, for I have promised to give half my kingdom to the man who killed Anodo and it is yours," replied the king.

There was great rejoicing and dancing and the hunter was carried to the king's palace and feasted. A very bedraggled figure then appeared; his clothes were torn and one of his boots was missing. It was Oni.

"Ah," said the king, "here is the stranger who calls himself Oni and who came yesterday to announce his intention of killing the eagle. You come too late, my friend, I fear."

"I killed Anodo. This man is an **impostor** and a liar," said Oni.

There was whispering between the king and his chiefs. At last he said, "Very well, you claim to have killed Anodo. What proof have you got to offer?"

"You see my condition," replied Oni, "but if you require further proof, send your men out to clear away the dead eagle and the broken cotton tree. Somewhere underneath you will find one of my boots."

The king ordered his men to go at once and search for the boot. After some little time the men returned. They carried Oni's magic boot. "We found it underneath the dead eagle's wing," they announced to the king.

"Now if you are still undecided and disbelieve my story, will you ask everybody to try on the boot and see if it fits," said Oni.

The king ordered everybody to try to see if they could fit the boot to their feet. Strange to relate, although it looked a perfectly normal boot, nobody could manage to put it on. When they had all tried without success, the boot was placed before the king and Oni stepped forward and said:

PREDICT

Pause at line 162. Will Oni challenge the person who claims to have defeated Anodo? Give reasons for your answer.

_____
_____
_____
_____
_____
_____

VOCABULARY

impostor (im·päs′tər) n.: person who pretends to be someone or something that he or she is not.

CONNECT

In lines 179–181, Oni proposes that the people of the kingdom try on the boot to see who it fits—to see who its rightful owner is. Can you think of a popular fairy tale that shares this **motif**?

_____
_____
_____
_____
_____
_____
_____

SUMMARIZE

Summarize what has happened in the story from the end of the battle to the end of the story.

_____

_____

_____

_____

_____

_____

_____

_____

Boot from Heaven—boot from Heaven,
Go on to your master's foot.

190 Immediately, the boot started to move from before the king and fitted itself onto Oni's foot of its own accord. The people and the king were convinced of the truth of Oni's claims and marveled greatly and were very delighted and grateful for his brave deed. The dishonest hunter was taken out and executed, and Oni received the promised reward.

That night, for the first time for many years, the bells of Ajo did not sound the curfew. Instead, the streets were full of happy, dancing people.

INTERPRET

This folk tale has a happy ending for both Oni and the people of Ajo. What has Oni gained through his deeds? What have the people of Ajo gained?

_____

_____

_____

_____

_____

_____

_____

Founders Society Purchase, Friends of African Art Fund. Photograph © 1995 The Detroit Institute of Arts accession number 77.71.

Epa cult mask.

Oni and the Great Bird

Motif Map Character types, events, and other features common to stories from around the world are called **motifs.** "Oni and the Great Bird" contains many motifs, among them the motif of the superhero. The graphic that follows lists several characteristics of the superhero. Locate story details that relate to each characteristic, and write them in the circles below.

Literary Skills
Analyze the superhero motif.

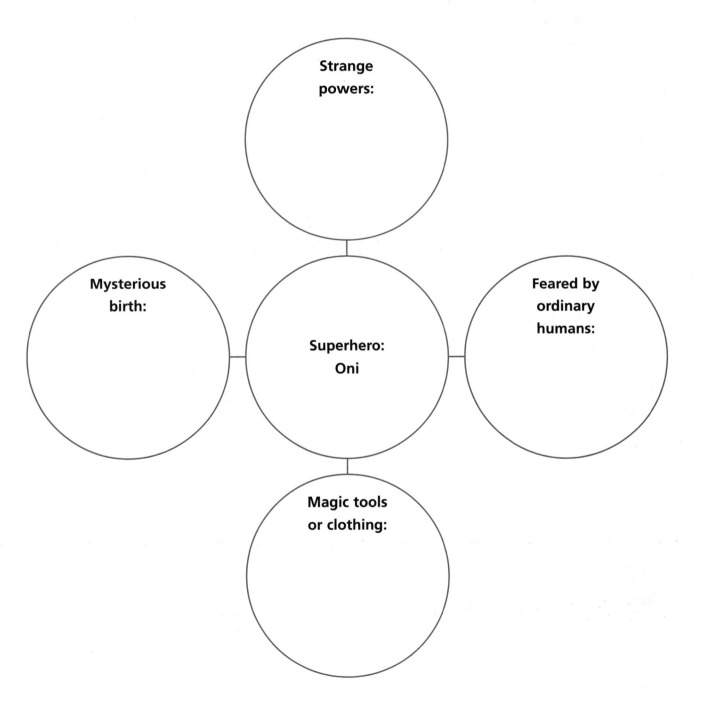

Strange powers:

Mysterious birth:

Superhero: Oni

Feared by ordinary humans:

Magic tools or clothing:

Skills Review

Oni and the Great Bird

VOCABULARY AND COMPREHENSION

A. Clarifying Word Meanings: Contrast   Fill in the blanks with the correct Word Bank word. Use contrast clues to help you.

1. Impossible to defeat, the _____ warrior triumphed over his enemy.

2. Setting aside her pride, the starving woman _____ the town to provide hunger relief.

3. It was not over after all. The play had just _____ when we arrived.

4. Unlike most birds, which fly quickly by, this bird _____ just above my head.

5. "He's not the real hero," the people cried. "He's an _____!"

B. Reading Comprehension   Answer each question below.

1. Why is Oni forced to leave his village at the beginning of the story?

_____

_____

2. How does the king of Ajo react to Oni's offer to fight Anodo?

_____

_____

3. Who wins the fight between Oni and Anodo? _____

_____

4. How does Oni prove that the hunter who claims to have killed Anodo is an impostor? _____

_____

SKILLS FOCUS

Vocabulary Skills
Clarify meanings by using contrast.

Loo-Wit, the Fire-Keeper

retold by Joseph Bruchac

LITERARY FOCUS: FOLK TALES

Folk tales are stories that have been passed from generation to generation. Each time the story is told, it takes on new life, with subtle
changes—perhaps some exaggeration here or an added character
there. In some folk tales, we learn about the lives people lived and
the beliefs they held and valued. In other tales, we may get a glimpse
of their humor and learn about their wildest dreams and fantasies.

The folk tale "Loo-Wit, the Fire-Keeper" tells us about the origin of
several geographic features in the states of Washington and Oregon.
It also cautions us about the ill effects of greed and fighting.

READING SKILLS: IDENTIFYING AUTHOR'S PURPOSE

Storytellers tell stories for many reasons. They may want to make us
laugh, cry, learn a lesson about life, or simply entertain us. Some stories,
such as **origin myths,** teach us about how things in the world came to
be. They may, for example, explain to us why the world is round or how
the snail got its shell.

As you read the folk tale that follows, look for details that help you
figure out the author's purpose. You may want to fill out a chart like
this one as you read. The first entry has been completed for you.

Detail	Possible Purpose
The brothers quarreled over land.	To show us what effects quarreling can have

Literary Skills
Identify
characteristics of
folk tales.

Reading Skills
Identify an
author's purpose.

**Vocabulary
Skills**
Understand
figures of
speech.

VOCABULARY DEVELOPMENT

PREVIEW SELECTION VOCABULARY

Preview the following words from the story before you begin reading.

claim (klām) *n.:* demand for something; here, demand for land.

The town overturned the man's claim. They ruled that the land belonged to everyone.

arched (ärcht) *v.:* traveled in an arc, or overhead curve.

The arrow arched over the river and landed to the south in the valley of the Willamette River.

aware (ə·wer′) *adj.:* knowing; conscious.

Though she was asleep, Loo-Wit was still aware, the people said.

UNDERSTANDING FIGURES OF SPEECH

One thing that helps brighten our world is the use of **figures of speech** in speaking and writing. Through figures of speech we are able to make interesting comparisons between things that are not alike on the surface. Two of the most commonly used figures of speech are the simile and metaphor.

SIMILE: Comparison in which a connecting word such as *like* or *as* is used.

The new sports car that was parked in the driveway looked like a tiger sleeping in the sun.

METAPHOR: Comparison in which no connecting word is used.

Do you want to drive the tiger parked in the driveway?

As you read "Loo-Wit," look for figures of speech that enliven the story.

Loo-Wit, the Fire-Keeper

retold by Joseph Bruchac

BACKGROUND: Literature and Social Studies
"Loo-Wit, the Fire-Keeper" explains the origin of some of the natural features of Washington and Oregon. (See the map, page 224.) The river gorges, mountains, and American Indian peoples mentioned in this myth are all real. The Klickitat, one of the rival peoples in the myth, are now part of the Yakima Nation, a confederation of peoples in south-central Washington. Many of the Multnomah peoples mentioned in the myth were wiped out by an epidemic of measles in 1832.

When the world was young, the Creator gave everyone all that was needed to be happy.

The weather was always pleasant. There was food for everyone and room for all the people. Despite this, though, two brothers began to quarrel over the land. Each wanted to control it. It reached the point where each brother gathered together a group of men to support his **claim.** Soon it appeared there would be war.

The Creator saw this and was not pleased. He waited
10 until the two brothers were asleep one night and then carried them to a new country. There a beautiful river flowed and tall mountains rose into the clouds. He woke them just as the sun rose, and they looked out from the mountaintop to the land below. They saw what a good place it was. It made their hearts good.

INFER

Who is the Creator (line 1)?

_____

_____

_____

_____

_____

IDENTIFY

Re-read lines 1–8. Underline the problem that begins the story.

VOCABULARY

claim (klām) *n.:* demand for something; here, demand for land.

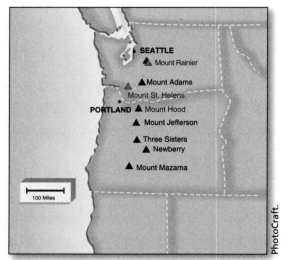

The Cascade Range in the United States.

CLARIFY

Pause at line 20. How is the brothers' problem solved?

_____

_____

_____

_____

_____

_____

_____

_____

_____

VOCABULARY

arched (ärcht) *v.:* traveled in an arc, or overhead curve.

INTERPRET

Pause at line 32. Why is a bridge a good symbol of peace between two nations?

_____

_____

_____

_____

_____

_____

_____

_____

_____

"Now," the Creator said, "this will be your land." Then he gave each of the brothers a bow and a single arrow. "Shoot your arrow into the air," the Creator said. "Where your arrow falls will be the land of your people, and you

20 shall be a great chief there."

The brothers did as they were told. The older brother shot his arrow. It **arched** over the river and landed to the south in the valley of the Willamette River. There is where he and his people went, and they became the Multnomahs. The younger brother shot his arrow. It flew to the north of the great river. He and his people went there and became the Klickitats.

Then the Creator made a Great Stone Bridge across the river. "This bridge," the Creator said, "is a sign of peace. You

30 and your peoples can visit each other by crossing over this bridge. As long as you remain at peace, as long as your hearts are good, this bridge will stand."

For many seasons the two peoples remained at peace. They passed freely back and forth across the Great Stone Bridge. One day, though, the people to the north looked south toward the Willamette and said, "Their lands are better than ours." One day, though, the people to the south looked north toward the Klickitat and said, "Their lands are more beautiful than ours." Then, once again, the people

40 began to quarrel.

The Creator saw this and was not pleased.

The people were becoming greedy again. Their hearts were becoming bad. The Creator darkened the skies and took fire away. Now the people grew cold. The rains of autumn began and the people suffered greatly.

"Give us back fire," they begged. "We wish to live again with each other in peace."

Their prayers reached the Creator's heart. There was only one place on Earth where fire still remained. An old

50 woman named Loo-Wit had stayed out of the quarreling and was not greedy. It was in her lodge only that fire still burned. So the Creator went to Loo-Wit.

"If you will share your fire with all the people," the Creator said, "I will give you whatever you wish. Tell me what you want."

"I want to be young and beautiful," Loo-Wit said.

"That is the way it will be," said the Creator. "Now take your fire to the Great Stone Bridge above the river. Let all the people come to you and get fire. You must keep the fire burn-

60 ing there to remind people that their hearts must stay good."

The next morning, the skies grew clear and the people saw the sun rise for the first time in many days. The sun shone on the Great Stone Bridge, and there the people saw a young woman as beautiful as the sunshine itself. Before her, there on the bridge, burned a fire. The people came to the fire and ended their quarrels. Loo-Wit gave each of them fire. Now their homes again became warm and peace was everywhere.

TEXT STRUCTURE

Repetition is often used in myths and fairy tales. Underline the two quotations in lines 33–40. Here, the repetition creates a rhythm. It also stresses the idea that each group is doing and saying the same thing.

RETELL

Pause at line 45. How are the people behaving? What does the Creator do?

_____

_____

_____

_____

_____

_____

_____

IDENTIFY

According to lines 48–60, why is Loo-Wit rewarded?

_____

_____

_____

FLUENCY

Read the boxed passage aloud, timing yourself. Then, read the passage aloud a second time, aiming to improve your speed.

How does the Creator solve
the brothers' latest quarrel
(lines 76–81)?

_____

_____

_____

_____

_____

_____

_____

_____

_____

IDENTIFY

What is the myth explaining
in the paragraph beginning
on line 76?

_____

_____

_____

_____

_____

_____

_____

_____

_____

American Museum of Natural History, New York.

Northwest Coast Indian mask.

70
One day, though, the chief of the people to the north
came to Loo-Wit's fire. He saw how beautiful she was and
wanted her to be his wife. At the same time, the chief of the
people to the south also saw Loo-Wit's beauty. He, too,
wanted to marry her. Loo-Wit could not decide which of
the two she liked better. Then the chiefs began to quarrel.
Their peoples took up the quarrel, and fighting began.

When the Creator saw the fighting, he became angry.
He broke down the Great Stone Bridge. He took each of the
two chiefs and changed them into mountains. The chief of
the Klickitats became the mountain we now know as Mount
80
Adams. The chief of the Multnomahs became the mountain
we now know as Mount Hood. Even as mountains, they
continued to quarrel, throwing flames and stones at each
other. In some places, the stones they threw almost blocked

the river between them. That is why the Columbia River is so narrow in the place called The Dalles° today.

Loo-Wit was heartbroken over the pain caused by her beauty. She no longer wanted to be a beautiful young woman. She could no longer find peace as a human being.

The Creator took pity on her and changed her into a
90 mountain also, the most beautiful of the mountains. She was placed so that she stood between Mount Adams and Mount Hood, and she was allowed to keep the fire within herself which she had once shared on the Great Stone Bridge. Eventually, she became known as Mount St. Helens, and she slept peacefully.

Though she was asleep, Loo-Wit was still **aware,** the people said. The Creator had placed her between the two quarreling mountains to keep the peace, and it was intended that humans, too, should look at her beauty and remember
100 to keep their hearts good, to share the land and treat it well. If we human beings do not treat the land with respect, the people said, Loo-Wit will wake up and let us know how unhappy she and the Creator have become again. So they said, long before the day in the 1980s when Mount St. Helens woke again.

INTERPRET

In lines 86–95, we have the **climax** of the story. Based on what you know about Mount St. Helens, what do you think the "fire within herself" stands for?

_____

_____

_____

_____

_____

VOCABULARY

aware (ə·wer′) *adj.:* knowing; conscious.

INFER

What does the teller of this myth suggest is the reason Mount St. Helens exploded in the 1980s? Why might the author have chosen to share this story with us?

_____

_____

_____

_____

_____

_____

_____

° **The Dalles** (dalz): town in Oregon on the steep, rocky banks of the Columbia River.

Loo-Wit, the Fire-Keeper

Author's Purpose   Stories are written for a purpose: to teach, to entertain, or perhaps to warn us about something. Think about "Loo-Wit, the Fire-Keeper" and what its purpose might be. Then, write that purpose in the first box of the chart below. Go through the story, and list details from the story that support its purpose.

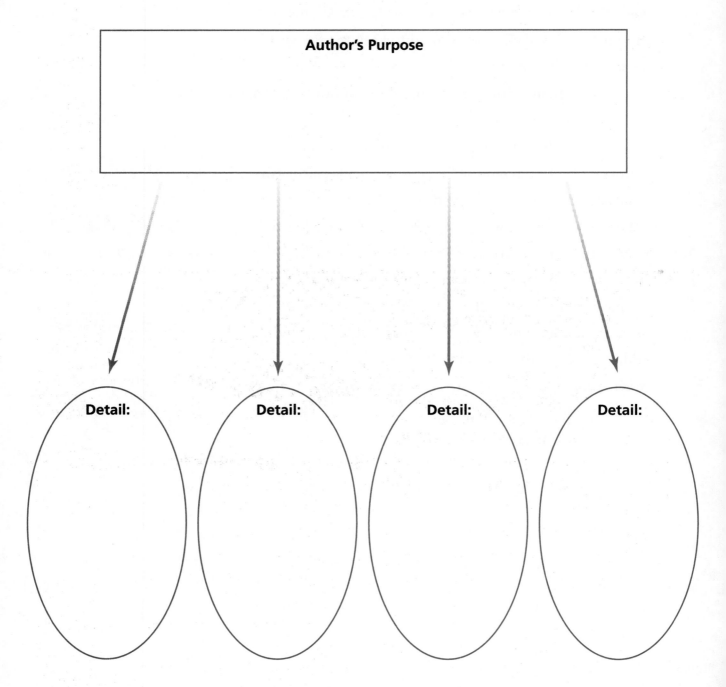

Author's Purpose

Detail: **Detail:**   **Detail:**   **Detail:**

Skills Review

Loo-Wit, the Fire-Keeper

VOCABULARY AND COMPREHENSION

Word Bank

Word Bank

claim

arched

aware

A. Understanding Figures of Speech   Read each sentence below. Fill in the blanks with the correct Word Bank word. Then, underline the figure of speech in each sentence.

1. The arrow _____ so high it looked like a silver rainbow.

2. The brother's _____ was nothing but a castle in the sky. It was worthless.

3. We were all _____ that fighting fate was like fighting the tide.

B. Reading Comprehension   Answer the questions below.

1. Why is the Creator angry with the brothers at the beginning of the story? _____

_____

2. What does the Creator do to solve the dispute between the brothers? Does the problem stay fixed for long? Explain. _____

_____

3. Who is Loo-Wit? Why does the Creator reward her? _____

_____

4. What problem does Loo-Wit's new appearance cause? _____

_____

_____

5. What becomes of the two brothers and Loo-Wit at the story's end?

_____

_____

SKILLS FOCUS

Vocabulary Skills
Understand figures of speech.

Literary Criticism:
Where I Stand

Academic Vocabulary for Collection 7

These are the terms you should know
as you read and analyze the stories in this collection.

Legend An old story passed down from generation to generation. Legends combine historical facts with made-up events. The stories about King Arthur's Camelot are some of the most famous legends in the English language.

Quest A long, dangerous journey in search of something of great value. The hero of the quest usually faces many hardships and trials. The hero often has to solve a **riddle**—a puzzling question or problem—before continuing on the quest.

Metamorphosis A change from one shape or form to another. In myths, humans are commonly changed to animals, and animals to humans.

● ● ●

Foreshadowing The use of clues to suggest events that will occur later in the story. Foreshadowing creates suspense and helps the reader make predictions about what will happen.

King Arthur: The Sword in the Stone

by Hudson Talbott

LITERARY FOCUS: LEGEND—A LITTLE FACT, A LOT OF STORY

How much do you know about your family history? Have stories about your ancestors been passed down from one generation to the next? As time passes and stories are passed along, events and characters may become exaggerated, and details may be added to spice up the accounts. These stories are a lot like legends in literature. A **legend** is a very old story that has been passed down from one generation to the next. Legends usually have some connection to a historical person or event, but they also contain a lot of made-up, sometimes fantastic, events.

READING SKILLS: RETELLING

Stories that are long or that have complicated plots can be difficult to follow. One good way to keep up with a story is to use a reading strategy called retelling. As you read this story, stop now and then to **retell** what you have read in your own words. Retelling will help you identify the major story events and keep all the information straight in your mind.

SKILLS FOCUS

Literary Skills
Understand legends.

Reading Skills
Retell a story.

Vocabulary Skills
Recognize Latin and Anglo-Saxon roots.

© Royalty-Free/CORBIS.

LEGEND

VOCABULARY DEVELOPMENT

PREVIEW SELECTION VOCABULARY

Before you read *King Arthur: The Sword in the Stone*, spend a few minutes previewing these vocabulary words.

turbulent (tur′byə·lənt) *adj.:* wild; disorderly.

> *King Arthur restored peace to a turbulent land.*

tournament (toor′nə·mənt) *n.:* series of contests.

> *Sir Kay hoped to show his bravery during the tournament.*

integrity (in·teg′rə·tē) *n.:* honesty; uprightness.

> *A knight's integrity kept him from wrongdoing.*

congregation (kän′grə·gā′shən) *n.:* gathering.

> *The king spoke to a congregation of villagers.*

LATIN AND ANGLO-SAXON ROOTS

English is made up of words borrowed from other languages. Many of these words come from Anglo-Saxon and French (the languages of two peoples that conquered England). English words taken from Anglo-Saxon are often short. They tend to be common words that you use all the time, such as *book, house,* and *yes.* Words taken from French, most of which were derived from Latin, tend to be longer and "fancier." Here are some examples.

Anglo-Saxon Words
deer, pig, cow, man, wife, foot, for, the, in, is

Words from Latin	
turbulent	*turba,* meaning "crowd"
tournament	*tornare,* meaning "turn"
messenger	*mittere,* meaning "send"

King Arthur: The Sword in the Stone   233

KING ARTHUR:
THE SWORD IN THE STONE

Hudson Talbott

BACKGROUND: Literature and Social Studies
The hero behind the legend of King Arthur probably lived about A.D. 500. The real Arthur is believed to have been a military leader of people called the Britons. In the first century B.C., the Romans invaded Britain, and they ruled for about four hundred years. After the armies of Rome pulled out of England in A.D. 410, several tribes tried to seize control. According to the earliest legends, a leader named Arthur united the Britons and led them to victory against one of those invading tribes, the Saxons. After Arthur's death the Saxons and the Angles, another tribe, conquered the Britons, but stories about the warrior king's unusual courage and goodness lived on among his people through the telling of legends.

IDENTIFY

Re-read lines 1–6. Underline information in the passage that sounds as if it might be factual.

_____

_____

_____

_____

_____

_____

_____

In ancient times, when Britain was still a wild and restless place, there lived a noble king named Uther.[1] After many years of turmoil, Uther defeated the invading barbarians and drove them from the land. For this triumph, his fellow British lords proclaimed him their high king, or Pendragon, meaning "Dragon's Head."

Soon after his coronation,[2] Uther Pendragon met and fell in love with the beautiful Lady Igraine,[3] a widow whose husband Uther had killed in battle. Uther married Igraine
10 and adopted her two young daughters, Margaise[4] and

---

1. **Uther** (y$\overline{oo}$′thər).
2. **coronation** n.: ceremony for crowning a king or a queen.
3. **Igraine** (ē·grān′).
4. **Margaise** (mär·gāz′).

Morgan le Fay. The price for this love was a high one, however. In his passion, the king had asked for the help of his sorcerer, Merlin, in winning the hand of Lady Igraine. In return Uther had agreed to give up their firstborn son. Merlin had foreseen great evil descending upon the king and felt that he alone could protect a young heir in the dangerous times ahead.

Before long, a beautiful boy child was born. But the joy surrounding the birth was brief, for Merlin soon appeared
20 to take the child away.

"But the child was just born!" exclaimed Uther. "How did you find out so quickly?"

Silently, the old sorcerer led the king to a balcony and pointed upward. There overhead was a great dragon formed by the stars. Its vast wings arched over the countryside, and its tail swept north beyond the horizon. "You see by this sign, my lord, that it is not I who calls for your son, but destiny."

Sadly, the king gave up his son, for Merlin convinced
30 him that the child's great future was threatened. Indeed, Uther Pendragon died within a year from a traitor's poison and Britain was once again plunged into darkness.

After the death of the high king, the struggle for leadership tore Britain to pieces. The great alliance King Uther had forged was shattered into dozens of quarreling, petty kingdoms—leaving no united force to oppose foreign invasion. Barbarians swept in once again and order gave way to chaos. Marauding knights roamed the countryside, taking what they wanted and burning the rest. No one was safe at
40 home, and travel was even more dangerous, with outlaws ruling the roads. Fear was a constant companion of those who managed to stay alive.

RETELL

Re-read lines 11–20. What deal was made between King Uther and Merlin?

_____

_____

_____

_____

_____

_____

_____

_____

_____

_____

_____

_____

_____

_____

WORD STUDY

Marauding (mə·rôd′iŋ), in line 38, means "raiding or plundering." It comes from the French *maraud,* meaning "vagabond."

IDENTIFY CAUSE & EFFECT

What effect did King Uther's death have on Britain (lines 33–42)? Underline that information.

Knights and horse (detail) (13th century) from Stained Glass Program at Sainte-Chapelle in Paris, France.

VOCABULARY

turbulent (tʉr'byə·lənt) *adj.:* wild; disorderly.

INTERPRET

Re-read lines 51–60 carefully. Circle the word *sun* each time it appears, and underline the word *son.* Why does Merlin deliberately play with the words *sun* and *son* in his discussion with the archbishop?

_____

_____

_____

WORD STUDY

Heir (er), in line 58, is derived from the Latin *heres.* Both *heir* and *heres* mean "person who inherits title or property from someone who dies."

RETELL

What has happened in lines 43–68? Retell the events briefly and clearly.

_____

_____

_____

_____

_____

_____

_____

After sixteen **turbulent** years, the archbishop of Canterbury[5] summoned Merlin to help restore order. Although the two men were of different faiths, they had great respect for each other and shared much wisdom between them.

"I am at a loss, Sir Wizard!" confided the archbishop. "I don't know how to help the people, and they are suffer-
50 ing more each day. If only Uther Pendragon were here!"

"I share your concerns, my lord, but I have good news," said Merlin. "Although the end of King Uther's reign left us in the dark for many years, it is at last time for the sun to return to Britain. A brilliant sun, my lord. Perhaps the brightest that Britain will ever know."

"But the sun was out this morning, sire," said the arch-bishop. "What has the weather to do with this?"

"I speak of the son of Uther Pendragon, the true heir of royal blood who lives in a distant land and must now be
60 summoned forth to keep his date with destiny."

_____

5. archbishop of Canterbury: even today, the highest-ranking bishop of the Church of England.

"His date with who?" asked the archbishop. "But the king had no heirs! Alas, that is our problem!"

"I wish to prove otherwise, my lord," replied Merlin. "If I have your leave to use my magic, I shall create an event to bring forth this young heir and prove to the world that he is the true and rightful high king of Britain."

The delighted archbishop agreed immediately, and Merlin withdrew to devise his scheme.

On a Sunday morning in late November the great cathedral of London was filled to capacity. As Mass was being said, a sudden murmur rippled through the crowd on the cathedral steps. Turning to see the cause of the commotion, the archbishop stopped in midprayer and walked toward the door. In the churchyard he discovered a block of white marble with an anvil sitting on top. Driven into the anvil, gleaming in the pale winter sun, was a sword. Its blade was of flawless blue-white steel, and the hilt was of highly wrought gold, inlaid with rubies, sapphires, and emeralds. Engraved in the marble block were these words:

WHOSO PULLETH OUT THIS SWORD

FROM THIS STONE AND ANVIL IS RIGHTWISE

KING BORN OF ENGLAND.

Ah, so this is Merlin's plan! thought the archbishop, smiling to himself. A group of barons and knights suddenly pushed their way through the crowd, each stating loudly that he should be the first to try. A few managed to leap onto the stone and give the sword an unsuccessful yank before the archbishop stopped them.

"Order! Order!" he shouted, raising his hands to quiet the crowd. "I hereby proclaim that on Christmas morning, one month from today, all those who consider themselves

PREDICT

Pause at line 68. Based on what you know about the King Arthur legend, what event might Merlin be planning?

_____

_____

_____

_____

_____

_____

_____

_____

_____

_____

_____

_____

_____

_____

_____

_____

WORD STUDY

The word *wrought* (line 78) is an alternative past tense or past participle of *work*. Here, *highly wrought* means "highly decorated."

CLARIFY

Pause at line 94. What test will prove who the rightful king is?

_____

_____

_____

_____

VOCABULARY

tournament (tŏŏr′nə·mənt) *n.:* series of contests.

INFER

Who is the boy that Sir Ector and his wife adopted as an infant (lines 105–113)?

_____

_____

_____

_____

_____

_____

_____

_____

_____

_____

_____

_____

worthy of attempting to pull this sword from the stone and anvil will be given the opportunity. He who wins the sword, thereby wins the kingdom."

A mighty roar of approval rose from the crowd. Some even danced and stomped their feet. Noticing how pleased they were, the archbishop went further. "And to celebrate this momentous occasion, a **tournament** shall be held on Christmas Eve."

100 With this, the delighted parishioners swept the flustered archbishop onto their shoulders and carried him jubilantly around the stone several times before setting him down. They hadn't had such cause for celebration in a long, long time.

To all parts of the kingdom, messengers rushed out, carrying the archbishop's proclamation.[6] Every castle and village was alerted, from Sussex to Cornwall and, finally, to the dark forest of Wales. There lived a certain gentle knight by the name of Sir Ector Bonmaison[7] with his two sons.

110 The elder was a handsome, robust youth, recently knighted and now known as Sir Kay. The younger was a gentle blond lad of about sixteen whom Sir Ector and his wife had adopted as an infant. His name was Arthur. Although Arthur was not of his blood, Sir Ector loved both sons equally and devoted himself to their upbringing.

Sir Kay was the first to hear the news of the great events in London, for as usual, he was in the courtyard polishing his helmet when the messenger arrived.

"A tournament! At last, a tournament!" he shouted.

120 "We must set out for London at once! Father, you know what this means to me."

"Yes, son, I do," said Sir Ector, bringing the weary messenger a bowl of food. "I was young and hotblooded

---

6. **proclamation** *n.:* official public announcement.
7. **Bonmaison** (bōn′mā·zōn′): This name is French for "good house."

once, too, and eager to show the world my worthiness of knighthood. But this sword-pulling contest—do you wish to be king, as well?" he asked Kay with a smile.

"I make no pretense about that, sir. To prove myself on the field of battle is my dream."

"Please remember that, my son," said Sir Ector.
130 "Pursuing one's goals with **integrity** is all that matters. Now go find Arthur so that we may prepare to leave. London is a long way off."

Arthur had wandered off alone, as he often did after finishing his chores. He was as devoted as ever to being a good squire for his brother. But, after all, Kay was *Sir* Kay now, and he rarely had anything to say to his younger brother except to bark orders at him. Arthur didn't mind, though. He was happy just to watch Kay practice his jousting and to dream of someday riding beside him in battle.
140 In the meantime, he had to content himself with his other companions—Lionel and Jasper, his dogs; Cosmo, his falcon; the orphaned fox cubs he kept hidden in the hollow log; and the deer that came to the edge of the woods when he whistled. He was in the woods now, patiently holding out a handful of oats for the deer, when Kay came bounding through the meadows to find him.

"Arthur, come quickly!" he shouted. "We're leaving for London at once! There's a big tournament. Here's your chance to show me what a good squire you can be! Hurry!"
150 Arthur stood silently for a moment. He had never been more than a few miles from his home. Was he daydreaming? Or was he really going to London to help Sir Kay bring honor and glory to their family as the whole world looked on? He ran back home, doubting his own ears until he reached the courtyard and saw Sir Ector preparing their horses for the journey.

VOCABULARY

integrity (in·teg′rə·tē) *n.*: honesty; uprightness.

WORD STUDY

Knights who are jousting (joust′in), lines 138–139, are engaging in combat using lances while on horseback. The word *joust* derives from Latin *juxtare*, meaning "to approach."

COMPARE & CONTRAST

In lines 133–146, what differences do you see in Arthur and his brother, Sir Kay?

_____
_____
_____
_____
_____
_____
_____
_____
_____
_____
_____
_____
_____
_____

CLARIFY

Pause at line 162. Why were so many people coming to London Town for Christmas?

_____

_____

_____

_____

_____

_____

_____

_____

_____

_____

_____

_____

_____

_____

_____

_____

_____

_____

IDENTIFY

Re-read lines 157–167. Do you see anything that **foreshadows,** or gives you a clue about, what might happen later in the story? Draw a box around the passage that helps you predict what will happen.

All of Britain seemed to be making its way to London Town that Christmas. Kings and dukes, earls and barons, counts and countesses funneled into the city gates for the
160   great contest. Sir Ector was pleased to see old friends and fellow knights. Sir Kay was eager to register for the jousting. And Arthur was simply dazzled by it all.

As Sir Ector and his sons made their way through the city streets, a glint of sunlight on steel caught Arthur's eye. How odd, he thought. A sword thrust point first into an anvil on top of a block of marble, sitting in a churchyard— surrounded by guards! London is so full of wonders!

Dawn arrived with a blare of trumpets, calling all con- testants to the tournament. In Sir Ector's tent, Arthur buck-
170   led the chain mail[8] onto Sir Kay and slipped the tunic of the Bonmaison colors over his brother's head. Sir Ector stood and watched until the preparation was complete and his son stood before him in all his knightly glory. Silently they embraced, mounted their horses, and headed for the tournament grounds.

© The Palma Collection/Getty Images.

8. **chain mail** *n.:* flexible armor made of thousands of tiny metal links.

The stadium for the event was the grandest ever built. Never had there been such a huge **congregation** of lords and ladies in the history of England. The stands surrounded a great meadow, swept clean of all snow, with the com-
180 batants' tents at either end. In the central place of honor sat the archbishop. Patiently, he greeted each king and noble as they came forth to kiss his hand. "I should do this more often," he chuckled to himself.

The first event was the mock battle, or *mêlée*. The contestants were divided into two teams—the Reds and the Greens. Sir Kay was with the Reds, who gathered at the southern end of the field, while their opponents took the north. They all readied their lances and brought down their helmet visors in anticipation of combat. Everyone looked
190 to the archbishop for a signal. Slowly, he raised his handkerchief, paused, and let it flutter to the ground. From either end of the field, the thunder of thousands of horse hooves rolled forward, shaking the earth, rattling the stands—louder and louder until a terrifying crash of metal split the air. A shower of splintered lances rained down in all directions. The audience gasped, and a few ladies fainted. Nothing had prepared them for this scale of violence.

Sir Kay performed admirably, for he charged ahead of his teammates and unseated two of the Greens. He was
200 already winning accolades[9] as he wheeled his charger around to aid a fellow Red.

As the teams withdrew, they revealed a battleground strewn with fallen warriors, some struggling to rise under the weight of their armor, others lying ominously still. Bits and pieces of armor and broken lances littered the field.

The next charge was to be undertaken with swords. Sir Kay was appointed captain of his team for having done so

---

9. accolades *n.*: words of praise.

VOCABULARY

congregation
(kän′grə·gā′shən) *n.*: gathering.

WORD STUDY

The word *mêlée* (mā′lā′), in line 184, is a French word meaning "hand-to-hand combat."

CONNECT

Re-read lines 184–205. Do you think this kind of sport would be acceptable today? Why or why not?

_____

_____

_____

_____

_____

_____

_____

_____

_____

_____

_____

_____

_____

_____

Magnificent (line 210) is from the Latin *magnus,* meaning "great," and *facere,* meaning "to do." What does Arthur mean when he tells Sir Kay he was magnificent?

_____

_____

_____

_____

_____

_____

_____

_____

PREDICT

Pause at line 235. Where will Arthur get a sword for Sir Kay?

_____

_____

_____

_____

_____

_____

_____

_____

_____

_____

_____

well in the first round. He trotted over to Arthur and handed down his lance.

210   "Kay! You were magnificent!" gushed Arthur, wiping down the steaming war horse. "You've brought great honor to our house this day!"

    "I need my sword, Arthur," said Sir Kay, struggling to take his helmet off.

    "Your sword, of course!" said Arthur brightly. He turned to get it, but then stopped suddenly. Where was the sword? His eyes scanned the little tent with its collection of weaponry. Spear, halberd, mace, bludgeon[10] . . . but no sword.

    "Excuse me, Kay," said Arthur, "could you use a
220 battle axe?"

    "Arthur, please! My sword!" said Sir Kay. "We haven't much time."

    "Of course, Kay! But just a moment—I'll finish polishing it," said Arthur, slipping out through the slit in their tent. With one great leap, he landed on his pony's back and galloped madly through the deserted streets, rushing back to their camp.

    "Sword. Sword. Where did I put that *sword*?" he muttered, desperately searching through the chests and bags.
230 But to no avail.

    How could this happen? he thought. Kay without a sword . . . and the whole world watching!

    He paced back and forth, and then a thought struck him: Kay will not be without a sword today. I know where I can get one!

    A few minutes later, he trotted into the churchyard where the sword in the anvil stood on the marble block. There wasn't a guard in sight—even they had gone to the tourney. Quietly, he brought his pony up to the stone and
240 tugged on the reins.

---

10. **halberd** (hal′bərd), **mace** (mās), **bludgeon** (bluj′ən): weapons.

"OK, Blaze. . . . We'll just see if this sword can be unstuck," he whispered. He stretched out his arm until his fingers touched the hilt.

"Hey, it's looser than I thought. . . . Steady, Blaze! Steady, boy!" As the pony stepped back a few paces, the sword glided out of the anvil's grip, unbalancing Arthur. He regained his seat and looked down in wonder at the mighty blade in his hand.

"This isn't just *any* sword. . . . Perhaps it's something
250 the church provides for needy strangers. Yes, that must be it! Well, I'll return it after the tournament. Someone else may need it. Thank you, sword, for saving me," he said, pressing its cross to his lips. "Wait until Kay sees this!"

He flung his cloak around the great sword and drove his little horse back to the tournament with lightning speed.

By now, Sir Kay had dismounted and was rather chafed.[11]

"Arthur, where have you been?" he shouted. "You . . ."

He caught himself as Arthur dropped to one knee and
260 opened the cloak.

"Your sword, my lord," Arthur said confidently. But his smile quickly disappeared when he saw Sir Kay's reaction. Frozen in place, his face white as milk, Sir Kay stared at the sword. Finally, he spoke.

"Where did you get this?" he asked Arthur, although he knew the answer.

Arthur confessed that he had searched in vain for Sir Kay's sword and had borrowed this one instead.

"Get Father at once, and tell no one of this!" said Sir
270 Kay sternly.

Arthur thought he must be in terrible trouble. Surely he could return the sword without his father knowing. Why

CLARIFY

In lines 244–253, does Arthur realize what he has just done? What does Arthur think the sword's purpose is?

_____
_____
_____
_____
_____
_____
_____
_____

INFER

Why is Sir Kay so disturbed when he sees the sword (lines 261–270)?

_____
_____
_____
_____
_____
_____
_____
_____

11. **chafed** (chāft) *v.* used as *adj.*: annoyed.

INFER

Why do beads of sweat form on Sir Kay's brow when he explains the situation to his father (lines 282–284)?

_____

_____

_____

_____

_____

RETELL

How does Sir Kay attempt to become king of all Britain (lines 278–300)?

_____

_____

_____

_____

_____

_____

_____

_____

_____

_____

_____

_____

_____

_____

_____

did Father have to be told? Nevertheless, he obeyed his brother and returned quickly with Sir Ector.

Sir Kay closed the curtains of the tent and opened the cloak, revealing the sword to his father.

Sir Ector gasped when he saw it. "How can this be?"

"Father, I am in possession of this sword," said Sir Kay nervously. "That is what matters. Therefore, I must be king
280 of all Britain."

"But how came you by it, son?" asked Sir Ector.

"Well, sire, I needed a sword . . . and we couldn't find mine . . . so, I decided to use this one!" said Sir Kay. Beads of sweat formed on his brow.

"Very well, lad. You drew it out of the stone. I want to see you put it back. Let's go," said Sir Ector.

"But _I have the sword_!" said Sir Kay. "Isn't that enough?"

"No," replied Sir Ector, as he mounted his horse and headed toward the cathedral. Arthur rode close behind and,
290 ever so slowly, Sir Kay mounted and followed.

The churchyard was still deserted when the three arrived. "Put the sword back in the anvil," said Sir Ector bluntly. "I must see it."

"Father, I . . ."

"Just do it, Kay, and you shall be king. If that's what you want." Sir Kay climbed onto the block. Sweat was now pouring off him. He raised the mighty sword over his head and plunged it downward. But the sharp point skidded across the surface of the anvil, causing Sir Kay to fall
300 headfirst off the block.

"Now, son, tell me. How came you by this sword?" asked Sir Ector again.

"Arthur brought it to me," said Sir Kay, dusting himself off. "He _lost_ my other one."

Suddenly a fear gripped Sir Ector's heart. "Arthur, my boy," he said quietly, "will you try it for us?"

"Certainly, Father," said Arthur, "but do we have to tell anyone about this? Can't we just . . ."

"Son, please," said Sir Ector solemnly. "If you can put the sword in that anvil, please do so now."

With a pounding heart, the lad took the sword from Sir Kay's hand and climbed slowly onto the block of marble. Raising it with both hands over his head, he thrust it downward, through the anvil, burying the point deep within the stone. Effortlessly he pulled it out again, glanced at his stunned father, and shoved the sword into the stone, even deeper this time.

Sir Ector shrieked and sank to his knees. His mouth moved, but no words came out. He put his hands together as in prayer. Silently, Sir Kay knelt and did the same.

"Father! What are you doing?" cried Arthur, leaping down from the stone. "Please! Get up! Get up! I don't understand!"

"Now I know!" sputtered Sir Ector, choking back tears. "Now I know who you are!"

"I'm your son, Father!" said the bewildered lad, crouching down by his father and putting his head to Sir Ector's chest.

After a few deep breaths, Sir Ector regained his composure. He smiled sadly down at Arthur and stroked his head.

"Fate would have it otherwise, my boy. Look there behind you." He pointed to the gold lettering on the marble block, which stated the purpose of the sword and the anvil.

Arthur sat in silence and stared at the words in the marble.

"Although you were adopted, I've loved you like my own child, Arthur," said Sir Ector softly. "But now I realize

INFER

Pause at line 306. Why does fear grip the heart of Sir Ector? What does his emotional reaction reveal to you about his character?

_____

_____

_____

_____

_____

IDENTIFY

Re-read lines 311–317. Underline the fantastic elements that identify this story as a legend.

CLARIFY

Sir Kay has until now treated Arthur as a servant. Why does Sir Kay kneel before Arthur (line 320)?

_____

_____

_____

_____

_____

_____

IDENTIFY

Re-read lines 341–349. In what way does Arthur seem like a child? In what way does he show his maturity?

_____

_____

_____

_____

_____

_____

_____

_____

_____

CLARIFY

Re-read lines 355–370. Did Merlin's scheme work as expected? How did Arthur surprise the wizard?

_____

_____

_____

_____

_____

_____

_____

_____

_____

_____

you have the blood of kings in you. To discover your birthright is the true reason we came to London. You are now our king and we your faithful servants."

At this, Arthur broke into tears. "I don't want to be king. Not if it means losing my father!" he sobbed.

"You have a great destiny before you, Arthur. There's no use avoiding it," said Sir Ector.

Arthur wiped his eyes with his sleeve. He straightened up so he could look Sir Ector in the eyes. A few minutes passed.

"Very well," Arthur finally said slowly. "Whatever my destiny may be, I am willing to accept it. But I still need you with me."

"Then so it shall be, lad. So it shall be," said Sir Ector.

They sat quietly for a time, comforting each other, until they felt another presence. From across the yard a hooded figure quietly floated into the fading light of the winter afternoon and knelt down beside them.

"Merlin," said Sir Ector, bowing his head to the famous enchanter.

"I've been waiting for you, Arthur," said the wizard.

"You know me, my lord?" asked Arthur.

"I put you in this good man's care many years ago and have kept an eye on you ever since."

"How did you do that, sire? We live far from here."

"Oh, I have my ways," replied Merlin. "But you still managed to surprise me. The sword-pulling contest isn't until tomorrow, and you pulled it out today!" he said with a chuckle.

"But what is to become of me now?" asked Arthur.

"Well, let us start with tomorrow," replied the old sorcerer. "We must still have the contest to prove to the world that you are the rightful heir. I will come for you when the time is right."

"But after that, sire, what is my future?" asked the boy.

Merlin weighed this question carefully. He wasn't at all sure whether the boy was prepared for his answer. Finally, he spoke. "I can tell you only what my powers suggest—and they point to greatness. Greatness surrounds you like a golden cloak. Your achievements could inspire humankind for centuries to come. But you alone can fulfill this destiny and then only if you wish it. You own your future. You alone."

Arthur breathed deeply and cast his eyes downward. He thought of all the goodbyes he would have to say. He thought of his fishing hole, and the birds that ate seeds from his hand. He thought of the deer that came when he called them.

"What time tomorrow, sire?" he asked.

"After all have tried and failed, whenever that may be," replied Merlin.

"I will be ready, sire," said Arthur. Then he rose, bade Merlin farewell, and silently returned to his tent.

On Christmas morning, the archbishop said Mass for the largest gathering he had seen in years. The grounds surrounding the cathedral were also filled—with those seeking to make history or watch it being made. As soon as the service ended, those who wished to try for the throne formed a line next to the marble block.

Leading the line was King Urien of Gore, husband to Margaise, Uther Pendragon's adoptive daughter. Ever since the high king's death, Urien had claimed loudly that he was the rightful heir. Indeed, he took his position on the marble block with a great sense of authority and gave the sword a confident tug, then another, and another. Urien was sweating and yanking furiously when finally asked to step down.

Next came King Lot of Orkney, husband to Morgan le Fay. King Lot felt certain that his wife's magical powers

CLARIFY

According to the information in lines 372–378, what has to happen for Arthur's future to be great? What must Arthur do?

_____

_____

_____

_____

_____

_____

WORD STUDY

Bid is an old-fashioned word, meaning "tell." Locate and circle the past tense of *bid* in lines 387–388.

INFER

Pause at line 388. Is Arthur excited about becoming king? Explain.

_____

_____

_____

_____

_____

_____

How are these men who try
to pull the sword from the
stone different from Arthur
(lines 395–415)?

_____

_____

_____

_____

What might the word *waned*
(line 414) mean? Look for
and underline context clues
that help you figure out the
meaning of this word.

_____

_____

Pause at line 435. What kind
of reaction would you expect
Merlin's announcement to
have on the archbishop and
the listening crowd?

_____

_____

_____

_____

_____

_____

would assure his victory. But pull and tug as he might, he couldn't move the sword. After that, King Mark of Cornwall, King Leodegrance of Cameliard, and King Ryence of North Wales all took their place on the stone—and failed. The dukes of Winchester, Colchester, Worcester, and Hamcester did not fare any better. Some thought the longer they wait-

410 ed, the looser the sword would become, thereby improving their chances. But this wasn't the case, for the sword never budged, not even slightly. Kings, dukes, earls, counts, and knights all left that marble block empty-handed. Finally, as the day waned and the line neared its end, the crowd grew impatient for a winner. Merlin went for Arthur.

Sir Ector and Sir Kay opened the curtains of their tent when they saw Merlin approaching.

"Your hour has come, my lord," said the old wizard to Arthur, who was standing alone in the center of the tent.

420 Silently, the boy walked forth as one in a dream.

The crowd made way for them as they entered, for Merlin was still revered by all. But who could these other people be? Especially that young blond lad dressed all in red. What was he doing here?

Merlin brought Arthur before the archbishop and bowed deeply. Arthur dropped to one knee.

"My lord," said Merlin, "I present to you a most worthy candidate for this contest. Has he your permission to attempt to pull yonder sword from the stone?"

430 The archbishop gazed down at the handsome lad. "Merlin, we are not familiar with this youth, nor with his credentials. By what right does he come to this place?"

"By the greatest right, my lord," said Merlin. "For this is the trueborn son of King Uther Pendragon and Queen Igraine."

The crowd broke into a loud clamor at hearing this. The startled archbishop raised his hands, but order was not easily restored.

"Merlin, have you proof of this?" asked the archbishop.

440 "With your permission, sire," blurted Arthur suddenly, "perhaps I can prove it by handling yonder sword in the anvil."

"Very well then, lad," said the archbishop, admiring Arthur's youthful boldness. "You have my permission. If what Merlin says is true, may God be with you."

Arthur rose and stepped up onto the marble block. He grabbed hold of the mighty golden hilt with both hands. A surge of sparkling warmth traveled up his arms, across his shoulders, and throughout his body. With one mighty tug, 450 he freed the sword from the anvil and lifted it heavenward. The blade flashed like lightning as he swung it around his head for all to see. Then, turning the point downward again, he drove it back into the anvil with equal ease.

© Richard T. Nowitz/CORBIS.

WORD STUDY

Clamor (line 436) is from the Latin *clamare,* meaning "to cry out."

PREDICT

Pause at line 453. How do you think the crowd will react now that Arthur has pulled the sword from the stone?

_____

_____

_____

_____

_____

_____

_____

_____

_____

_____

_____

_____

FLUENCY

Read the boxed passage to yourself a few times. Take note of its meaning and the words the writer has chosen to bring that scene to life. Then, take turns reading the passage aloud with a partner.

The entire gathering stood dumbstruck for a long moment, trying to comprehend what they had just seen. Arthur looked about for reassurance. He looked to Sir Ector, then Merlin, and then the archbishop. They all simply stared at him, with eyes wide in amazement. A child giggled and clapped his hands in glee, then so did another,

460 and another. Cheers began to ring out as people found their voices again. Suddenly, a thunder of shouting and clapping rose up around Arthur. Amidst the tumult, he closed his eyes and whispered, "Thank you, Father."

Then he grabbed the sword's hilt for a second time and withdrew it. As he brought it above his head, a thousand swords throughout the crowd were raised in solidarity.[12] Arthur drove the sword back into the anvil and pulled it out once again. This time, as he lifted the great blade to the sky, more swords and halberds were raised, along with

470 brooms, rakes, and walking sticks, as counts and common folk alike saluted their newfound king.

Not everyone was overjoyed at this turn of events, however. Although all had seen the miracle performed, several kings and dukes were unwilling to recognize Arthur's right to the throne. Loudest among the grumblers were King Lot and King Urien, Arthur's brothers-in-law. "How dare this beardless, unknown country boy think he can be made high king to rule over us!" they said. "Obviously, Merlin is using the boy to promote himself!"

480 But these malcontents[13] gained no support from those around them and were quickly shouted down. So they gathered themselves together and stormed away in a huff of indignation.[14]

---

12. **solidarity** (säl′ə·dar′ə·tē) *n.:* unity among a group.
13. **malcontents** (mal′kən·tents′) *n.:* discontented or unhappy people.
14. **indignation** *n.:* righteous anger.

To everyone else, the day belonged to Arthur. All the other kings and nobles rushed forth to show their acceptance, for they trusted Merlin and were grateful to have a leader at last. They hoisted the young king-to-be above their heads to parade him through the streets of London.

As the noisy procession flowed out of the churchyard, the archbishop hobbled over to Merlin to offer congratulations for a successful plan.

"Thank you, my lord, but I think we are not yet finished," said the wizard.

The archbishop looked puzzled.

"I fear that King Lot and King Urien and those other discontented souls will leave us no peace until they have another chance at the sword," continued Merlin. "We must offer them a new trial on New Year's Day."

And so they did. But again, no one could budge the sword but Arthur. These same troublesome kings and dukes still refused to acknowledge his victory, though. So another trial took place on Candlemas,[15] and yet another on Easter.

By now, the people had grown impatient, for they had believed in Arthur all along and had grown to love him. The idea of having a fresh young king inspired hope and optimism. The world suddenly felt young again.

Finally, after the trial held on Pentecost,[16] they cried out, "Enough! Arthur has proven himself five times now! We will have him for our king—and no other!"

The archbishop and Merlin agreed. There was proof beyond dispute at this point. So the coronation was set for May Day in the great cathedral of London.

Upon arriving that morning, Arthur stepped up on the block and pulled the sword from the anvil for the last time.

---

15. **Candlemas** (kan′dəl·məs): church feast on February 2.
16. **Pentecost** (pen′tə·kôst′): Christian festival on the seventh Sunday after Easter, celebrating the "birthday" of the Christian Church.

A procession (line 489) is a sort of formal or ceremonial parade. The word *procession* comes from the Latin prefix *pro–*, meaning "forward," and the Latin word *cedere*, meaning "to go."

RETELL

In lines 495–509, how is it officially settled that Arthur is the rightful king of Britain?

_____

_____

_____

_____

_____

_____

_____

_____

_____

_____

_____

_____

_____

_____

_____

_____

With the blade pointing heavenward, he entered the church, walked solemnly down the central aisle, and laid the sword upon the altar. The archbishop administered the holy sacraments[17] and finally placed the crown upon Arthur's head.

520 Ten thousand cheers burst forth as the young king emerged from the cathedral. At Merlin's suggestion, Arthur stepped up on the marble block to speak to the people. A hush fell over the masses as he raised his hands to address them.

"People of Britain, we are now one. And so shall we remain as long as there is a breath in my body. My faith in your courage and wisdom is boundless. I ask now for your faith in me. In your trust I shall find my strength. For your good I dedicate my life. May this sword lead us to our destiny."

---

17. **sacraments** *n.:* rituals instituted by the church, such as baptism, Holy Communion, and penance.

King Arthur: The Sword in the Stone

Retelling Chain   **Legends** are stories that are based on a real person or event. Complete the chart below with events from *King Arthur: The Sword in the Stone*. Then, indicate whether each event is likely to be based on actual historic events or on the writer's imagination. To do this, place a check mark under events you think are based on real events.

Literary Skills
Analyze legends.

Reading Skills
Retell a story.

Event	Event	Event	Event

Event	Event	Event	Event

Event	Event	Event	Event

Skills Review

King Arthur: The Sword in the Stone

VOCABULARY AND COMPREHENSION

Word Bank

turbulent
tournament
integrity
congregation

A. Latin and Anglo-Saxon Roots   Match the Word Bank words with their roots.

_____ **1.** congregation

_____ **2.** turbulent

_____ **3.** tournament

_____ **4.** integrity

a. *integer*, meaning "untouched" or "whole"

b. *congregatio*, meaning "an assembling"

c. *tourner*, meaning "turn"

d. *turba*, meaning "crowd"

B. Reading Comprehension   Answer each question below.

1. What agreement does King Uther make with Merlin in order to win the hand of Lady Igraine? _____

_____

2. What scheme does Merlin come up with in order to reveal Britain's new king? _____

_____

3. Why do Sir Kay and Arthur go to London Town for Christmas Eve?

_____

_____

4. Why does Arthur pull the sword out of the anvil and stone the first time? Why is that event so important? _____

_____

5. How do King Lot and King Urien feel about Arthur's becoming king of all Britain? _____

_____

SKILLS FOCUS

Vocabulary Skills
Recognize Anglo-Saxon and Latin roots.

254   Part 1   **Collection 7 / Literary Criticism: Where I Stand**

Sir Gawain and the Loathly Lady

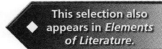

This selection also appears in *Elements of Literature.*

retold by Betsy Hearne

LITERARY FOCUS: THE QUEST

What makes a legend a legend? An important part of being a legend is doing something no one else is capable of doing. In most legends, therefore, the hero embarks on a long, dangerous journey called a **quest.** During the quest, the hero faces horribly difficult tasks or some kind of temptation.

Not only does a hero have to endure tests of strength and bravery but in many legends the hero must also display intelligence and cunning. Very often, the hero is presented with a riddle while on a quest. A **riddle** is a puzzling question or problem. Before the quest can resume, the riddle must be solved.

READING SKILLS: PREDICTING

Legends are a lot of fun to read. Although they have familiar elements, such as heroes and quests, you never know what fantastic event will happen next. As you read "Sir Gawain and the Loathly Lady," make predictions about where the story will take you. Here are some tips to help you out.

- Look for clues that hint at, or **foreshadow,** what will happen.
- As the story develops and builds suspense, guess at possible outcomes. Think about where the story might lead.
- Ask yourself questions as you read the story, and revise your predictions as necessary.
- Use your own experiences and knowledge to make predictions.

SKILLS FOCUS

Literary Skills
Understand the quest.

Reading Skills
Make predictions.

Vocabulary Skills
Understand French word origins.

VOCABULARY DEVELOPMENT

PREVIEW SELECTION VOCABULARY

Get to know the vocabulary words below before you read "Sir Gawain and the Loathly Lady."

chivalry (shiv'əl·rē) *n.:* code that governed knightly behavior, such as courage, honor, and readiness to help the weak.

Chivalry required knights to help those in need.

countenance (koun'tə·nəns) *n.:* face; appearance.

Under his visor, the knight's countenance revealed his fear.

loathsome (lōth'səm) *adj.:* disgusting.

Dame Ragnell's appearance was loathsome. It made it hard for her to find a suitor.

sovereignty (säv'rən·tē) *n.:* control; authority.

King Arthur had sovereignty over all of Britain.

CLARIFY WORD MEANINGS: THE FRENCH INFLUENCE

The English language contains words from many other languages. At one time, England was ruled by French-speaking Normans. As a result, French was spoken by government, church, and court officials, and French words worked their way into the English language.

Vocabulary words that come from French are boldface in the story excerpts below.

- "For you are my king and I am your friend—it is my part to save your life, or else I am a false knight and a great **coward.**" (from *couard,* meaning "with tail between the legs")

- "Thank you, **courteous** Gawain," said the lady. (from *corteis,* meaning "court")

- "In all his country there was nothing but **chivalry,** and knights were loved by the people." (from *chevaler,* meaning "knight")

Sir Gawain and the Loathly Lady

retold by Betsy Hearne

© Royalty-Free/CORBIS.

Now if you listen awhile I will tell you a tale of Arthur the King and how an adventure once befell him.

Of all kings and all knights, King Arthur bore away the honor wherever he went. In all his country there was nothing but **chivalry,** and knights were loved by the people.

One day in spring King Arthur was hunting in Ingleswood with all his lords beside him. Suddenly a deer ran by in the distance and the king took up chase, calling back to his knights, "Hold you still every man, I will chase this one myself!" He took his arrows and bow and stooped low like a woodsman to stalk the deer. But every time he came near the animal, it leapt away into the forest. So King Arthur went a while after the deer, and no knight went with him, until at last he let fly an arrow and killed the deer. He had raised a bugle to his lips to summon the knights when he heard a voice behind him.

10

"Sir Gawain and the Loathly Lady" from *The Oryx Multicultural Folktale Series: Beauties and Beasts* by Betsy Hearne. Copyright © 1993 by The Oryx Press. Reproduced by permission of **Greenwood Publishing Group, Inc.,** **Westport, CT.**

VOCABULARY

chivalry (shiv'əl·rē) *n.*: code that governed knightly behavior, such as courage, honor, and readiness to help the weak.

INFER

Pause at line 16, and think about what you've learned about King Arthur so far. What sort of personality does he seem to have?

_____

_____

_____

_____

_____

WORD STUDY

Locate and circle the two words in lines 26–32 that are no longer in common use. What might those words mean?

_____

_____

_____

_____

_____

_____

FLUENCY

Read the boxed passage silently several times. Concentrate on pronouncing the knight's French name correctly, and read the passage as smoothly as you can. Then, take turns reading the passage with a partner.

IDENTIFY

Pause at line 46. What **riddle** is presented to King Arthur?

_____

_____

_____

_____

_____

_____

_____

"Well met, King Arthur!"

Though he had not heard anyone approach, the king turned to see a strange knight, fully armed, standing only 20 a few yards away.

"You have done me wrong many a year and given away my northern lands," said the strange knight. "I have your life in my hands—what will you do now, King Alone?"

"Sir Knight, what is your name?" asked the king.

"My name is Gromer Somer Joure."[1]

"Sir Gromer, think carefully," said the king. "To slay me here, unarmed as I am, will get you no honor. All knights will refuse you wherever you go. Calm yourself—come to Carlyle and I shall mend all that is amiss."

30 "Nay," said Sir Gromer, "by heaven, King! You shall not escape when I have you at advantage. If I let you go with only a warning, later you'll defy me, of that I'm sure."

"Spare my life, Sir Gromer, and I shall grant you whatever is in my power to give. It is shameful to slay me here, with nothing but my hunting gear, and you armed for battle."

"All your talking will not help you, King, for I want neither land nor gold, truly." Sir Gromer smiled. "Still . . . if you will promise to meet me here, in the same fashion, on a day I will choose . . ."

40 "Yes," said the king quickly. "Here is my promise."

"Listen and hear me out. First you will swear upon my sword to meet me here without fail, on this day one year from now. Of all your knights none shall come with you. You must tell me at your coming what thing women most desire—and if you do not bring the answer to my riddle, you will lose your head. What say you, King?"

"I agree, though it is a hateful bargain," said the king. "Now let me go. I promise you as I am the true king, to

---

1. Gromer Somer Joure (grō·mer′ sō·mer′ zho͞or).

come again at this day one year from now and bring you
your answer."

The knight laughed, "Now go your way, King Arthur.
You do not yet know your sorrow. Yet stay a moment—do
not think of playing false—for by Mary[2] I think you would
betray me."

"Nay," said King Arthur. "You will never find me an
untrue knight. Farewell, Sir Knight, and evil met. I will come
in a year's time, though I may not escape." The king began to
blow his bugle for his knights to find him. Sir Gromer turned
his horse and was gone as quickly as he had come, so that the
lords found their king alone with the slain deer.

"We will return to Carlyle," said the king. "I do not like
this hunting."

The lords knew by his **countenance** that the king met
with some disturbance, but no one knew of his encounter.
They wondered at the king's heavy step and sad look, until
at last Sir Gawain[3] said to the king, "Sire, I marvel at you.
What thing do you sorrow for?"

"I'll tell you, gentle Gawain," said Arthur. "In the forest
as I pursued the deer, I met with a knight in full armor, and
he charged me I should not escape him. I must keep my
word to him or else I am foresworn."[4]

"Fear not my lord. I am not a man that would dishonor you."

"He threatened me, and would have slain me with
great heat, but I spoke with him since I had no weapons."

"What happened then?" said Gawain.

"He made me swear to meet him there in one year's
time, alone and unarmed. On that day I must tell him what
women desire most, or I shall lose my life. If I fail in my
answer, I know that I will be slain without mercy."

---

2. **by Mary:** a mild oath.
3. **Gawain** (gä′wān).
4. **foresworn** adj.: untrue to one's word; shown to be a liar.

RETELL

Pause at line 60. What must
King Arthur do before he
returns to meet the knight
in one year?

_____

_____

_____

_____

_____

_____

VOCABULARY

countenance (koun′tə·nəns)
n.: face; appearance.

INFER

Re-read lines 63–71. Why
does the king confide in
Sir Gawain?

_____

_____

_____

_____

_____

_____

_____

_____

WORD STUDY

The word _tidings_ (line 100) is not often used anymore. What might it mean?

_____

_____

_____

_____

PREDICT

Pause at the end of the complete sentence in line 113. What do you think the ugly lady might tell King Arthur?

_____

_____

_____

_____

_____

_____

_____

"Sire, make good cheer," said Gawain. "Make your horse ready to ride into strange country, and everywhere you meet either man or woman, ask of them the answer to the riddle. I will ride another way, and every man and woman's answer I will write in a book."

"That is well advised, Gawain," said the king. They made preparations to leave immediately, and when both were ready, Gawain rode one way and the king another— each one asked every man and woman they found what

90   women most desire.

Some said they loved beautiful clothes; some said they loved to be praised; some said they loved a handsome man; some said one, some said another. Gawain had so many answers that he made a great book to hold them, and after many months of traveling he came back to court again. The king was there already with his book, and each looked over the other's work. But no answer seemed right.

"By God," said the king, "I am afraid. I will seek a little more in Ingleswood Forest. I have but one month to my set

100   day, and I may find some good tidings."

"Do as you think best," said Gawain, "but whatever you do, remember that it is good to have spring again."

King Arthur rode forth on that day, into Ingleswood, and there he met with a lady. King Arthur marveled at her, for she was the ugliest creature that he had ever seen. Her face seemed almost like that of an animal, with a pushed-in nose and a few yellowing tusks for teeth. Her figure was twisted and deformed, with a hunched back and shoulders a yard broad. No tongue could tell the foulness of that lady.

110   But she rode gaily on a palfrey[5] set with gold and precious stones, and when she spoke her voice was sweet and soft.

"I am glad that I have met with you, King Arthur," she said. "Speak with me, for your life is in my hand. I know of

---

5. **palfrey** (pôl′frē) _n._: gentle riding horse.

your situation, and I warn you that you will not find your answer if I do not tell you."

"What do you want with me, lady?" said the king, taken aback by the lady's boldness.

"Sir, I would like to speak with you. You will die if I do not save you, I know it very well."

120 "What do you mean, my lady, tell me," stammered the king. "What is your desire, why is my life in your hand? Tell me, and I shall give you all you ask."

"You must grant me a knight to wed," said the lady slowly. "His name is Sir Gawain. I will make this bargain: If your life is saved another way, you need not grant my desire. If my answer saves your life, grant me Sir Gawain as my husband. Choose now, for you must soon meet your enemy."

"By Mary," said the king, "I cannot grant you Sir Gawain. That lies with him alone—he is not mine to give. I can only

130 take the choice to Sir Gawain."

"Well," she said. "Then go home again and speak to Sir Gawain. For though I am foul, yet am I merry, and through me he may save your life or ensure your death."

"Alas!" cried the king. "That I should cause Gawain to wed you, for he will not say no. I know not what I should do."

"Sir King, you will get no more from me. When you come again with your answer I will meet you here."

"What is your name, I pray you tell me?"

"Sir King, I am the Dame Ragnell, that never yet

140 betrayed a man."

"Then farewell, Dame Ragnell," said the king.

Thus they departed, and the king returned to Carlyle again with a heavy heart. The first man he met was Sir Gawain. "Sire, how did you fare?" asked the knight.

"Never so ill," said the king. "I fear I will die at Sir Gromer's hand."

RETELL

Re-read lines 112–127. What does Dame Ragnell offer to King Arthur? What does she want in return?

_____

_____

_____

_____

_____

_____

_____

_____

INFER

Why does Arthur return to Carlyle with a heavy heart (lines 142–143)?

_____

_____

_____

_____

_____

_____

_____

_____

_____

_____

_____

INFER

Pause at line 158. What does Sir Gawain's response reveal about the code of chivalry?

_____

_____

_____

_____

_____

VOCABULARY

loathsome (lō*th*′səm) *adj.*: disgusting.

PREDICT

Pause at line 176. Will Dame Ragnell give King Arthur the answer he needs? Explain.

_____

_____

_____

_____

_____

_____

IDENTIFY

Locate and underline Dame Ragnell's answer to the riddle (lines 177–185).

"Nay," said Gawain. "I would rather die myself I love you so."

"Gawain, I met today with the foulest lady that I ever saw. She said she would save my life, but first she would have you for her husband."

"Is this all?" asked Gawain. "Then I shall wed her and wed her again! Though she were a fiend, though she were as foul as Beelzebub,[6] her I shall marry. For you are my king and I am your friend—it is my part to save your life, or else I am a false knight and a great coward. If she were the most **loathsome** woman that ever a man might see, for your love I would spare nothing."

"Thank you, Gawain," said King Arthur then. "Of all knights that I have found, you are the finest. You have saved my life, and my love will not stray from you, as I am king in this land."

The day soon came when the king was to meet the Dame Ragnell and bear his answer to Sir Gromer. Gawain rode with him to the edge of Ingleswood Forest, but there the king said, "Sir Gawain, farewell. I must go west, and you must go no further."

"God speed you on your journey. I wish I rode your way," said Gawain.

The king had ridden but a mile or so more when he met the Dame Ragnell. "Ah, Sir King, you are welcome here bearing your answer."

"Now," said the king, "since it can be no other way, tell me your answer, save my life, and Gawain shall you wed; so he has promised. Tell me in all haste. Have done, I may not tarry."[7]

"Sire," said the Dame Ragnell, "now you will know what women desire most, high and low. Some men say we desire

---

6. **Beelzebub** (bē·el′zə·bub′): the devil; Satan.
7. **tarry** *v.*: linger; delay.

to be fair, or to wed, or to remain fresh and young, or to
180 have flattery from men. But there is one thing that is every
woman's fantasy: We desire of men, above all other things,
to have **sovereignty,** for then all is ours. Therefore go on
your way, Sir King, and tell that knight what I have said to
you. He will be angry and curse the woman who told you,
for his labor is lost. Go forth—you will not be harmed."

The king rode forth in great haste until he came to the
set place and met with Sir Gromer.

"Come, come, Sir King," said the knight sternly. "Now
let me have answer, for I am ready."

190 The king pulled out the two books for Sir Gromer to
see. "Sir, I dare say the right one is there."

Sir Gromer looked over them, every one, and said at
last, "Nay, nay, Sir King, you are a dead man."

"Wait, Sir Gromer," said the king. "I have one more
answer to give."

"Say it," said Sir Gromer, "or so God help me you shall
bleed."

"Now," said the king, "here is my answer and that is
all—above all things, women desire sovereignty, for that is
200 their liking and their greatest desire; to rule over any man.
This they told me."

Sir Gromer was silent a moment with rage, but then he
cried out, "And she that told you, Sir Arthur, I pray to God
I might see her burn in a fire, for that was my sister, Dame
Ragnell. God give her shame—I have lost much labor. Go
where you like, King Arthur, for you are spared. Alas that I
ever saw this day, for I know that you will be my enemy and
hunt me down."

"No," said King Arthur, "you will never find me an
210 attacker. Farewell." King Arthur turned his horse into the
forest again. Soon he met with the Dame Ragnell, in the

VOCABULARY

sovereignty (säv′rən·tē) *n.:*
control; authority.

CLARIFY

Pause at line 208. Why was
Dame Ragnell able to give
King Arthur the correct
answer to the riddle?

_____
_____
_____
_____
_____
_____
_____
_____
_____
_____
_____
_____
_____
_____
_____
_____
_____
_____
_____

INFER

Pause at line 233. What does Gawain's behavior toward Dame Ragnell reveal about his character?

_____

_____

_____

_____

_____

_____

_____

_____

_____

_____

_____

INFER

Why does Dame Ragnell insist on having a grand wedding (lines 237–245)?

_____

_____

_____

_____

_____

_____

_____

_____

same place as before. "Sir King," she said. "I am glad you have sped well. I told you how it would be, and now since I and none other have saved your life, Gawain must wed me."

"I will not fail in my promise," said the king. "If you will be ruled by my council, you shall have your will."

"No, Sir King, I will not be ruled," said the lady. "I know what you are thinking. Ride before, and I will follow to your court. Think how I have saved your life and do not disagree with me, for if you do you will be shamed."

220 The king was ashamed to bring the loathly lady openly to the court, but forth she rode till they came to Carlyle. All the country wondered when she came, for they had never seen so foul a creature, but she would spare no one the sight of her. Into the hall she went, saying, "Arthur, King, fetch in Sir Gawain, before all the knights, so that you may troth[8] us together. Set forth Gawain my love, for I will not wait."

Sir Gawain stepped forward then, and said, "Sir, I am ready to fulfill the promise I made to you."

230 "God have mercy," said the Dame Ragnell when she saw Gawain. "For your sake I wish I were a fair woman, for you are of such goodwill." Then Sir Gawain wooed her[9] as he was a true knight, and Dame Ragnell was happy.

"Alas!" said the Queen Guinevere, and all the ladies in her bower.[10] "Alas!" said both king and knights, that the beautiful Gawain should wed such a foul and horrible woman.

She would be wedded in no other way than this— openly, with announcements in every town and village, and she had all the ladies of the land come to Carlyle for the feast. 240 The queen begged Dame Ragnell to be married in the early morning, as privately as possible. "Nay," said the lady. "By heaven I will not no matter what you say. I will be wedded openly, as the king promised. I will not go to the church until

---

8. **troth** (trôth) _v._: engage to marry.
9. **wooed her**: said romantic things; spoke of love.
10. **bower** (bou′ər) _n._: old-fashioned word for a private room.

Queen Guinevere
(1858) by William Morris.
Oil on canvas.
© Tate Gallery, London/Art Resource, NY.

IDENTIFY

How do Sir Gawain's friends react at the wedding feast (lines 246–253)?

High Mass time,[11] and I will dine in the open hall, in the midst of all the court."

At the wedding feast there were lords and ladies from all estates, and Dame Ragnell was arrayed in the richest manner—richer even than Queen Guinevere. But all her rich clothes could not hide her foulness. When the feasting began, only Dame Ragnell ate heartily, while the knights and squires sat like stones. After the wedding feast, Sir Gawain and the Lady Ragnell retired to the wedding chamber that had been prepared for them.

"Ah, Gawain," said the lady. "Since we are wed, show me your courtesy and come to bed. If I were fair you would be joyous—yet for Arthur's sake, kiss me at least."

Sir Gawain turned to the lady, but in her place was the loveliest woman that he had ever seen.

"By God, what are you?" cried Gawain.

"Sir, I am your wife, surely. Why are you so unkind?"

"Lady, I am sorry," said Gawain. "I beg your pardon, my fair madam. For now you are a beautiful lady, and today you were the foulest woman that ever I saw. It is well, my lady, to have you thus." And he took her in his arms and kissed her with great joy.

"Sir," she said, "you have half-broken the spell on me. Thus shall you have me, but my beauty will not hold. You

CLARIFY

Pause at line 265. What magical event has just happened?

---

11. **High Mass time:** main Mass of Sunday morning. People of the highest class would attend High Mass.

may have me fair by night and foul by day, or else have me fair by day, and by night ugly once again. You must choose."

270   "Alas!" said Gawain. "The choice is too hard—to have you fair on nights and no more, that would grieve my heart and shame me. Yet if I desire to have you fair by day and foul by night, I could not rest. I know not in the world what I should say, but do as you wish. The choice is in your hands."

"Thank you, courteous Gawain," said the lady. "Of all earthly knights you are blessed, for now I am truly loved. You shall have me fair both day and night, and ever while I live as fair. For I was shaped by witchcraft by my step-mother, God have mercy on her. By enchantment I was to

280   be the foulest creature, till the best knight of England had wedded me and had given me the sovereignty of all his body and goods. Kiss me, Sir Gawain—be glad and make good cheer, for we are well." The two rejoiced together and thanked God for their fortune.

King Arthur came himself to call them to breakfast the next day, wondering why Gawain stayed so late with his loathly bride. Sir Gawain rose, taking the hand of his lady, and opened the door to greet the king.

The Dame Ragnell stood by the fire, with her pale

290   lovely skin and red hair spilling down to her knees. "Lo," said Gawain to the king, "this is my wife the Dame Ragnell, who once saved your life." And Gawain told the king the story of the lady's enchantment.

"My love shall she have, for she has been so kind," said the king. And the queen said, "You will have my love for-ever, Lady, for you have saved my Lord Arthur." And from then on, at every great feast, that lady was the fairest, and all his life Gawain loved the Lady Ragnell.

Thus ends the adventure of King Arthur and of the

300   wedding of Sir Gawain.

Sir Gawain and the Loathly Lady

Shield of Legend   Take a look at the "knight's shield" below. Each section of the shield lists one element of a legend. For each element, list related details from "Sir Gawain and the Loathly Lady."

Literary Skills
Analyze a quest story.

Hero:	**The quest:**
The riddle:	**Temptations or tasks:**

Sir Gawain and the Loathly Lady

VOCABULARY AND COMPREHENSION

Word Bank

chivalry
countenance
loathsome
sovereignty

A. Clarify Word Meanings: The French Influence   Three of the four vocabulary words are borrowed from French. The original French word for each French-influenced vocabulary word is listed below, along with its meaning. Write the correct word from the Word Bank on the line next to each.

1. *souveraineté,* meaning "above; over" _____

2. *chevaler,* meaning "knight" _____

3. *contenance,* meaning "bearing; conduct" _____

B. Reading Comprehension   Answer each question below.

1. Why does Sir Gromer Somer Joure want to kill King Arthur? _____

_____

2. What riddle does Sir Gromer Somer Joure present to King Arthur?

_____

_____

3. What quest do King Arthur and Sir Gawain undertake? _____

_____

4. What does Dame Ragnell ask of King Arthur in return for saving his life?

_____

_____

5. What caused Dame Ragnell to be so ugly? What caused her to

become beautiful? _____

_____

SKILLS FOCUS

Vocabulary Skills
Understand French word origins.

The Changing of the Shrew

by Kathleen Kudlinski

LITERARY FOCUS: LEGENDS

When you think of a legend, do you think of Michael Jordan? a historical figure such as Abraham Lincoln? or even a story about a great tragedy, such as the sinking of the *Titanic*? A **legend** is simply a very old story passed down from one generation to the next. The story may be based on a real person or event, but often it contains information that is exaggerated or completely made up.

So, although stories about Michael Jordan, Abraham Lincoln, and the sinking of the *Titanic* might have some elements of a legend, the stories about them are still mostly factual. The stories may have to be retold for a few hundred more years before they qualify as actual legends! If you can't wait that long, read "The Changing of the Shrew," based on the popular characters from Arthurian legend.

READING SKILLS: USING TEXT CLUES

Chances are that when you read a story, you don't think of how great its punctuation is or how terrifically its text is styled. Nonetheless, without those text clues your understanding of the story would probably suffer. When we talk about **text clues,** we are talking about punctuation, as well as the use of italics, boldface, and capitals. As you read "The Changing of the Shrew," you'll notice that the writer uses italics for a couple of different reasons.

- When a single word or only a few words are italicized, the writer is calling out their importance or emphasizing them.
- Italics sometimes are used to set off one or more complete sentences in a passage. When an italicized passage is not in quotation marks but sounds like a character speaking, the passage is revealing a character's unspoken thoughts.
- Using full capital letters in a passage indicates that the passage should be given extreme emphasis, even more than if it had been italicized.

SKILLS FOCUS

Literary Skills
Identify characteristics of legends.

Reading Skills
Use text clues.

Vocabulary Skills
Use word roots and affixes to clarify meaning.

VOCABULARY DEVELOPMENT

PREVIEW SELECTION VOCABULARY

Take a few minutes to preview these words before you read "The Changing of the Shrew."

progression (prō·gresh′ən) *n.:* sequence; order of events or things.

Arthur studied the progression of the planets to better understand the seasons.

visible (viz′ə·bəl) *adj.:* able to be seen.

When Arthur's wiggling nose became visible, Merlin knew Arthur wanted some cheese.

predators (pred′ə·tərz) *n.:* those who capture and feed upon other animals.

Merlin turned Arthur into a mouse, but he was worried that Arthur would be eaten by one of the predators.

emphatically (em·fat′ik·lē) *adv.:* forcefully; insistently.

Nodding his head emphatically, Arthur told Merlin that he greatly enjoyed being a mouse.

USING AFFIXES

An affix is a word part added to the beginning or end of a word to change its meaning. If you know the meaning of a word's affix, you can often figure out the word's meaning. Here are some common affixes you should get to know.

Affix	Meaning
pro–	"before"
dis–	"lack of" or "opposite of"
–ly	"in the manner of"

The Changing of the Shrew

Kathleen Kudlinski

"We will study planetary **progression** today, Arthur, because *that* is the lesson I have prepared." Merlin pushed a damp lock of gray hair off his forehead.

"But it's spring!" Arthur stood with his arms spread to catch the sunshine as it poured over the cold stone windowsill. "Can't we just study spring, instead?"

The wizard looked over Arthur's shoulder at the first soft green on the far hillside pasture. "If you know the heavens well," he tried to tell the boy, "you'll know the

10 seasons." Merlin wondered if the first fenny snakes were out basking in that warm sunshine. Curing a rash of winter fevers in the drafty castle had burned up nearly all of his snake tongues.

"Please, Merlin. For once can't we do something that isn't planned?"

"I suppose you'd rather play games," he said harshly. *But, Jove! It did sound good. This truly must be spring.* "How about a race to the far hilltop?"

The boy's eyes reflected disbelief, then surprise, joy,

20 then anger. "No fair. You'll fly!"

And that is what the wizard did. Spreading his arms wide, he placed the tips of his thumbs against the second joints of his third fingers. Humming a perfect A-flat, he stepped out through the window and drifted toward the kitchens below.

He flattered the cook into packing a hearty lunch for them, wheedled the dairy maid into giving up two crocks

---

VOCABULARY

progression (prō·gresh'ən) *n.:* sequence; order of events or things.

WORD STUDY

The term "fenny snakes" (line 10) refers to "snakes from the fens." A *fen* is a bog or wetland.

IDENTIFY

Pause at line 13. Who are the story's main characters? Underline their names.

INTERPRET

Underline the words in italics (line 17). The writer uses italics to show Merlin's inner thoughts, which Arthur doesn't hear. How does this technique help readers understand Merlin?

_____

_____

_____

_____

_____

_____

COMPARE & CONTRAST

Re-read lines 21–30. Circle the actions of Merlin that seem ordinary or human. Then, put a box around the actions that come from his use of magic.

INTERPRET

What does Merlin mean when he says he was "thinking on his feet" (line 46)?

_____

_____

_____

_____

_____

_____

_____

INFER

Pause at line 57. What can you infer about Arthur from his words and actions?

_____

_____

_____

_____

_____

_____

_____

of buttermilk, and, floating on a lovely breeze up the hillside, charmed a dozen snakes into parting with their

30 tongues. *A good morning's work,* he thought, shaking the cool spring air out from under his robes. But it had scarcely given him time to plan a lesson for a future king. *What to do with the boy?*

"Well, what shall we study?" Arthur panted as he finally crested the hill.

"Precisely." Merlin nodded sagely. "I thought we'd discuss it over lunch." He patted the cloth spread beside him, hoping the boy would sit quietly and let him think.

"Oh, Merlin. It's too early to eat. What can you show

40 me about spring? Couldn't we do something magic?"

Why couldn't Arthur be in a growth spurt this spring, Merlin wondered, *instead of an intellectual stage?* He toyed with the idea of casting a growth spell, but decided against it. Cook hadn't packed enough food for that.

"Well?"

"All right, Arthur." Merlin was thinking on his feet, which was hard, for he was seated on the grass and quite winded from his flight. *Spring fancies were for younger men,* he reminded himself. *Or should be.* "Perhaps I'll try

50 something with you that I hadn't intended to do for several more years."

"I'm ready." Arthur plopped down beside the wizard.

"I'm not so sure you are. There may be some danger." As he heard his own words, Merlin could have kicked himself. A threat of danger never discouraged any ten-year-old.

Arthur jumped back to his feet, shouting, "On with it, then!"

"Very well," Merlin said, though he knew that was not the case at all. "Listen closely, for I shall not be with you

60 after I cast the spell." Arthur quieted down as Merlin knew
he would. He'd not used magic on the boy as yet, and it had
frightened him. *As it should.*

"I am going to cast you into an animal's body. While
you are there you must fend for yourself, for I cannot go
with you."

Arthur clapped and shouted, "Oh, make me an eagle!
Perhaps a lion? Or a stallion? . . ."

Merlin knew now he'd made an error. The boy was
clearly too young, but it was too late to change courses.
70 *What to do?*

"How about a griffon?[1] Oh, could I be a dragon? Or
maybe a . . ."

They both glanced down as a tiny animal scampered
across the picnic cloth toward the cook's basket.

"A mouse!" Merlin roared, considerably relieved.

Arthur stopped in the middle of his heroic list. "You're
going to make me into a mouse?"

"Yes. Do you have any questions?"

"Couldn't it be something more, well, grand?"

80 Merlin shook his head, hoping the boy would decide
to skip the whole lesson.

Arthur sat silently for a moment. "Will I be able to
read the mouse's mind while I'm inside his body?"

"No. *His* mind will be in *your* body, beside me here
on the picnic cloth." Merlin was beginning to regret the
whole idea.

"So you get to talk to a giant mouse?" Arthur
laughed aloud.

Merlin looked at the sky and began chanting.

90 As he finished the spell, Merlin watched the boy
closely. Although Arthur looked the same to him, from

---

1. **griffon:** mythical animal that is part eagle and part lion.

INFER

Why do you think Merlin says that magic *should* frighten Arthur (lines 61–62)?

_____
_____
_____
_____
_____
_____
_____
_____
_____

PREDICT

Pause at line 86. What might Arthur learn from being changed into a mouse?

_____
_____
_____
_____
_____
_____
_____
_____

WORD STUDY

Underline "mouse-in-Arthur" and "boy-shaped mouse" (lines 96 and 99). The writer uses these terms to emphasize to readers that Arthur is still under Merlin's spell.

VOCABULARY

visible (viz′ə·bəl) *adj.:* able to be seen.

Visible comes from the Latin word *videre,* meaning "see," and the Latin suffix *–ible,* meaning "capable of being."

RETELL

Pause at line 121. Then, explain what has happened to Arthur and the mouse.

_____

_____

_____

_____

_____

_____

_____

_____

_____

_____

_____

_____

_____

_____

his tangled brown hair to his worn leather boots, Merlin knew that a mouse's mind was taking over the strong young body. Soon the boy's muscles began to tremble. His eyes jerked wide open, and he jumped to his feet.

"Oh, my!" the mouse-in-Arthur whimpered as he tried to hide Arthur's body behind the lunch basket.

"Easy, easy," Merlin said gently. "I won't hurt you."

"But you are so big!" said the boy-shaped mouse,
100 wringing his hands.

"Look at yourself, mouse. You, too, are big now." Moving slowly so he wouldn't frighten the timid animal, Merlin pointed toward Arthur's body. "I've played somewhat of a trick on you. You will be a boy for a few moments while I use your body for some magic."

The mouse-in-Arthur's eyes widened. When he opened his mouth, Merlin expected a yowl of terror. Instead, the giant mouse squeaked, and ran to hide behind a small tree.

"Really, now, old fellow," Merlin called to him. "There
110 is nothing to worry about." The boy's shoulders stuck out on both sides of the sapling, but he did not move. "I'll protect you," Merlin promised.

Now Arthur's nose was **visible** on one side of the tree trunk. It was wiggling.

"I have some cheese in the basket," Merlin coaxed. "Come closer and I'll show you."

The mouse-in-a-boy hurried back, glancing over his shoulder as he came.

At the distant scream of a hawk, he grabbed the
120 edge of the cloth and dove under it, upsetting the cheese, the sausage pasties,[2] the wine, and the wizard.

_____

2. **sausage pasties:** sausage pies.

Merlin sighed deeply and dusted off his robes. As he began picking up the scattered dinner, a whisper came through the cloth. "Do you have food?"

"Yes. Will you come out and share a bite?"

A moment passed and Merlin repeated his offer. "Did you hear me?" he asked the quivering cloth.

"Yes," the boy-shaped mouse whispered. "You mustn't speak so loudly. They'll find us."

130 "Who?" Merlin found himself whispering back.

"Don't jest about the Deaths," came the offended reply.

"Someone wants to kill you?" Merlin knew that Arthur's mind was somewhere near, planted in this mouse's tiny body. If that body died, so would Arthur. "Just how much danger is there for you?" he prodded.

The boy-mouse picked up the edge of the cloth and waved Merlin in. The old wizard looked around the field before he, too, climbed under the picnic cloth.

"The sky is full of danger," the mouse whispered in a
140 sing-song voice. "Hawks and herons by day and owls by night. The grass crawls with danger: snakes and lizards and spiders." Merlin felt himself crouching further as he listened. "Danger pads on quiet paws: ferrets and weasels, badgers and foxes, cats and . . ." the mouse's whisper dropped to a hiss, ". . . shrews."

A cow mooed and the mouse-in-Arthur's-body stopped breathing.

"Are you all right?" Merlin whispered quickly.

The boy-mouse looked at him angrily and put his
150 hand over Merlin's mouth.

When a few moments of silence had passed, the mouse continued, "The water swims with danger: bullfrogs and bass, turtles . . ."

INTERPRET

Re-read lines 132–153. Circle the word *danger* each time it appears. What effect does this repetition have on your reading experience? Explain.

_____

_____

_____

_____

_____

_____

_____

_____

_____

_____

_____

_____

_____

_____

_____

_____

_____

_____

_____

_____

IDENTIFY

Why does Arthur say he
liked being small (line 169)?
Underline his explanation.

"Don't mice think of anything besides being eaten?"
Merlin wondered aloud.

"No," the mouse answered. "What else is there?"

"Enough!" Merlin shouted, throwing the cloth off
their heads. He had to get the real Arthur back before he
was eaten by one of these **predators.** As the mouse-in-
160 Arthur's-body cowered in the grass at his feet, Merlin
chanted the spell of undoing.

With the last words, the boy's body trembled. "Not
now!" he whispered angrily. "I had almost reached the
cheese in safety!"

Merlin looked at their picnic, once again spilled about
on the grass.

"Oh, do get up," the wizard said. "We don't need to
learn any more about mice."

"But I liked being small," Arthur answered. "I could
170 hide anywhere."

"You kept yourself hidden?"

Arthur nodded **emphatically.** "It was so exciting to
know there could be enemies everywhere. I still can feel
that thrill."

© Martha Paulos/Getty Images.

Merlin wondered if he hadn't acted too quickly. Knowing how to hold a keen edge of caution could certainly help the future king in his court.

"Please make me a mouse again," Arthur begged. "I'll be perfectly safe." Merlin's eyebrows rose. "Well, I will be
180 very careful. And I learned so much."

Merlin nodded, stroking his chin. They both had. "You want to be small again?"

Arthur nodded.

"But what shall you be? We must choose something safer than a mouse."

"Could I be a cat, Merlin? How about a falcon?"

"Hush, child, let me think." Which was the most dreaded animal on the mouse's list? Quiet and frightened, the mouse's voice came back to him: *Badgers and foxes,*
190 *cats and SHREWS.*" That was it. "Would you like to learn about shrews?" he asked, though he already knew the answer.

"What a wonderful idea! They are bloody good fighters, Merlin. And they even have a poison bite. Can I start right off?"

Merlin again began the chant. Again there was no change to be seen in Arthur's body as the shrew's mind took over. As before, the eyes were the first clue that the change was complete. This time, they opened clear and
200 alert. When they found Merlin, the shrew-in-Arthur's eyes narrowed.

"Oh, dear," muttered the wizard, backing off the cloth.

The boy-sized shrew sprang at him, caught his hand and sunk his teeth into Merlin's finger.

"Oh, do stop," Merlin cried. "This is all wrong." He tried to pull the boy's head away from his throbbing finger.

WORD STUDY

A shrew (line 190) is a tiny animal that has a long, pointed snout and is related to a mole. Some types of shrews are poisonous.

_____

_____

_____

_____

_____

_____

_____

_____

_____

_____

_____

_____

_____

_____

_____

_____

_____

WORD STUDY

Release (line 219) comes from the Latin _relaxare,_ meaning "relax" or "set free." In this context, _release_ is used as a noun meaning "act of freeing."

The boy-sized shrew just ground his teeth in more deeply and watched Merlin's distress with obvious glee.

"Freeze!" Merlin shouted, and every living thing
210 stopped. Bird song was stilled. The cows froze in place. Butterflies stopped flapping and fell to the soft grass. It was the only spell Merlin could think of on such short notice, and it hadn't quite solved the problem. He looked at the shrew-in-Arthur locked to his finger with astonishingly sharp teeth.

"Listen, shrew. You are, like it or not, a boy for a while. I am going to lift the spell and you will try to behave like a boy."

Merlin cast a release over the meadow. Bird and insect
220 song filled the air. A rainbow's worth of butterflies flew up from the grasses. The cows again chewed their cud. And the shrew-in-Arthur gave one last crunch to the wizard's finger before he released his bite.

"Let's just sit here quietly, shrew, shall we? And wait for it all to be over." Merlin still didn't like the look in those wild eyes, but he was relieved to see the boy's body settling at the far corner of the picnic cloth.

"I am simply starving," said the shrew. "And you will provide my lunch."
230 "No, I think not," said Merlin. "Cook packed just enough for Arthur and me."

"You mistake me," said the shrew. "You've had your turn to hold me still. Now it is my turn." He pointed to Merlin's bloody finger. "My bite is poisonous. In moments you won't be able to move. It doesn't hurt to be eaten that way. At least none of my other victims have complained."

Merlin just smiled and waited.

The shrew-in-Arthur hummed tunelessly for a moment. "I am simply starving. Can you still move?" He looked hopefully at Merlin.

The magician raised his hand and waved at him.

"You know, if I don't eat every four hours, I shall die. I am quite truly starving. That is how we shrews are." He shrugged and looked hungrily at the cows grazing, then back at the wizard. "I say, aren't you feeling the least bit stiff yet?"

Merlin simply waved and grinned. "It is as I said. You are no more a shrew than I am. You are a boy."

The shrew-in-Arthur blinked once. "What do these boys eat?"

"For one thing, boys do not eat wizards." The idea left Merlin chuckling until he noticed the look on the shrew's face. He added firmly, "Never."

The wizard hoped this lesson was going more smoothly for his student. He had a sudden rush of affection for Arthur, a boy with such a quick, open mind and loving heart.

"Don't you ever think of anything besides eating?" he asked the shrew.

"No," the shrew answered. "What else is there?"

In the uneasy silence that followed, Merlin saw a tiny furry body in the grass beside the cloth. Before he could move he saw the shrew-in-Arthur grab the little animal and bite its head off.

Merlin yelped in surprise. Then he froze, staring at the small, headless body in horror. *What if the shrew-in-Arthur had just eaten Arthur-in-the-shrew? Was the real Arthur dead? What would become of Britain with this brutal creature as its king?*

240

250

260

FLUENCY

Read the boxed passage expressively, showing the difference in the characters' ages and the humor in their words.

COMPARE & CONTRAST

Circle the word *eating* (line 258). How would you compare what it was like being a shrew with what it was like being a mouse? What do you think the author is trying to say?

_____

_____

_____

_____

_____

_____

IDENTIFY

Re-read lines 265–269. What word in the story's climax would you choose that tells what Merlin fears? Why? Put a box around the word.

_____

_____

_____

_____

_____

270   "Mouse," the shrew-in-Arthur said, offering the limp, headless body to Merlin. "Care to try a bite?"

Merlin gagged and shook his head no. He watched, horrified, as the shrew-in-Arthur finished the morsel and picked his teeth. Finally he had to ask, "Are you sure that was a mouse?"

"Yes, quite. Meadow mouse, by the taste of it. Deer mice are sweeter. I'll catch that one over by the basket, if you'd like to try it."

"No!" cried Merlin. "Lessons are quite over for the
280   morning." He raced through the spell of undoing.

At the last word, Arthur's glance darted quickly left, then right. "Where is that mouse!" he said. "I almost had him."

"Arthur," Merlin said gently. "We do not eat mice." He watched the boy's eyes cloud with confusion, then clear.

"I would actually have eaten a mouse?"

"Yes. Raw."

Arthur's face twisted and he swallowed hard. "I don't think I want to study any more today."

290   Merlin reached across the cloth and hugged the boy fiercely. Then they unpacked the cheeses, pasties, and buttermilk.

Arthur grabbed a morsel, crying, "I am simply starving!"

Merlin looked at him sharply. The boy grinned. "No, I guess I'm not *that* starving. But I'll never forget how real hunger feels." He appeared to be lost in thought. "Having a poison bite made everything different. It felt so powerful to know that if I could just make the first move, I would be in
300   control of things. I wonder if that works with people, too?" His grin faded as he noticed the bloody tooth marks in Merlin's finger.

INTERPRET

Read lines 295–310 carefully. What did Arthur learn when he became a shrew?

"The shrew, or rather, *I* did that to you?" he asked, in a tiny voice. And in a tinier voice still, "I would actually have eaten you?"

"Yes. Raw." Merlin magicked away the wound and smiled kindly at the future king. "But you didn't."

Arthur was quiet a moment. "I guess that getting in the first move isn't a good idea until you're sure you're not hurting a friend."

310

Merlin nodded, then asked, "Would you mind if I don't plan this sort of lesson again for some time?"

"Fine." Arthur grinned at him. "Only, Merlin, when we do study this way, shouldn't we hold the lessons *after* lunch?" Without waiting for an answer, he bit into the cheese.

INTERPRET

Think about what Arthur learned in the story. How does what he learned reveal the story's **theme,** or message about life?

_____

_____

_____

_____

_____

_____

_____

_____

_____

_____

_____

_____

_____

_____

_____

_____

_____

The Changing of the Shrew

SKILLS FOCUS

Reading Skills
Recognize characteristics of legends.

Fact/Imagination Chart   A **legend** is a story based on an actual person or event. As the story is retold, it takes on a life and personality of its own. With each new teller, characters may become bolder and braver, their journeys ever more perilous, and events more fantastic. Fill in the chart below with details from "The Changing of the Shrew" that are examples of fact and fiction.

Story Details That May Be Based on History or Fact	Story Details That Come from the Author's Imagination

Skills Review

The Changing of the Shrew

VOCABULARY AND COMPREHENSION

A. Using Affixes   Fill in the blanks below with the correct words from the Word Bank. Then, circle the words in the paragraph that contain an affix meaning "opposite of."

Merlin told Arthur that he had to study planetary

(1) _____, but Arthur was disinterested. When Merlin

changed him into a mouse, the mouse-in-Arthur was afraid of being

eaten by (2) _____. He tried to disappear, but his nose

was (3) _____ from behind a tree. Merlin changed

Arthur into a shrew before he released him from his spell. Arthur said

(4) _____ that he was excited when he was a shrew.

B. Reading Comprehension   Answer each question below.

1. Why doesn't Arthur want to study planetary progression?

   _____

   _____

2. Does Merlin think it is a good idea to transform Arthur into various

   animals? Why or why not? _____

   _____

3. Why is the mouse-in-Arthur so afraid? _____

   _____

4. Why does the shrew-in-Arthur bite Merlin's finger? Does the bite

   have its desired effect? _____

   _____

5. What does Arthur learn from his experience? _____

   _____

Vocabulary Skills
Use word roots and affixes to clarify meaning.

Reading for Life

Academic Vocabulary for Collection 8

These are the terms you should know
as you read and analyze the selections in this collection.

———

Consumer documents Informational documents used in the buying and selling of products. Instruction manuals, warranties, and contracts are examples of consumer documents.

Workplace documents Informational documents used in offices, factories, and other work sites. Memos, schedules, and project guidelines are examples of workplace documents.

Public documents Informational documents that inform the public. Voter-registration packets, swimming regulations at a public pool, and weather bulletins are all examples of public documents.

Technical directions Documents used to explain or establish procedures for using technology. How-to instructions and installation manuals provide technical directions.

This selection also appears in *Elements of Literature.*

Casting Call / Hollywood Beat/Application

READING FOCUS: ANALYZING PUBLIC DOCUMENTS

We, the public, get a lot of information from public documents. Any document (printed or electronic) that gives information to the public is referred to as a **public document.** Public documents may be issued by schools, places of worship, government agencies, the courts, libraries, and fire and police departments, to name just a few. Following are some examples of public documents:

Type of Public Document	Purpose
Elevator certificate	To inform public when elevator inspection was last performed and by whom
Calendar of local events	To inform townspeople of community events and services
Evacuation booklet	To inform public of emergency procedures in the event of a disaster

IDENTIFYING TEXT STRUCTURES

Unlike novels, stories, and poems, which are often read for enjoyment, public documents are read for one reason: to get information. It's your job as a reader to locate the information you need and to clarify its meaning. Use text-structure clues to find and make sense of the information in public documents.

COMMON TEXT STRUCTURES

- headings (capture main point of text that follows)
- bulleted lists (give information in logical order)
- numbered lists (give information in a specific sequence)
- charts, graphs, and illustrations (capture information visually)
- captions (describe visuals)
- boldface and italics (give emphasis to text; highlight important ideas)

SKILLS FOCUS

Reading Skills
Analyze information in public documents; identify text structures.

Reading an Announcement

Let's follow one person's experience in finding information she needs by using some pubic documents. Meet Sam (Miss Samantha Sallyann Lancaster). Sam is smart, and she can beat anyone, anytime, anywhere on her BMX bike. Imagine Sam's excitement when she comes across this **announcement** in her favorite biking magazine:

Casting Call

If you've been looking for the right break to get into motion pictures, this may be your chance. Street-Wheelie Productions is casting fresh talent for an upcoming action movie.

To audition, you must
- be a charismatic, awesome, off-the-wall male or female individualist
- be an expert at making your BMX-type bike do whatever you want it to do
- have your own bike
- look like you're between the ages of twelve and fifteen
- meet the requirements for a permit to work in the entertainment industry if you are under age eighteen
- be living in or near San Francisco during July and August 2004

Auditions will be held in
Golden Gate Park, San Francisco
Saturday, May 25, 2004
10:00 A.M. to 5:00 P.M.

Bring your bike.

See you in the movies!

IDENTIFY

Pause at line 4. Underline the name of the company making the casting call.

_____

_____

_____

_____

_____

_____

INFER

Re-read the requirements for an audition (lines 5–15). Why do you think applicants must be living in or near San Francisco during July and August?

_____

_____

_____

_____

_____

IDENTIFY

Circle the city where the auditions will take place. What should someone who wants to audition bring to the audition? Underline that information.

Pause at line 7. What kind of movie will Sam be auditioning for?

_____

_____

_____

_____

_____

_____

_____

INFER

Underline what makes the BMX bike an important part of the movie (lines 8–13).

RETELL

Re-read lines 8–13. Retell what the movie is about.

_____

_____

_____

_____

_____

_____

_____

Locating Information: An Article

Sam thinks, "Cool!" This may be for her, but she wants more information. An **Internet search** using the key words *StreetWheelie Productions* and *San Francisco* yields this **article** from *Hollywood Beat,* a newsmagazine.

Hollywood Beat

Shhhhhh!

Here's a little secret for you. Remember Bilbo Baggins, the lovable little hobbit who saved Middle Earth from the Powers of Darkness in J.R.R. Tolkien's classic novel? Well, that little hobbit's about to get radical. *Hollywood Beat* has discovered that StreetWheelie Productions is developing an out-of-sight version of this tale, and Middle Earth will never be the same.

Set in San Francisco, the hobbits are bike-riding dudes who, in order to save their world, oppose an
10   endless stream of baddies who ride BMX bikes. The principal character, Bilbo, is a nerdy innocent who finds himself at the center of (Middle) Earth–shaking events. The result? Batman meets Mr. Rogers.

Sources close to the production say that there is some big talent interested in the project. As of yet, nobody's talking, but remember . . . you'll hear all about it first on *Hollywood Beat.*

Filling Out the Application

Study the application below to find out what Sam will need to do to get permission to work in a movie.

STATE OF CALIFORNIA
Division of Labor Standards Enforcement

APPLICATION FOR PERMISSION TO WORK
IN THE ENTERTAINMENT INDUSTRY

THIS IS NOT A PERMIT ❑ NEW ❑ RENEWAL

PROCEDURES FOR OBTAINING WORK PERMIT
1. Complete the information required below.
2. School authorities must complete the School Record section below.
3. For minors 15 days through kindergarten, please attach a certified copy of the minor's birth certificate. See reverse side for other documents that may be accepted.
4. Mail or present the completed application to any office of the Division of Labor Standards Enforcement for issuance of your work permit.

Name of Child	Professional Name, if applicable

Permanent Address Number Street City State Zip Code	Home Phone No.

School Attending	Grade

Date of Birth	Age	Height	Weight	Hair Color	Eye Color	Sex

Statement of Parent or Guardian: It is my desire that an Entertainment Work Permit be issued to the above-named child. I will read the rules governing such employment and will cooperate to the best of my ability in safeguarding his or her educational, moral, and physical interest. I hereby certify, under penalty of perjury, that the foregoing statements are true and correct.

Name of Parent or Guardian (print or type)	Signed	Daytime phone #

SCHOOL RECORD

❑ I certify that the above-named minor meets the school district's requirements with respect to age, school record, attendance, and health.
❑ Does not meet the district's requirements and permit should not be issued.

Authorized School Official	Date	
School Address	School Telephone	[School Seal or Stamp]

HEALTH RECORD

COMPLETE THIS SECTION IF INSTRUCTED TO DO SO
OR IF INFANT UNDER ONE MONTH OF AGE

Name of Doctor   Address   Telephone Number

I certify that I am Board Certified in pediatrics and have carefully examined

and, in my opinion: He/She is physically fit to be employed in the production of motion pictures and television. If less than one month, infant is at least 15 days old, was carried to full term, and is physically able to perform.

_____ M.D. _____
Signature   Date
Approved DLSE 277 Rev. 03/99

INFER

Who needs to fill out this application?

_____

_____

_____

_____

IDENTIFY

Who needs to fill in the section titled "School Record"?

_____

_____

_____

_____

_____

DRAW CONCLUSIONS

Underline the two things a doctor has to certify. Why is this an important part of the application?

_____

_____

_____

_____

Casting Call / Hollywood Beat / Application

SKILLS FOCUS

Reading Skills
Analyze public documents.

Information-Locator Wheel   The documents you just read contain a lot of information. Write the number of each item from the Information Bank in the area that shows where each piece of information can be found.

Information Bank

1. age of character Sam might play

2. age at which you can work in entertainment in California

3. how the actor playing the part should look

4. title of the book that StreetWheelie Productions is making into a movie

5. name of a main character in the movie

6. types of people who must declare that Sam can work in the entertainment industry

7. requirements for trying out for a part in the movie

8. Sam's birth date

9. time and place of audition

10. the city where the movie will be set

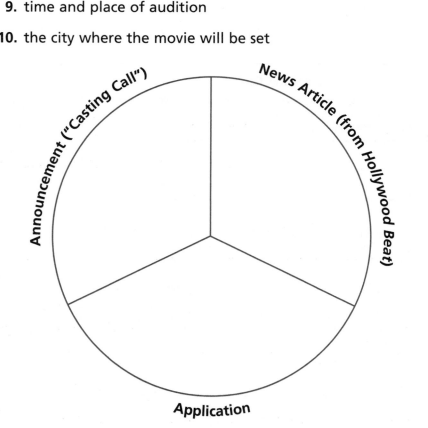

Skills Review

Casting Call / Hollywood Beat / Application

COMPREHENSION

Reading Comprehension   Answer the questions that follow.

1. Why is Sam interested in the "Casting Call" announcement?

   _____

   _____

   _____

2. Where and when will the auditions for the movie be held?

   _____

   _____

   _____

3. What special talent must people have to audition for the movie?

   _____

   _____

   _____

4. What will the movie be about?

   _____

   _____

   _____

5. Why does Sam have to fill out an application?

   _____

   _____

   _____

How to Locate the Big and Little Dippers by Bill Kramer

READING FOCUS: ANALYZING TECHNICAL DIRECTIONS

The purpose of **technical directions** is to guide the reader through a series of steps in order to achieve a goal (software installation, assembly of a product, and so on). Although directions may not be the most exciting things to read, they can be real timesavers—and even lifesavers—when written effectively and followed correctly.

Effective directions, no matter their subject matter, contain the same basic features:

- a complete list of supplies, tools, or ingredients
- a series of steps, numbered or lettered to indicate sequence
- diagrams or charts to illustrate complex steps
- clearly labeled warnings

IDENTIFYING TEXT STRUCTURES

Just as you learned to read words like *a* and *the* when you were quite young, you should learn to recognize text structures. Many informational texts, especially those containing technical directions, are formatted in certain ways to make information stand out more clearly. The more familiar you are with these features and structures, the better you'll be able to locate and digest the information within these texts.

Common Text Structures

- headings (capture main point of text that follows)
- bulleted lists (give information in logical order)
- numbered lists (give information in a specific sequence)
- charts, graphs, and illustrations (capture information visually)
- captions (describe visuals)

SKILLS FOCUS

Reading Skills
Analyze technical directions; identify text structures.

Vocabulary Skills
Recognize affixes.

VOCABULARY DEVELOPMENT

PREVIEW SELECTION VOCABULARY

Preview the following words before you read the selection.

hemisphere (hem'i·sfir') *n.:* area that lies within a specific half-section of earth.

Canada lies in the Northern Hemisphere of earth.

horizon (hə·rī'zən) *n.:* line where the sky seems to meet the earth.

At sunset the sun dips below the horizon.

degree(s) (di·grēz) *n.:* one 360th part of the circumference of a circle.

The roads met at an angle of ninety degrees.

essentially (ə·sen'shə·lē) *adv.:* basically.

The two illustrations of the Milky Way were essentially the same; one had slightly more detail than the other.

RECOGNIZING AFFIXES

An **affix** is something that is added (affixed) to a word to alter its meaning. Prefixes are affixes added to the front of words (*nonviolent; unrealistic*). Suffixes are affixes added to the end of words (*payment; respectfulness*). Becoming familiar with affixes and their meanings will help you unlock the meanings of many unfamiliar words you encounter when reading.

Get to know these common affixes.

Affix	Meaning	Examples
hemi–	half	hemisphere; hemistich
tele–	far off	telescope; telephone
–ly	in a manner or direction	essentially; practically
–ness	state or quality of being	brightness; greatness

_____
_____
_____
_____
_____
_____
_____

_____
_____
_____
_____
_____

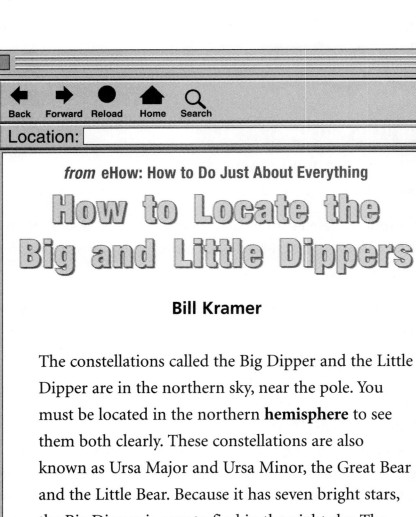

from eHow: How to Do Just About Everything

How to Locate the Big and Little Dippers

Bill Kramer

The constellations called the Big Dipper and the Little Dipper are in the northern sky, near the pole. You must be located in the northern **hemisphere** to see them both clearly. These constellations are also known as Ursa Major and Ursa Minor, the Great Bear and the Little Bear. Because it has seven bright stars, the Big Dipper is easy to find in the night sky. The Little Dipper is harder to see because it's made up of fainter stars.

© Roz Woodward/Getty Images.

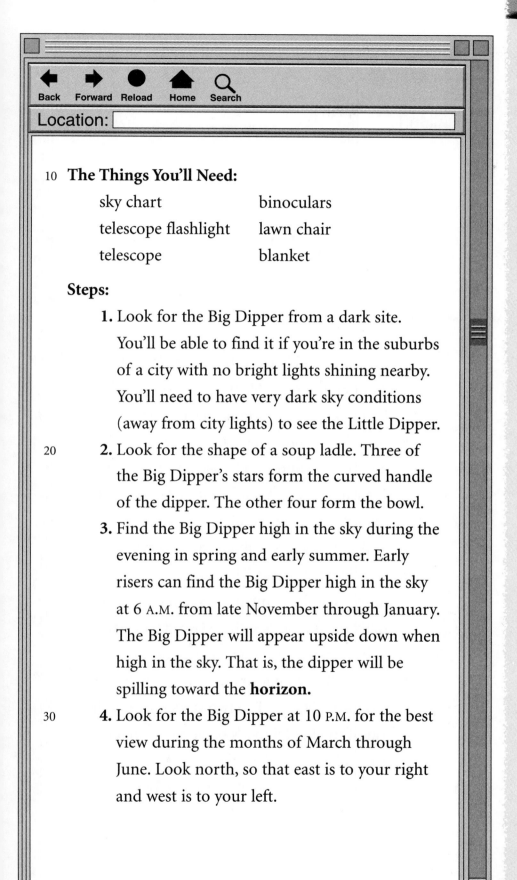

The Things You'll Need:

10

sky chart   binoculars

telescope flashlight   lawn chair

telescope   blanket

Steps:

1. Look for the Big Dipper from a dark site. You'll be able to find it if you're in the suburbs of a city with no bright lights shining nearby. You'll need to have very dark sky conditions (away from city lights) to see the Little Dipper.

20

2. Look for the shape of a soup ladle. Three of the Big Dipper's stars form the curved handle of the dipper. The other four form the bowl.

3. Find the Big Dipper high in the sky during the evening in spring and early summer. Early risers can find the Big Dipper high in the sky at 6 A.M. from late November through January. The Big Dipper will appear upside down when high in the sky. That is, the dipper will be spilling toward the **horizon.**

30

4. Look for the Big Dipper at 10 P.M. for the best view during the months of March through June. Look north, so that east is to your right and west is to your left.

IDENTIFY

Circle the list of things you'll need before you can follow the step-by-step directions.

INFER

Why do you think you need to be in a dark place to see the stars in the sky (lines 15–19)?

_____

_____

_____

_____

_____

_____

_____

_____

_____

_____

_____

_____

_____

_____

VOCABULARY

horizon (hə·rī′zən) *n.:* line where the sky seems to meet the earth.

What or whom do you think the stars are named after (lines 39–40)?

_____

_____

_____

_____

_____

_____

_____

_____

_____

_____

_____

_____

_____

_____

_____

essentially (ə·sen′shə·lē) *adv.:* basically.

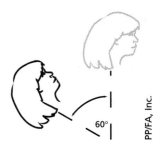

PP/FA, Inc.

5. Tilt your head back until you're looking up about 60 **degrees.** The seven stars making up the Big Dipper should be clearly visible.

6. Identify the individual stars of the Big Dipper. Start at the handle and go around the bowl. Their names are Alkaid, Mizar, Alioth, Megrez,

40   Phad, Merak, and Dubhe.

7. Look through a small telescope or pair of binoculars at Mizar. This star is seen as a double star. Its companion's name is Alcor. Many people can see these two stars clearly with the naked eye once they're pointed out.

8. Use the Big Dipper to locate the North Star and Little Dipper. The two stars forming the end of the Big Dipper's bowl point directly at the North Star. The Little Dipper has

50   **essentially** the same shape as the Big Dipper, but its handle is curved the other way.

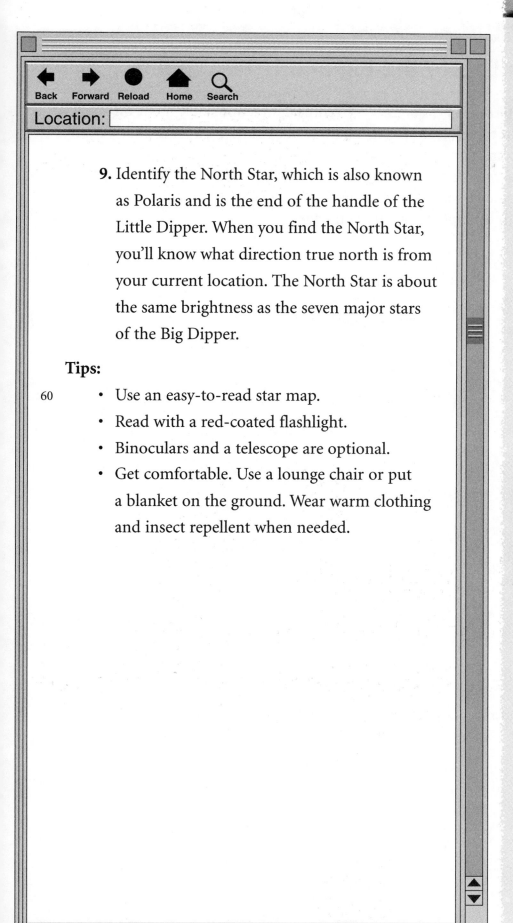

9. Identify the North Star, which is also known as Polaris and is the end of the handle of the Little Dipper. When you find the North Star, you'll know what direction true north is from your current location. The North Star is about the same brightness as the seven major stars of the Big Dipper.

Tips:

60
- Use an easy-to-read star map.
- Read with a red-coated flashlight.
- Binoculars and a telescope are optional.
- Get comfortable. Use a lounge chair or put a blanket on the ground. Wear warm clothing and insect repellent when needed.

Why do you think sailors use Polaris to navigate (lines 54–56)?

_____

_____

_____

_____

_____

_____

_____

_____

_____

ANALYZE

Do the tips in lines 60–65 have to be followed in a specific order? Explain.

_____

_____

_____

_____

_____

_____

_____

_____

_____

_____

How to Locate the Big and Little Dippers

Technical Directions Organizer   Technical directions may focus on any number of topics, from fixing a hard disk to building a hang glider. Most technical directions, however, contain common features and text structures to make accessing the information predictable and easy. Read through "How to Locate the Big and Little Dippers." Then, fill in the organizer below with examples taken from the text.

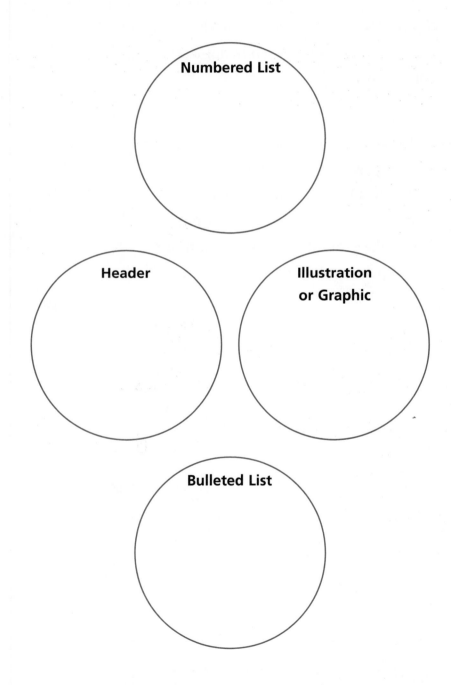

Numbered List

Header

Illustration or Graphic

Bulleted List

Skills Review

How to locate the Big and Little Dippers

VOCABULARY AND COMPREHENSION

A. Affixes Fill in the paragraph below with words from the Word Bank. Then, circle the two Word Bank words that contain affixes.

Of all the constellations, the Big Dipper is one of the brightest. You cannot see it in the southern half of the globe; you can only see it in the Northern (1) _____. Where the sky seems to meet the earth, the Big Dipper looks like a giant ladle spilling over the (2) _____. Away from city light, tilt your head back sixty (3) _____ toward the sky. (4) _____, the Little Dipper has the same shape as the Big Dipper.

B. Reading Comprehension Answer the questions that follow.

1. By what other names are the Big Dipper and Little Dipper known?

_____

2. Under what heading do you learn what equipment you'll need?

_____

3. Which two steps explain the best time to find the Big and Little Dippers? _____

_____

4. Who or what are Alkaid, Mizar, Alioth, Megrez, Phad, Merak, and Dubhe? _____

_____

5. Why is the information in the Tips section presented in a bulleted list rather than a numbered list? _____

_____

Vocabulary Skills Recognize affixes.

Part Two

Reading Informational Texts

Academic Vocabulary for Part 2

These are the terms you should know as you read
and analyze the informational selections in this section.

_____

Main Idea The most important point in a text or section of text.

Summary A brief restatement of the main events or ideas in a text.

Comparison Description of how two or more things are alike.

Contrast Description of how two or more things are different.

Cause An event that makes something happen.

Effect What happens as a result of a cause.

Argument A position supported by evidence.

Evidence Details a writer uses to support his or her position.

● ● ●

Text Features Special type, such as boldface, italics, and capitals, and
bullets that call attention to important information.

Headings Titles at the tops of pages or sections.

Illustrations Drawings, photos, art, graphs, maps, or other visuals.

Captions Descriptions of art, illustrations, charts, or maps. A caption
usually appears beneath or next to the visual it describes.

Footnotes Definitions and/or examples of difficult terms within the
text. Footnotes are numbered and usually appear at the bottom
of the text page.

Guide to Mammals

edited by Sydney Anderson

READING SKILLS: UNDERSTANDING TEXT STRUCTURES

Text structures help us locate and understand information we read in articles and books. As you read this excerpt from *Guide to Mammals*, look for how the following structures are used.

- **Main headings and subheads** Words or short phrases that give the main idea of the text that follows. A main heading may be followed by one or more subheadings that go into more detail about the topics.
- **Captions** Descriptions of art, illustrations, charts, or maps. A caption usually appears beneath the visual it describes.
- **Footnotes** Definitions and/or examples of difficult terms within the text. Footnotes usually appear at the bottom of the page.
- **Illustrations** Art, photographs, drawings, charts, or maps that accompany a text.

VOCABULARY DEVELOPMENT: PREVIEW SELECTION VOCABULARY

Before you read the *Guide to Mammals* excerpt, get to know the following vocabulary words:

habitat (hab′i·tat′) *n.:* region where a plant or an animal naturally grows or lives.

Indian elephants live in a varied habitat that includes forests and plains.

maturity (mə·choor′ə·tē) *n.:* state of being full grown; adulthood.

Female elephants reach maturity—adulthood—at nine to fifteen years of age.

dissipate (dis′ə·pāt′) *v.:* break up and scatter; make disappear.

If the elephant's large ears didn't help dissipate its body heat, the elephant would have difficulty staying cool. Mammals have to be able to get rid of their body heat.

matriarchal (mā′trē·är′kəl) *adj.:* ruled by a mother or highly respected older woman.

Elephants live in family groups that have a matriarchal structure, meaning the head of the family is an elderly female.

SKILLS FOCUS

Reading Skills
Understand text structures.

from Simon & Schuster's
Guide to Mammals

edited by Sydney Anderson

335 Elephas maximus[1] *(Indian elephant)*

Classification: Order Proboscidea,[2] Family Elephantidae.[3]

Description: They are usually gray and may have light
blotches over the body. There are only a few long,
stiff hairs present on the body; the tip of the tail,
however, has a tuft of hairs. The forehead is flat. Its
long trunk, formed of upper lip and nose, has a single
process at the tip. Compared with the African
elephant, the Indian elephant has much smaller ears,

10
4 nails on each hind foot instead of 3, and 19 pair of
ribs instead of 21; the tusks, present only in some
males, are generally shorter. Length of head and body
including trunk up to 6.5 m (21.3 ft), shoulder height
2.5–3.2 m (8.2–10.5 ft), weight up to 5400 kg (5.9 t);
females somewhat smaller.

Distribution: India, the Indochinese peninsula, Sumatra, and
Sri Lanka.

Habitat: Varied; from forests to plains.

Behavior: The Indian elephant lives in groups of 10–30,

20
although groups of this size are becoming increasingly
rare. The group is made up of individuals which are
closely related, and is led by an elderly female. It rests
during the hottest hours of the day and frequently
sprays dirt over itself to keep away insects. When the

---

1. **Elephas maximus** (el′ə·fəs maks′ə·məs): Latin for "largest elephant."
2. **Proboscidea** (prō′bō·sə·dā′ə): Latin for "long flexible snout"
   or "trunk."
3. **Elephantidae** (el′ə·fən·tē′dī).

From *Simon & Schuster's Guide to Mammals* by
Luigi Boitani and Stefania Bartoli, edited by
Sydney Anderson. Copyright © 1983 by **Simon
& Schuster.** Reproduced by permission of the
publisher.

TEXT STRUCTURE

The entries in this field guide
are numbered and begin
with the scientific name of
the mammal followed by its
more common name. What
five categories of information does each entry provide?

_____

_____

_____

_____

_____

_____

_____

_____

_____

_____

_____

_____

VOCABULARY

habitat (hab′i·tat′) *n.:* region
where a plant or an animal
naturally grows or lives.

VOCABULARY

maturity (mə·chŏŏr′ə·tē) *n.:*
state of being full grown;
adulthood.

WORD STUDY

Read the sentence containing the word *gestation*
(line 25). Underline the
words that provide a clue
to its meaning.

IDENTIFY

Two types of information are
provided in lines 31–42.
What are they? Circle the
text that clued you in.

VOCABULARY

dissipate (dis′ə·pāt′) *v.:*
break up and scatter;
make disappear.

WORD STUDY

Two words on pages 304 and
305 contain the prefix *sub–*.
Sub– can mean "under," or it
can indicate a division into
smaller parts. With this
knowledge, what might *subspecies* (line 38) and *Sub-
Saharan* (line 43) mean?

_____

_____

_____

_____

_____

_____

_____

CORBIS.

Indian elephant.

herd travels, it usually does so in single file. Gestation
lasts for 18–22 months and a single young is born
(although twins are not unknown), which weighs
about 220 pounds at birth. Females reach **maturity** at
9–15 years of age, males at about 15 years. The life

30   span is about 70–80 years.

336   Loxodonta[4] africana *(African elephant)*

Classification: Order Proboscidea, Family Elephantidae.

Description: This is the largest living terrestrial mammal. Its
enormous ears serve to **dissipate** body heat and brush
away insects from its eyes. The upper incisors form
tusks, which average about 1.5 m (5 ft) long and weigh
about 16 kg (35 lb). The trunk has two fingerlike
processes at the tip. The forest subspecies of this
elephant is smaller than the savanna race. Length of

---

4. **Loxodonta** (läks′ə·dän′tə): *Loxodonta* is a generic name for elephants.
Loxo and *donta* are from the Latin, meaning "lozenge" and "tooth."
The name refers to the lozenge-shaped ridges on elephants' molars.

40 head and body including trunk up to 7.5 m (24.8 ft); shoulder height to 4 m (13 ft); weight may exceed 6000 kg (6.6 t).

Distribution: Sub-Saharan Africa except southern Africa.

Habitat: From semidesert to forest at different altitudes.

Behavior: This elephant is a social creature living in family groups which have a **matriarchal** structure. The head of the group is an elderly female; she makes decisions about when and where to move, and keeps the peace.
50 Groups of African elephants can number more than 100 individuals in periods of drought. The groups are constantly moving when the animals are feeding. The elephant must drink daily and enjoys bathing in waterholes. Breeding occurs all year, but a female will only give birth once every 4 years. Gestation lasts 22–24 months, at the end of which a single offspring is born, weighing about 220 pounds. It nurses for 2–3 years.

CORBIS.

African elephant.

COMPARE & CONTRAST

This field guide contains photographs. Compare the photograph of the African elephant with that of the Indian elephant. What is the most obvious difference between these two creatures?

_____
_____
_____
_____
_____
_____
_____
_____
_____
_____
_____
_____
_____
_____
_____
_____
_____
_____

VOCABULARY

matriarchal (mā′trē·är′kəl) *adj.:* ruled by a mother or highly respected older woman.

Guide to Mammals

Text Structures Chart   You can use the text structures of informational writing to find different kinds of information. Read through the *Guide to Mammals* excerpt, and fill in the chart below with examples of the types of text structures it contains.

Title of Text:

_____

_____

_____

_____

**Illustrations and Captions
(What Are They About?):**

_____

_____

_____

_____

Headings (What Are They?):

_____

_____

_____

_____

Main Idea:

_____

_____

_____

_____

Skills Review

~~~~~~~~~~~~~~~~~~~~~~~~~~~~~~~~~

Guide to Mammals

VOCABULARY AND COMPREHENSION

A. Selection Vocabulary   Write words from the Word Bank to complete the paragraph below.

The (1) _____ of most elephants is India or

Africa. The social order of elephants is (2) _____; that

is, they are led by females. When they reach (3) _____,

the elephant females become heads of their families. To

(4) _____ any fear elephants may experience,

the elephant leaders display calmness and strength.

> **Word Bank**
>
> **habitat**
> **maturity**
> **dissipate**
> **matriarchal**

B. Reading Comprehension   Answer each question below.

1. What two mammals are described in this article? Give their scientific

   names as well as their informal names. _____

   _____

2. What kind of information is given following the subhead

   "Distribution"? _____

   _____

3. What does *loxodonta* mean? (Hint: Look at footnote 4.) _____

   _____

   _____

4. Which of the mammals discussed lives in the semidesert or forest?

   _____

   _____

Top Ten Languages

from The World Almanac for Kids

READING SKILLS: ANALYZING COMPARISON AND CONTRAST

When you compare two things, you look for ways in which they are alike. When you contrast two things, you look for ways in which they are different. Look at the examples in the chart below.

Cantaloupe and Honeydew

Comparison	Contrast
• both fruits • both melons • both roundish • both have rinds • both taste sweet	• Cantaloupe has a rough green-gray rind; honeydew has a smooth green rind. • Cantaloupe has bright orange flesh; honeydew has light green flesh.

Read "Top Ten Languages," and then compare and contrast the information you find in it.

VOCABULARY DEVELOPMENT: PREVIEW SELECTION VOCABULARY

Preview these words before you begin reading "Top Ten Languages."

principal (prin′sə·pəl) *adj.:* first in rank or importance.

The most important language in China is Mandarin, which is also the principal language in the world.

immigrants (im′ə·grənts) *n.:* people who settle in a new country or region.

Immigrants, people who moved to the United States from other countries, brought their native languages with them.

census (sen′səs) *n.:* official, periodic count of population and recording of economic status, age, gender, and so on.

The last time the government took a census to record information about the country's people, Spanish was the second most common language.

SKILLS FOCUS

Reading Skills
Understand comparison-and-contrast texts.

from The World Almanac for Kids
Top Ten Languages

PhotoDisc, Inc.

Would you have guessed that Mandarin, the **principal** language of China, is the most common spoken language in the world? You may find more surprises in the chart below, which lists languages spoken in 1999 by at least 100,000,000 native speakers (those for whom the language is their

10

first language, or mother tongue) and some of the places where each one is spoken.

VOCABULARY

principal (prin′sə·pəl) *adj.:* first in rank or importance.

IDENTIFY

Pause at line 12. When were these two surveys of languages done? Underline the dates. Why are dates important to note in surveys like these?

_____

_____

_____

_____

_____

_____

_____

_____

_____

_____

_____

TOP TEN WORLD LANGUAGES 1999

Language	Where Spoken	Native Speakers
Mandarin	China, Taiwan	885,000,000
Hindi	India	375,000,000
Spanish	Spain, Latin America	358,000,000
English	U.S., Canada, Britain	347,000,000
Arabic	Arabian Peninsula	211,000,000
Bengali	India, Bangladesh	210,000,000
Portuguese	Portugal, Brazil	178,000,000
Russian	Russia	165,000,000
Japanese	Japan	125,000,000
German	Germany, Austria	100,000,000

20

TEXT STRUCTURE

What are the column headings of the chart at left? Circle them.

Which Languages Are Spoken in the United States?

Since the beginning of American history, **immigrants** have come to the United States from all over the world and brought their native languages with them.

30 The table below lists the most frequently spoken languages in the United States, as of the 1990 **census,** starting with English. The number for English is the number of people who speak only English at home.

TOP TWENTY LANGUAGES IN THE U.S. 1990

Language Used at Home	Speakers over 5 Years Old
1. English only	198,601,000
2. Spanish	17,339,000
3. French	1,702,000
4. German	1,547,000
5. Italian	1,309,000
6. Chinese	1,249,000
7. Tagalog	843,000
8. Polish	723,000
9. Korean	626,000
10. Vietnamese	507,000
11. Portuguese	430,000
12. Japanese	428,000
13. Greek	388,000
14. Arabic	355,000
15. Hindi, Urdu, related languages	331,000
16. Russian	242,000
17. Yiddish	213,000
18. Thai	206,000
19. Persian	202,000
20. French Creole	188,000

40 (line marker)

50 (line marker)

Top Ten Languages

Comparison-and-Contrast Chart   Compare and contrast information from the tables in "Top Ten Languages" by completing the Venn diagram below. Compare only the top ten languages. (Hint: Chinese and Mandarin can be considered the same language.)

SKILLS FOCUS

Reading Skills
Analyze comparison-and-contrast texts.

Top Ten World Languages 1999:

Both:

Top Twenty Languages in the U.S. 1990:

Skills Review

Top Ten Languages

VOCABULARY AND COMPREHENSION

A. Selection Vocabulary   Write words from the Word Bank to complete the paragraph below.

The (1) _____ taken last year has revealed new information about the U.S. population. One thing I find interesting is that the number of (2) _____ is increasing. According to a recent survey, the (3) _____ reason immigrants give for moving here is the chance at a better quality of life.

B. Reading Comprehension   Answer each question below.

1. What is the most common spoken language in the world? How many people were native speakers of this language in 1999?

   _____

   _____

2. Why are so many languages spoken in the United States?

   _____

   _____

3. What was the second most common language in the United States in 1990? What was the worldwide rank of this language in 1999?

   _____

   _____

4. What languages were more common worldwide than English in 1999?

   _____

   _____

Before You Read

NONFICTION

from Words from the Myths

by Isaac Asimov

READING SKILLS: ANALYZING CAUSE AND EFFECT

You know that putting money in a vending machine **causes** a certain **effect**—you will get your snack or drink. Informational texts commonly use cause-and-effect organizational patterns to explain how something came to be the way it is. In the excerpt from *Words from the Myths,* Isaac Asimov explores cause-and-effect relationships. He discusses how some English words got their meanings from Greek mythology. The signal words below may help you locate causes and effects in text.

Words That Signal Causes	Words That Signal Effects
because, due to, were caused by, came to be, given that, results from, as	therefore, thus, consequently, so, as a result, for that reason, then

VOCABULARY DEVELOPMENT: PREVIEW SELECTION VOCABULARY

Take some time to preview the words below.

plague (plāg) *v.:* torment or trouble.

Many ills plague human beings.

insolent (in'sə·lənt) *adj.:* disrespectful in speech or behavior.

Myths often warn against pride, which can lead to insolent behavior.

retribution (re'trə·byo͞o'shən) *n.:* punishment for evil done or reward for good done.

The gods punished disrespectful humans. The retribution sometimes was harsh.

boastful (bōst'fəl) *adj.:* inclined to brag.

Sometimes the gods would repay humans with bad fortune because the humans had become boastful, bragging about their good fortune.

membrane (mem'brān') *n.:* thin, soft, pliable sheet or layer, especially of animal or vegetable tissue.

The spinal cord is covered by a double membrane, two very thin layers of tissue.

SKILLS FOCUS

Reading Skills
Analyze cause and effect.

from **Words from the Myths**

Isaac Asimov

> **BACKGROUND: Informational Text and Language**
> Before you read this article, you should know
> that Prometheus (prō·mē′thē·əs) and Epimetheus
> (ep·ə·mē′thē·əs) are brothers. Zeus, king of the
> gods, is very angry at Prometheus because
> Prometheus has just disobeyed Zeus's orders
> and given humanity the gift of fire. To get
> revenge on Prometheus and to punish human-
> ity, Zeus tricks Epimetheus, the weaker brother.
> Here is Zeus's trick.

COMPARE & CONTRAST

Use the description of
Pandora in lines 1–4 to
visualize her. Then, study the
painting of Pandora on the
next page. How is your vision
of Pandora similar to or
different from Rossetti's?

_____

_____

_____

_____

_____

VOCABULARY

plague (plāg) *v.:* torment or
trouble.

Zeus created a beautiful woman to whom all the gods
gave gifts of beauty, grace, wit, melody, and so on. She was
called *Pandora* (pan·dôr′ə), from Greek words meaning
"all-gifted." She was then given to Epimetheus for a wife.
Because of her beauty, Epimetheus accepted her, although
Prometheus had warned him against taking any gift
from Zeus.

Along with Pandora, Epimetheus received a box which
Pandora was forbidden to open. At her first opportunity,
10 she opened the box to see what was in it and out flew the
spirits of old age, death, famine, sickness, grief, and all the
other ills that **plague** human beings. Only hope was left at
the bottom of the box and, when finally let out, was all that
kept human beings alive under the weight of their misery.

AFP/CORBIS.

Pandora Holding Her Box by Dante Gabriel Rossetti.

IDENTIFY CAUSE & EFFECT

In lines 8–14, Asimov uses causes and effects to explain the story of Pandora's box. Underline the action Pandora takes. What happens because of her action?

_____

_____

_____

WORD STUDY

Underline the **metaphor** in line 14. What is misery compared to here? Why is this a good way to describe unhappiness?

_____

_____

_____

_____

WORD STUDY

Continually means "happening over and over again." Knowing this, explain the torture of Prometheus (lines 21–22).

_____

_____

_____

_____

Thus, anything which is harmless when undisturbed, but which lets loose many troubles when interfered with, is called a "Pandora's box."

Not satisfied with having his revenge on humanity, Zeus also punished Prometheus directly. He chained him

20 to a rock in the Caucasus Mountains which, to the ancient Greeks, represented the eastern end of the world. There he was continually tortured by an eagle.

insolent (in'sə·lənt) *adj.*: disrespectful in speech or behavior.

retribution (re'trə·byoō'shən) *n.*: punishment for evil done or reward for good done.

boastful (bōst'fəl) *adj.*: inclined to brag.

WORD STUDY

Underline the word *hubris* (hyoō'bris) in line 33. Circle the words in context that define hubris.

IDENTIFY
CAUSE & EFFECT

Pause at line 33. What is the effect of hubris?

_____

_____

_____

_____

WORD STUDY

Underline the word *nemesis* (nem'ə·sis) in line 43. Circle the words in context that define nemesis. If you say, "Tests are my nemesis," what do you mean?

_____

_____

_____

_____

_____

The story of Pandora is actually a moral tale, a kind of fable intended to teach people how to behave. For instance, Epimetheus is a warning against careless action taken without due consideration of possible consequences. Pandora herself is a warning against foolish curiosity.

Many mythical warnings were against the kind of pride which made people consider themselves above the
30 law. Such pride led to **insolent** behavior and a disregard of the rights of others. In the Greek myths, it usually involved defying the gods—the sort of pride the Greeks called "hubris."

When that happened, the gods saw to it that the proud individual was dealt with by *Nemesis,* the goddess of **retribution.** The name comes from Greek words meaning to "distribute." In other words, Nemesis sees to it that matters are distributed evenly. If a person has so much good fortune that he or she becomes **boastful,**
40 proud, and insolent, Nemesis sees to it that this person has a corresponding amount of bad fortune to even things out.

Since most of the Greek myths involve matters evened out by bad fortune, rather than by good fortune, "nemesis" has come to mean, in our language, an unavoidable doom.

Pride is still considered the most serious of the seven deadly sins. It was through pride that Lucifer fell, according to our own stories. We still have this old Greek feeling about pride when we speak of "the jealous gods" who won't allow anyone to be too lucky. That is why we say that "pride
50 goeth before a fall" and knock on wood when talking about how fortunate we are, or how well off. That is supposed to keep off Nemesis.

An example of such a pride-goeth-before-a-fall myth is the story of *Arachne* (ə·rak′nē). She was a girl of the kingdom of Lydia (in western Asia Minor) who was very skilled at weaving. She was so proud of her skill that she boasted that even Athena, the goddess of the practical arts, including that of weaving, could not do better, and challenged Athena to a contest. (There was hubris.)

60   Athena accepted the challenge and both wove tapestries. Athena wove into hers all sorts of glorious stories about the gods, while Arachne wove into hers unflattering stories about them. Arachne's work was excellent but Athena's was perfect. In anger at Arachne's subject matter, Athena tore Arachne's weaving to shreds and Arachne, struck with terror, hanged herself. (There was nemesis.)

Athena, who was not a cruel goddess, didn't want things to go that far, so she loosened the rope and changed Arachne into a spider. As a spider, Arachne continued 70 spinning threads and weaving beautiful webs, and she also continues to hang from a strand of gossamer as though still trying to hang herself. Of course, "arachne" is the Greek word for "spider" and the idea of the myth surely came from watching spiders at work. But it does teach a moral: Avoid hubris.

In zoology, the name of the girl lives on, since spiders and its relatives are put in the class "Arachnida."

Furthermore, anything as filmy and delicate as a spider's web is said to be "arachnoid." For instance, the 80 brain and spinal cord are enclosed by a double **membrane** for protection. In between the two parts of the double membrane is a third membrane which is very thin and filmy. This is called the "arachnoid membrane."

IDENTIFY CAUSE & EFFECT

Asimov tells Arachne's story in a series of causes and effects (lines 53–72). Underline the words that tell how Arachne feels about her weaving skill. What does Arachne's pride cause her to do?

_____

_____

_____

_____

_____

FLUENCY

Read the boxed passage aloud. Before you begin, look again at the pronunciation of the name *Arachne* so that the flow of your reading is not interrupted by an unfamiliar word.

WORD STUDY

Underline the words in context (lines 78–79) that define *arachnoid*. What does that word mean?

_____

_____

_____

VOCABULARY

membrane (mem′brān′) *n.*: thin, soft, pliable sheet or layer, especially of animal or vegetable tissue.

IDENTIFY CAUSE & EFFECT

What cause and effect does Asimov describe in lines 91–97? Circle the sentence that describes the cause, and underline the sentence that describes the effect.

_____

_____

_____

_____

_____

_____

_____

_____

_____

COMPARE & CONTRAST

What character traits do Phaethon and Arachne share? Use the word *hubris* in your answer.

_____

_____

_____

_____

_____

_____

_____

_____

_____

Greek bowl showing Helios in his chariot.

Araldo de Luca/CORBIS.

Another example of this sort of myth is that of *Phaethon* (fā′ə·thän), the mortal son of Helios. He was so proud of being the son of the sun god, that he felt he could drive the sun (which was pictured as a gleaming chariot drawn by wild, gleaming horses) across the sky. He tricked his father into promising to let him do so.

90 (That was hubris.)

Phaethon drove the sun but found he could not control the horses, which went out of their course and swooped too near the earth. The Greeks supposed the burning sands of the Sahara showed where the swooping sun chariot had scorched the earth. To save the earth from destruction, Zeus was forced to kill Phaethon with a thunderbolt. (That was nemesis.)

from Words from the Myths

Cause-and-Effect Chart   Fill in the chart below with information from the *Words from the Myths* excerpt to complete each cause-and-effect relationship.

Reading Skills
Analyze cause and effect.

Cause	Effect
	Old age, death, famine, sickness, grief, and other ills trouble human beings.
A proud person defied the gods.	
Arachne challenged Athena to a weaving contest.	
	The Sahara was formed.

Skills Review

from Words from the Myths

VOCABULARY AND COMPREHENSION

A. Selection Vocabulary   Write words from the Word Bank to complete the paragraph below.

Arachne bragged and was (1) _____ about her skill at weaving tapestries. Her work was filmy and delicate, like the structure of a (2) _____. Arachne was arrogant; she even wove horrible stories about the gods into her work. Her (3) _____ behavior upset Athena. In (4) _____, Athena destroyed Arachne's weavings. It could have been worse. Athena could have chosen to (5) _____ all talented weavers!

B. Reading Comprehension   Answer each question below.

1. What does the expression *Pandora's box* mean in today's English?

   _____

   _____

2. How did Zeus directly punish Prometheus? _____

   _____

3. How did the word *nemesis* come to mean "unavoidable doom"

   in English? _____

   _____

4. Why did Arachne challenge Athena to a contest? What kind of

   contest was it? _____

   _____

5. Why did Zeus kill Phaethon with a thunderbolt? _____

   _____

Before You Read

from Miss Manners' Basic Training: Eating by Judith Martin

READING SKILLS: TRACING AN AUTHOR'S ARGUMENT

You may think of an argument as an angry discussion with someone, but it can also mean "debate." When a writer presents an **argument** in an informational text, he or she is simply trying to persuade you to agree with a certain point of view. The writer will probably use evidence in the form of facts, statistics, or quotations from experts to support the argument.

As you trace the **author's argument** in this excerpt from *Miss Manners' Basic Training: Eating,* keep these questions in mind:

- What is the subject of this text?
- What is the writer's point of view on the subject?
- What evidence does the writer use to support her argument?

VOCABULARY DEVELOPMENT: PREVIEW SELECTION VOCABULARY

Preview these vocabulary words before you begin reading.

affected (a·fekt'id) *adj.:* artificial; pretending to be something you are not.

Eating Asian foods with chopsticks isn't considered affected. If you use chopsticks in an Asian restaurant, no one will think you're trying to be something you're not.

incident (in'sə·dənt) *n.:* minor disturbance.

With practice, you will be able to use chopsticks without incident, but most minor mishaps by Westerners will be overlooked in Asian countries.

cultivate (kul'tə·vāt') *v.:* develop or acquire.

If you can't cultivate the skill to use chopsticks, you should ask for a fork.

communal (kə·myo͞on'əl) *adj.:* belonging to a group.

Food is often served in a communal bowl; everyone eats from the same bowl.

humiliate (hyo͞o·mil'ē·āt') *v.:* hurt someone's pride; make someone feel foolish.

Don't humiliate people by telling them they don't know how to set a table.

SKILLS FOCUS

Reading Skills
Understand an author's argument.

from Miss Manners' Basic Training: Eating

Judith Martin

American style of eating.

European style of eating.

TEXT STRUCTURE

Most of the text uses a question-and-answer format in the form of letters to and from Miss Manners. Circle the greeting in each letter from Miss Manners. How does Miss Manners address her readers? How do you feel about this greeting?

_____

_____

_____

_____

_____

_____

American and European Styles

Dear Miss Manners—Is it acceptable in the United States to use the European method of dining with the knife in the right hand and the fork in the left, cutting the food as you eat it?

Gentle Reader—Is it acceptable for someone in the United States to speak with, say, an English or French accent?

Certainly, if that person is a foreigner or foreign-born. Eating European style (keeping the fork in the left hand

10 and packing food onto the back of it with the knife) rather than American style (switching the fork to the right hand after cutting and bringing food to the mouth with the fork

facing upward) is acceptable in the United States for foreigners and the foreign-born. In anyone else, it is considered **affected.**

Chopsticks

Chopstick usage varies in different countries, as indeed do the implements[1] themselves. Here is the basic technique considered acceptable when practiced by Westerners:

20   Chopsticks are held as if you were using two pencils at once, except that the lower one is gripped between the thumb, at about knuckle level, and the end of the ring finger, while the upper chopstick is gripped between the end of the thumb and the end of the forefinger, with the assistance of the middle finger. This should provide enough leverage to grasp food by moving the upper chopstick down so that the tips hold it securely enough to get it to the mouth without **incident.**

         Of course, a lot depends on what we mean by "it."
30 Grains of rice? Slippery noodles? Tiny tofu squares that collapse under pressure?

         This may be the place for Miss Manners to mention that one may properly ask for a fork when dining in an Asian restaurant in the West—although they are usually already provided by restaurateurs, who have no desire to witness or clean up after ineptitude. Tourists attempting a difficult foreign custom should **cultivate** a look of appealing stupidity that will give their mistakes a sort of childish charm.

40   Things you may not do with your chopsticks include stabbing (food or people), putting the parts that have been in your mouth into a **communal** bowl (Chinese restaurants provide a spoon to get around this practice, and the

---

1. implements: tools.

IDENTIFY

Pause at line 15. How does the writer feel about Americans who use the European method of eating? Underline the answer.

VOCABULARY

affected (a·fekt'id) *adj.*: artificial; pretending to be something you are not.

incident (in'sə·dənt) *n.*: minor disturbance.

INFER

What do you think Miss Manners means by "without incident" (line 28)?

_____

_____

_____

WORD STUDY

What do you guess *ineptitude* means in line 36? Check the context.

_____

_____

_____

VOCABULARY

cultivate (kul'tə·vāt') *v.*: develop or acquire.

communal (kə·myo͞on'əl) *adj.*: belonging to a group.

An East-West trade-off.

Japanese method is to reverse one's sticks), parking them in the bowl crossed or pointing across the table (they are left on a chopstick holder or on the paper container in which they came), or doing any of those other nasty things imaginative children of all nations come up with.

The Soup Spoon

50 Dear Miss Manners—Where do you place your mouth and lips in relation to a soup spoon? A friend and I have a difference of opinion. I say you sip from the side, but if it's a thick type of soup with lots of items in it (such as pieces of vegetables), you place the tip of the spoon in your mouth so you can consume the liquid and whatever else at the same time.

Gentle Reader—Yours would be an excellent solution if the journey of food to mouth were merely a transportation problem, to be figured out on a practical basis. But if that
60 were the case, Miss Manners would also have to listen to

more efficient movers, who might point out that picking things out of the soup with the fingers would be even more practical, provided that the soup wasn't scalding.

One always pours soup, even goody-laden soup, into the mouth from the side of an oval soup spoon. Perhaps Miss Manners can make up for this bad news by telling you about the gumbo[2] spoon: It's large, it's proper for soups with a lot of things in them, and it's round, so it is less obvious if you slip from side to tip.

Extra Spoons (and Some Plates)

Dear Miss Manners—My boyfriend insists that when we are having company (unless it's a picnic), a spoon is to be set, along with whatever other flatware[3] is needed, even when there is nothing being served that requires a spoon. The dinner in question consisted of green salad, grilled halibut, wild rice, and bread. In addition, he felt that bread plates weren't necessary, as that created too many dishes on the table, in addition to dinner and salad plates.

Gentle Reader—Miss Manners appreciates the interest that both of you take in the properly set table and the opportunity she has to side graciously with both of you.

She is with you on the spoon. Contrary to popular fears, table settings are not tricks to **humiliate** people who can't see a relationship between the flatware and the food. The two are directly connected: What is set out is there to be used and is even placed (outside to inside) in order of use. A spoon is not set out unless it is needed—for grapefruit at breakfast, for example, or for soup at dinner. A dessert spoon would be placed above the plate, parallel to the table's edge. (Which reminds Miss Manners—

2. **gumbo:** thick soup made with okra.
3. **flatware:** knives, forks, and spoons.

EVALUATE

Underline Miss Manners' advice about eating soup. Do you agree with her?

_____

_____

_____

_____

_____

_____

_____

_____

_____

_____

_____

_____

IDENTIFY AUTHOR'S ARGUMENT

Re-read lines 79–98, in which Miss Manners presents two arguments—on the topics of spoons and plates. Locate and underline the author's arguments.

VOCABULARY

humiliate (hyo͞o·mil′ē·āt′) v.: hurt someone's pride; make someone feel foolish.

you didn't have any dessert, did you? Are all your friends on diets?)

However, she is with the gentleman in thinking that three plates for each person would make the table look like a china shop. Bread can always be placed on the edge of the main plate, or on the tablecloth (yes, surprisingly enough— as long as there is no butter involved to make grease stains). You could also serve the salad as a separate course.

The Knife

100 Dear Miss Manners—My niece, an educated and charming person, holds her knife and fork in a most awkward fashion. She holds her knife vertically while cutting her meat. Please comment.

Gentle Reader—She tries to cut meat while holding her knife in a completely vertical position? The poor lady. She will probably starve to death.

Packing the Fork

Dear Miss Manners—Is a person allowed to eat a small portion of potato and meat together from the same forkful 110 of food, or must they always be consumed separately?

Gentle Reader—Making a food package on the fork, such as using mashed potatoes to cement meat and peas onto it, is considered distasteful in America—to other diners, that is. However, those who find it tasty may absentmindedly allow the prongs of a meat-laden fork to drift idly into the potatoes on its way to the mouth. Or they can learn how to park meat in a discreet corner of the cheek until the potato delivery arrives on the next fork run.

FLUENCY

Read the boxed passage aloud. What attitude will you convey? Circle or underline words that you stumbled over. Then, read the passage again, paying careful attention to those problem words.

INTERPRET

What is Miss Manners' tone in lines 111–118—is she serious or humorous? Underline the words that give you a clue.

from Miss Manners' Basic Training: Eating

Argument Chart   In the excerpt from *Miss Manners' Basic Training: Eating,* the author presents arguments for the proper ways to eat and to set the table. Fill in the chart below to trace one of the author's arguments.

SKILLS FOCUS

Reading Skills
Analyze and trace an author's argument.

Argument or Perspective

_____

_____

_____

_____

_____

Detail That Supports Argument	**Detail That Supports Argument**	**Detail That Supports Argument**
_____	_____	_____
_____	_____	_____
_____	_____	_____
_____	_____	_____
_____	_____	_____
_____	_____	_____
_____	_____	_____

Skills Review

from Miss Manners' Basic Training: Eating

VOCABULARY AND COMPREHENSION

Word Bank

affected
incident
cultivate
communal
humiliate

A. Selection Vocabulary   Write words from the Word Bank to complete the paragraph below.

Miss Manners thinks Americans who eat European style seem snobby and (1) _____. Doing so may cause an embarrassing (2) _____. On using chopsticks, she suggests that inexperienced diners not (3) _____ themselves but request forks instead. Those who use chopsticks should not dip them into a (4) _____ dish. In short, Miss Manners advises that diners (5) _____ a considerate manner toward all.

B. Reading Comprehension   Answer each question below.

1. What is the European method of dining? Does Miss Manners think it is acceptable for someone born in the United States to use this method?

   _____

   _____

2. What does Miss Manners recommend you do if you're eating in an Asian restaurant in the West and you don't want to use chopsticks?

   _____

   _____

3. What are unacceptable ways of handling chopsticks?

   _____

   _____

4. According to Miss Manners, how should you always use a soup spoon?

   _____

   _____

ONLINE ARTICLE

Mexicans Resist Flight from "Friendly" Volcano by Tim Weiner

READING SKILLS: IDENTIFYING THE MAIN IDEA

When you tell someone what an informational text is about, you're describing its main idea. The **main idea** is the most important point the writer wants to get across to the reader—it's *why* the writer wrote the material. As you read "Mexicans Resist Flight from 'Friendly' Volcano," keep these main-idea questions in mind:

- Does the title of the text tell you the main idea or hint at it?
- Is there a sentence near the beginning or end of the selection that states the main idea?
- What main idea is suggested by the details in the text?

VOCABULARY DEVELOPMENT: PREVIEW SELECTION VOCABULARY

Get to know these words before you read the selection.

revered (ri·vird′) *v.* used as *adj.:* adored; loved.

> *The volcano was revered as a provider of rain and rich soil.*

benevolent (bə·nev′ə·lənt) *adj.:* kindly; good.

> *The volcano was more benevolent, or kind, than their own government.*

metropolis (mə·träp′ə·lis) *n.:* main city of a country, state, or region.

> *Many people live in central Mexico's metropolis, Mexico City.*

abrasive (ə·brā′siv) *adj.:* causing rubbing off or scraping; rough.

> *The volcano's abrasive soot was as rough as sandpaper.*

evacuation (ē·vak′yoo·ā′shən) *n.:* removal from, often because of danger.

> *The government ordered an evacuation, but many older people would not leave their village.*

futility (fyoo·til′ə·tē) *n.:* uselessness.

> *Once the government saw that it couldn't remove the whole population that lived near the volcano, it admitted the futility of its earlier attempts.*

SKILLS FOCUS

Reading Skills
Identify the main idea.

from The New York Times on the Web

Mexicans Resist Flight from "Friendly" Volcano

Tim Weiner

BACKGROUND: Informational Text and Social Studies

The volcano Popocatépetl (pō·pō′kä·te′pet′l) near Mexico City is one of the world's most dangerous volcanoes. The reporter Tim Weiner was on the scene during one of its most recent eruptions, on December 18, 2000. Weiner filed this eyewitness report the day after the eruption.

Here are some things to know before you read the article:

- On December 18, 2000, Popocatépetl erupted in its strongest explosion in over a thousand years.
- Popocatépetl is 17,945 feet high and can be seen by about thirty million people, most of whom live in Mexico City.
- The name *Popocatépetl* means "smoking mountain" in the Nahuatl language, the language of the ancient Aztec people.

Marco Ugate/Associated Press.

Residents of communities near the base of the volcano Popocatépetl try to keep warm as the volcano spews ash and smoke in the background.

Mexico City, Dec. 19—Every thousand years or so, the great Popocatépetl explodes with killing force, and as it rumbled and puffed this weekend, government officials monitoring geophysicists' instruments pleaded with thousands of villagers under the volcano to flee.

Few did. People fought to stay put, even after it erupted violently throughout Monday night and this morning, flinging glowing five-foot rocks for miles, in

10 what is believed to be its biggest bang in more than a millennium. They felt strongly that the volcano— their volcano, **revered** as the god of rain and giver of rich soil—was more **benevolent** a force than their government.

"The people in the villages consider Popo a friendly volcano, the beating heart of the land," said Homero Aridjis, a poet, former diplomat, and president of PEN, the international writers' association. "It's our Indian beliefs against European science."

20 Maybe they were right: Though the mountain is hurling incandescent bombs, potentially threatening everyone for 20 miles around, it has killed no one yet. But this clash of verities versus technology—or human nature against nature—is an old story. And since the volcano still is capable of an immense explosion, it is far from over.

Scientists and the government warned today that a full-blown eruption, pouring rivers of lava down Popocatépetl's slopes, could come at any time. The

metropolis (mə·träp′ə·lis) *n.:*
main city of a country, state,
or region.

abrasive (ə·brā′siv) *adj.:*
causing rubbing off or
scraping; rough.

evacuation
(ē·vak′yōō·ā′shən) *n.:*
removal from, often
because of danger.

The writer quotes three
different people to support
an important idea. Read the
boxed passage aloud, using
expression to show that
three different people are
speaking.

Use context clues to guess at
the meaning of *antiquities* in
line 51.

Location:

30 volcano, less than 40 miles east of Mexico City and its
nearly 20 million people, fumed billows of gray ash
all day. The wind carried it south, sparing the
metropolis and its international airport a coat of
abrasive soot.

  All day Monday and today, government sound
trucks went through villages near the volcano, blaring
warnings. Church bells rang out danger and army
commanders appeared with evacuation orders. But
thousands resisted the call. Vicente Jiménez, a

40 26-year-old corn farmer from Santiago Xanitzintla,
about seven miles from the flaming crater, heard all
the alarms and was unmoved.

  "We never left," he said today. "We don't feel
comfortable leaving our homes and everything we
own in the hands of the authorities. For many people
leaving was hard enough, but leaving our homes in
the hands of the police is even harder."

  A fellow farmer who stayed behind, Adolfo
Castro, 55, said, "This is a very old village. The church

50 is important to us, and there was no one guarding it.
There are antiquities inside that go back centuries."

  An army commander charged with carrying out
evacuation today shook his head. "It's too late to be
fighting with these people," he said. "They've shut
themselves in behind four locks. They are older
people who will never leave."

  More than 20,000 people appeared to have
turned down the government's offers of trans-

Location:

portation, food, and shelter. "Their resistance is
60 reasonable, based on their experience," said Luis
González y González, a historian at the National
College. "The people have nothing to identify with
but their families and their land."

After nearly seven decades of deep sleep,
17,945-foot Popocatépetl (pronounced poh-poh-
kah-TEH-peh-tel), became active again in December
1994. Since then, government scientists have erected
a world-class monitoring network of sensors around
it, measuring its internal pressure and recording its
70 smallest tremors.

The Mexican government also set up 1,232
shelters with room for more than 300,000 people.
It accurately predicted the eruption, broadcast the
warning clearly, and yet could not persuade people
to leave through reason alone.

Part of the resistance lies in village traditions.
People call the volcano Don Gregorio, or Don Goyo
for short, and see him as a living, giving creature.
Shamans in the villages communicate with him and
80 insist he will not hurt people unless people hurt him.

"People here still carry gifts up the mountain, a
stewpot of turkey with mole, a basket of fruits," said
Tomás Jiménez, Vicente's father, who said his family
has lived in Santiago Xanitzintla for centuries. "They
ask for a better harvest or more rain."

Part of the fight against flight has an even deeper
foundation, though.

DECODING TIP

In line 59, draw a vertical line between the root word *resist* and the suffix *–ance*. The suffix means "process or action of." What does *resistance* mean?

_____

_____

_____

_____

_____

_____

_____

_____

_____

_____

_____

_____

WORD STUDY

Mount St. Helens, a volcano, is sometimes **personified** as a sleeping giant. Underline words in lines 76–80 that show that the village people have personified Popocatépetl.

In the paragraph that begins on line 99, what important idea does Dr. Miller convey about the people's refusal to leave the area around Popo? Underline the examples he provides in the next paragraphs to support his opinion.

_____

_____

_____

_____

_____

_____

_____

_____

_____

_____

_____

_____

_____

_____

_____

_____

_____

_____

_____

Location: [   ]

"It's human nature," said Dan Miller, a research geologist and the chief of the United States Volcano
90 Disaster Assistance Program, which is based in Vancouver, Washington, who has worked in more than a dozen countries, throughout Latin America, Asia, and Africa.

"Wherever we go in the world we have met with the same kind of problem," said Dr. Miller, whose program is run by the United States Office of Foreign Disaster Assistance and the United States Geological Survey.

"People who live in high-risk zones around
100 volcanoes don't expect an eruption to take place, and if it did, they don't expect it to affect them. Government scientists in the U.S. and elsewhere meet with mistrust when they issue proclamations or recommendations. People don't understand or believe their warnings."

The same thing happened at the Mount St. Helens eruption in Washington State 20 years ago. "When Mount St. Helens woke up after 123 years, a fair number of people refused to be evacuated, and
110 many of the 57 people killed had illegally entered into closed-off and restricted areas," Dr. Miller said.

Late last year in Ecuador, at least 22,000 villagers were evacuated by the government when the 16,475-foot volcano called Tungurahua—"Throat of Fire" in the Quechua Indian language—showed signs that a violent explosion was coming. "Now 15 months have gone by and the predicted devastating events haven't occurred," Dr. Miller said. "And the people have fought their way through military barricades back 120 home. And they're there now, even though the eruptions continue."

This evening, though some villages were all but deserted, it appeared that roughly 30,000 people— slightly more than half of the 56,000 people the government wanted to protect—had accepted the offer of shelter, said the interior minister, Santiago Creel. Mr. Creel, who like the rest of the government of President Vicente Fox has been in power only 18 days, said he saw the **futility** of forcing the others 130 to leave.

"We don't think there's a clear way for us to remove the whole population," he said.

And Mr. Fox, touring Cholula, the largest town near the smoking cone of Popocatépetl, spoke for many of the villagers when he said the future under the volcano was as clear as the ashen cloud over it.

"We have to wait and see what Mr. Popocatépetl says," Mr. Fox observed. "Because he's the one setting the agenda here. Nobody else can."

VOCABULARY

futility (fyo͞o·til′ə·tē) *n.:* uselessness.

WORD STUDY

What does Mr. Fox mean in the **simile** "the future under the volcano was as clear as the ashen cloud over it" (lines 135–136)?

Mexicans Resist Flight from "Friendly" Volcano

SKILLS FOCUS

Reading Skills
Analyze the
main idea.

Main-Idea Chart   The **main idea** of a text is its most important idea.
Read through the article again, and jot down details from it that you find
important. Then, try out several statements of what you think is the main
idea of the article.

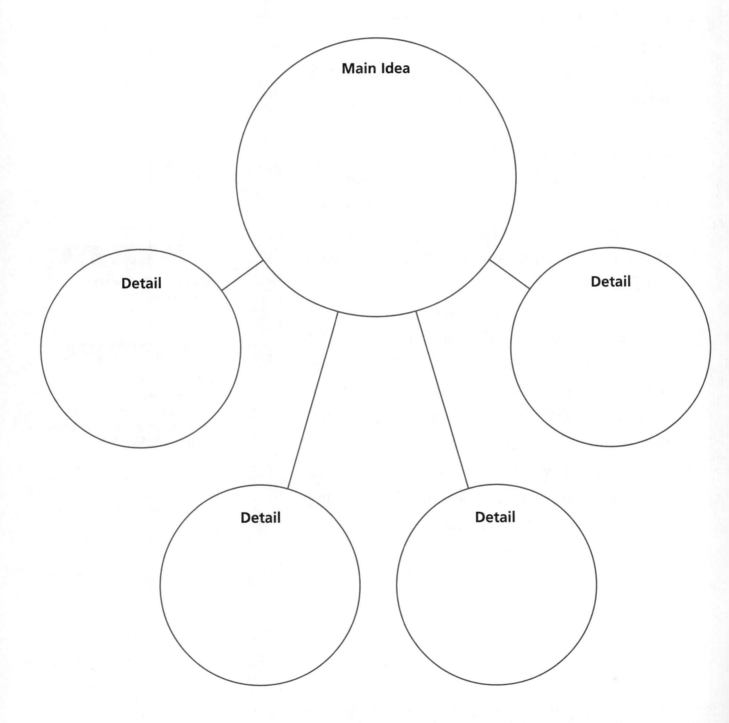

Main Idea

Detail

Detail

Detail

Detail

Skills Review

Mexicans Resist Flight from "Friendly" Volcano

VOCABULARY AND COMPREHENSION

A. Selection Vocabulary   Write words from the Word Bank to complete the paragraph below.

For many villagers, (1) _____ from their homes near the (2) _____ seems worse than living near an active volcano. For thousands of years, the Mexican people have (3) _____ their "friendly," or (4) _____, volcano "Don Goyo." Officials see the (5) _____ of forcing people to leave, even when (6) _____ soot and debris spew from the volcano.

B. Reading Comprehension   Answer each question below.

1. Why wouldn't people leave the villages around the volcano? _____

_____

2. Was Mexico City in danger from the volcano? Explain. _____

_____

3. How many people turned down the government's offer of free transportation, food, and shelter? According to the text, was their resistance reasonable?

_____

_____

4. Is it common for people to remain near a volcano when they're warned that it is about to explode? Why or why not? _____

_____

_____

How to Stay Fit for Life

by Ritu Upadhyay

READING SKILLS: SUMMARIZING

If you were to tell some friends about a trip you took, you probably wouldn't tell them every little detail. If you did, your friends would get pretty bored with your description. Instead, you would summarize your trip, telling your friends about the main events or high points of the journey. **Summarizing**—restating the main events or ideas of a text in a much shorter form than the original—is a great way to review the main events of a text. As you read "How to Stay Fit for Life," pause every so often to summarize what you've read.

VOCABULARY DEVELOPMENT: PREVIEW SELECTION VOCABULARY

Preview the words below before you read "How to Stay Fit for Life."

hectic (hek′tik) *adj.:* confused; excited.

> *Many kids' hectic schedules include school, activities with friends, and even music lessons, so it's hard to find time for exercise.*

obesity (ō·bē′sə·tē) *n.:* condition of being very overweight.

> *Obesity is becoming a common problem among kids. Because kids don't get regular exercise, more of them are becoming very overweight.*

pediatrician (pē′dē·ə·trish′ən) *n.:* doctor who specializes in treating children.

> *Doctors who treat children remind them that they only get one body. These pediatricians stress the importance of learning to take care of your body at an early age.*

yielding (yēl′diŋ) *v.* used as *n.:* producing.

> *In addition to yielding health benefits, regular exercise gives you more energy for your busy schedule.*

SKILLS FOCUS

Reading Skills
Summarize a text.

How to Stay Fit for Life

Ritu Upadhyay

© Royalty-Free/CORBIS.

Exercise Is Key to Staying Healthy

You know this fact better than anyone else does: kids are busier than ever before. The amount of homework has increased, and so has involvement in after-school activities. Kids feel pressure to do well in school and to keep up with music lessons and other activities. But health experts say most kids' **hectic** schedules leave out one of the most important activities: exercise.

"It's a myth that kids get enough physical activity," says gym teacher Andy Schmidt, who was named Teacher of the
10 Year by the National Association for Sport and Physical Fitness. "Kids' lives are busy, but they don't get the exercise time needed to stay healthy."

Alarming reports released last year by the U.S. Department of Health and Human Services show that

"How to Stay Fit for Life" by Ritu Upadhyay from *Time for Kids,* Spring, March 10, 2001. Copyright © 2001 by **Time Inc.** Reproduced by permission of the publisher.

SUMMARIZE

Pause at line 7. Circle the idea from this paragraph that you would include in a **summary.**

VOCABULARY

hectic (hek′tik) *adj.:* confused; excited.

IDENTIFY CAUSE & EFFECT

According to information in lines 8–12, why don't kids have time for exercise?

_____

_____

_____

_____

IDENTIFY

Re-read lines 13–20. Why do more than 25 percent of students get no physical education in school?

_____

_____

_____

_____

_____

_____

_____

_____

_____

_____

nearly half of all young people in America are not vigorously active on a regular basis. This trend is a big factor in the rising rate of **obesity** among kids. School budget cuts and more emphasis on preparing for tests have led many schools to cut down on gym and recess time. Now more

20 than 25% of students get no physical education in school.

Good for Your Mind and Body

Staying fit is a key element to maintaining your health. "We only get one body, so we have to learn to take care of it at an early age," says Dr. Charles Capetta, a **pediatrician** at the Dartmouth Hitchcock Clinic in Nashua, New Hampshire. Exercise helps build and maintain healthy bones, muscles and joints. It also prevents or delays the development of health problems that affect adults, including high blood pressure and heart disease.

30 Besides **yielding** medical benefits, staying fit means you have more energy to keep up with your packed daily

SUMMARIZE

In lines 21–29, what information would you include in a summary? Underline it.

VOCABULARY

obesity (ō·bē′sə·tē) *n.:* condition of being very overweight.

pediatrician (pē′dē·ə·trish′ən) *n.:* doctor who specializes in treating children.

yielding (yēl′diŋ) *v.* used as *n.:* producing.

FLASH FACT!
More than half of girls and one-quarter of boys ages 6 to 17 years cannot run a mile any faster than they can walk one.

© Royalty-Free/CORBIS.

schedule. Exercise can also help you relax, respond better to stress and build self-confidence.

It's not necessary to be involved in competitive sports to stay in shape. The good news: riding bikes or Rollerblading with your friends count too. "Have fun, and do what you enjoy," says Schmidt. "If you find an activity you really enjoy, you will stick with it."

IDENTIFY

Circle the **main idea** in lines 34–38.

IDENTIFY

According to the chart below, which kind of exercise should you do least often?

A FORMULA FOR STAYING FIT

Different parts of our bodies require different types of exercise. Read below to find out what combination you need to stay strong and flexible.

EXAMPLE	BENEFIT	AMOUNT
Aerobic Exercise Running, basketball, jumping rope, dancing	Aerobic exercise increases your heart rate, making you breathe harder. This strengthens your heart and lungs and improves the delivery of oxygen and blood throughout your body.	Thirty minutes a day, five days a week
Strength Training Pull-ups, sit-ups, push-ups, tugs-of-war	Muscle strength refers to the amount of work your muscles are able to do without getting tired. Endurance is the amount of time your muscles can work. Building both improves overall fitness.	Two or three days a week
Flexibility Training Sit and reach, yoga, gymnastics, tai chi	Flexibility is important because it allows you to move joints and stretch muscles in a full range of motion. Stretching before and after exercise helps protect you from injury.	Before and after any workout

How to Stay Fit for Life

SKILLS FOCUS

Reading Skills
Summarize
a text.

Summary Chart   Summarizing a text can help you remember its key details and determine its main idea. In a summary you use your own words to restate the main events or main details of the text. A summary is always much shorter than the text itself.

Fill out the chart that follows with details from "How to Stay Fit for Life." Then, write a summary of the article and its main idea in the boxes at the right.

Key Details

Summary

Main Idea

Skills Review

How to Stay Fit for Life

VOCABULARY AND COMPREHENSION

A. Selection Vocabulary   Write words from the Word Bank to complete the paragraph below.

My days were so (1) _____, so packed with activities, that I never used to go for walks. The last time I visited my (2) _____, however, she warned me that (3) _____ is a serious condition. She said doctors agree that being very overweight can lead to serious health problems. Now I'm on a regular exercise schedule. Besides (4) _____ better health, exercise has given me a lot more energy.

> **Word Bank**
> hectic
> obesity
> pediatrician
> yielding

B. Reading Comprehension   Answer each question below.

1. What percentage of kids in America do not get regular exercise? What health problem is increasing because of the lack of exercise?

   _____

   _____

2. What are some of the benefits of exercise? _____

   _____

   _____

3. Do you need to join a sports team in order to stay fit? Why or why not?

   _____

   _____

4. According to the article, what kind of exercise should you get most often? How much of this kind of exercise should you get each week?

   _____

   _____

ARTICLE

In Search of King Arthur

by Mara Rockliff

READING SKILLS: EVALUATING EVIDENCE

If someone told you that a magic potion would enable you to fly, would you believe it? You'd probably want evidence that the potion works before you'd try it out, right? In the same way, when you read an informational text, you need to evaluate its **evidence,** the details that a writer uses to support a position.

As you read "In Search of King Arthur," ask these questions about the evidence the writer uses:

- **Is the evidence adequate?** Is there enough evidence to support the writer's position?
- **Is the evidence accurate?** Are there mistakes or errors in the evidence that is presented? Does the evidence come from a source you can trust?
- **Is the evidence appropriate?** Does the evidence directly relate to the writer's conclusion?

VOCABULARY DEVELOPMENT: PREVIEW SELECTION VOCABULARY

A few words from "In Search of King Arthur" may be unfamiliar to you. Preview the words below before you start to read.

resistance (ri′zis·təns) *n.:* movement to oppose governing power.

Although the Celtic warriors put up resistance to the Anglo-Saxons, the invaders eventually conquered the Celts.

ruthless (rōōth′lis) *adj.:* pitiless; cruel.

The Anglo-Saxons were ruthless. They showed no pity toward the Celtic people.

excavations (eks′kə·vā′shənz) *n.:* things or places unearthed by exploratory digging.

Archaeologists dug up an interesting piece of slate during their excavations. It was from the sixth century, and it had the Latin name Artognou (pronounced ärth′nou) on it.

SKILLS FOCUS

Reading Skills
Evaluate evidence.

In Search of King Arthur

Mara Rockliff

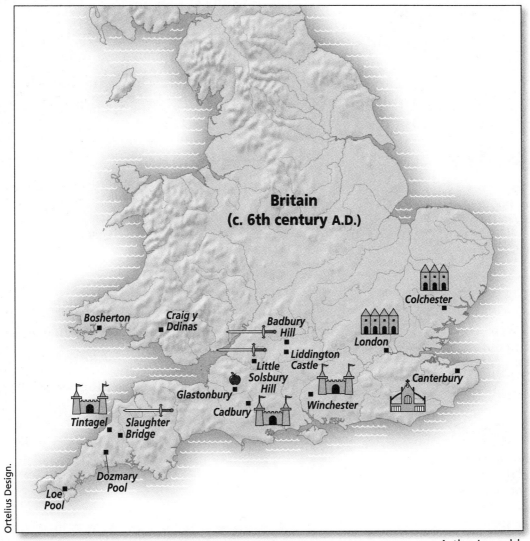

Britain
(c. 6th century A.D.)

Colchester

London

Canterbury

Bosherton

Craig y
Ddinas

Badbury
Hill

Liddington
Castle

Little
Solsbury
Hill

Glastonbury

Winchester

Tintagel

Slaughter
Bridge

Cadbury

Dozmary
Pool

Loe
Pool

Ortelius Design.

Arthur's world.

Stories tell us that King Arthur ruled with strength and wisdom from his court at Camelot. Stories also say that Arthur was badly wounded in battle and sailed to the Isle of Avalon to be healed. But who was this mysterious man, whose legend grew while written record of his reign vanished from the face of the earth?

Historical Evidence

Some historians believe that the real Arthur lived in the
sixth century A.D. He seems to have been a great Celtic
10 warrior who drove the Saxon invaders back at the Battle of
Badon Hill (possibly at the present-day Liddington Castle).
This warrior won his people forty years of peace before
their part of the country finally gave up its **resistance** to
the **ruthless** Anglo-Saxons. This Celtic warrior is mentioned by a sixth-century writer named Gildas and by a
ninth-century monk named Nennius. Both say that this
leader halted the Anglo-Saxons and won twelve battles for
the Britons. Gildas calls the warrior Ambrosius Aurelianus.
Nennius calls him Artorius (Latin for "Arthur").

20 ## Archaeological Evidence

Archaeologists have searched for solid evidence of Arthur's
existence. In 1998, it seemed they might have found it. At
Tintagel Castle, long believed by locals to be Arthur's birth-
place, **excavations** made by archaeologists produced a piece
of slate dating back to the sixth century. Inscribed on it in
Latin is the name Artognou, pronounced ärth′no͞u.

Is this Arthur's tomb?

Something else was dug up at the site: massive quantities of expensive sixth-century pottery imported from the Mediterranean. This find shows that during Arthur's time 30 *someone* very rich and powerful lived at Tintagel.

Where Was Camelot?

Sir Thomas Malory placed Camelot in Winchester, in his famous book *Le Morte d'Arthur* (*The Death of Arthur*), published in 1485. The proof hung in the Great Hall of Winchester Castle: the Round Table itself.

As it turns out, though, this could not be *the* Round Table. Measuring eighteen feet across and weighing 2,400 pounds, the round table at Winchester certainly is impressive. And it's old. But not that old. In 1976, tree-ring and carbon dating, 40 along with research into medieval carpentry, revealed that the table was built around 1270—perhaps for King Edward I, who was a huge fan of the Arthur legend.

So where was the real Camelot? Some say it was Colchester, an ancient British city whose Roman name could hint at a connection: Camulodunum. A more likely bet is Cadbury Castle. It's not what most people think of as a castle. Actually it's a hill—a high, steep hill—flat on top, but ringed by giant mounds that hide the hilltop from below. In Arthur's time, say archaeologists, it was a fortress. 50 They've dug up evidence: ruined fortifications, signs of a cobbled road that led through a wooden gatehouse, even the remains of a great timber hall for feasts. South Cadbury is near a village called Queen Camel—another possible source for the name Camelot.

IDENTIFY

What two facts in lines 20–30 could support the claim that Arthur lived at Tintagel?

_____

_____

_____

_____

_____

_____

_____

_____

_____

_____

_____

_____

_____

IDENTIFY

Underline the facts in lines 31–42 that prove that the Round Table at Winchester is not King Arthur's Round Table.

IDENTIFY

Underline the **archaeological evidence** in lines 43–54 that supports the claim that Camelot was at Cadbury Castle.

_____

_____

_____

_____

_____

_____

_____

_____

_____

IDENTIFY

Underline the **evidence** in lines 68–74 that suggests that Glastonbury Tor might be Avalon.

_____

_____

_____

_____

_____

_____

_____

_____

Where Is Arthur Buried?

The Welsh say that Arthur sleeps in Wales, beneath a giant rock called Craig y Ddinas. In 1191, however, the monks of Glastonbury Abbey claimed to have unearthed Arthur's grave. They dug up a cross of lead inscribed in Latin "Here

60 lies buried the renowned King Arthur with Guinevere, his second wife, in the Isle of Avalon." Digging deeper, they found a hollow tree trunk. Inside lay two skeletons, of a woman and a man.

Unfortunately even the cross has disappeared, and many experts now believe the finding was a fake. It might have been cooked up to lure pilgrims to the abbey, which needed funds following a disastrous fire.

Still, Glastonbury could be Avalon. It's not an island—in fact, it's miles from water—but towering above the abbey

70 is the rocky peak of Glastonbury Tor. Today farmland surrounds it; in Arthur's time, it was a soggy marsh. Rising from the mist, the tor may very well have seemed an enchanted isle. Long ago the tor was known as Inis Avalon, the apple-bearing island.

Will archaeologists ever find proof that Arthur did exist? No one knows. (It would certainly be hard to prove he didn't!) But man or myth, one thing is certain: In the hearts of those who cherish his heroic ideals, King Arthur lives— and will live forever.

In Search of King Arthur

Evidence Chart   Use the chart below to evaluate the adequacy, accuracy, and appropriateness of the evidence in the article "In Search of King Arthur." Go through the text, and make a list of the evidence the writer uses to support an idea or opinion. Then, in the columns next to each item of evidence, state whether the evidence is appropriate and accurate. Finally, in the box at the bottom of the chart, state whether you think the writer has used enough evidence to support her position.

Reading Skills
Evaluate
evidence.

Point Writer Is Making		
Evidence	Appropriate?	Accurate?
1.		
2.		
3.		
Is the evidence adequate? Explain.		

Skills Review

In Search of King Arthur

VOCABULARY AND COMPREHENSION

A. Selection Vocabulary   Write words from the Word Bank to complete the paragraph below.

     In bygone times, the Britons fought many battles. Eastern Britain was invaded by (1) _____ Anglo-Saxons in the sixth century. Arthur was a great warrior who led the (2) _____ against the invaders. His success in overcoming the Anglo-Saxons probably led to the legend of King Arthur. Historians think that the (3) _____ in Cadbury show a castle where the real Arthur may have lived.

B. Reading Comprehension   Answer each question below.

1. During what time period do historians think the real Arthur lived?

_____

_____

2. What evidence of Arthur's existence did archaeologists find in 1998? Where did they find it? _____

_____

3. What book placed Camelot in Winchester? When and by whom was the book written? _____

_____

4. In what two places is Arthur said to be buried? Is there solid evidence for either claim? _____

_____

Before You Read

California State Parks: Rules and Regulations by the California State Parks Commission

READING SKILLS: ANALYZING INFORMATION IN PUBLIC DOCUMENTS

What time does the city library open? When do lifeguards go on duty at the town pool? You can usually find answers to these kinds of questions in public documents. Although public documents may be issued by almost anyone (church officials, politicians, schools, parks committees, and so on), all these documents have one thing in common: They exist to inform us, the public. As you read "California State Parks: Rules and Regulations," use these tips to locate information quickly and easily:

- Look for a head or title to identify the purpose of the document.
- Scan the text for heads, subheads, and special features such as bulleted lists, words in capital letters, and boldface terms.
- Study diagrams, illustrations, footnotes, and glossary entries.
- Carefully re-read any information that seems confusing.

VOCABULARY DEVELOPMENT: PREVIEW SELECTION VOCABULARY

Take some time to preview these vocabulary words.

designated (dez′ig·nāt′əd) *v.:* specially marked for a purpose.

Firearms are allowed only in areas that have been designated for hunting.

hazard (haz′ərd) *n.:* dangerous condition.

Down wood can be a hazard because it provides fuel for wildfires.

facilities (fə·sil′ə·tēz) *n.:* places equipped for specific uses.

Fires are allowed in certain facilities, such as cabins with grills.

ejected (ē·jekt′əd) *v.:* thrown out.

People with pets that disturb others can be ejected from the park and not allowed to come back.

occupied (äk′yoo·pīd′) *v.:* inhabited; lived in; possessed; filled; in use.

A campsite must be occupied by campers or reserved in order to hold the site.

SKILLS FOCUS

Reading Skills
Analyze information in public documents.

California State Parks: Rules and Regulations

California State Parks Commission

BACKGROUND: Informational Text and Social Studies
With millions of visitors per year, how do state parks stay so beautiful and safe? A code of rules and regulations is one solution to the problem. These rules are made and enforced so that all visitors to state parks can enjoy the beauties of nature.

You're about to read a summary of the rules and regulations for California state parks. This information is made available to the public online as well as through the state government's Office of Communications.

ANALYZE INFORMATION

Who created this set of rules and regulations? How can you tell?

_____

_____

_____

_____

_____

VOCABULARY

designated (dez′ig·nāt′əd) *v.*: specially marked for a purpose.

Rules and regulations protect California State Parks for the enjoyment of future generations as well as for the convenience and safety of the park visitors. To ensure your visit is a pleasant one, please observe the following:

NATURAL SCENERY, PLANTS, AND ANIMAL LIFE are the principal attractions of most state parks. They are integral parts of the ecosystem and natural community. As such they are protected by Federal, State, and Park laws. Disturbance or destruction of these resources is strictly forbidden.

10   **LOADED FIREARMS AND HUNTING** are not allowed in units of the State Parks System. Possession of loaded firearms or air rifles is prohibited. Exceptions are for hunting in recreation areas that have been **designated** by the State Park and Recreation Commission.

DEAD AND DOWN WOOD is part of the natural condition. Decayed vegetation forms humus and assists the growth of trees and other plants. For this reason the gathering of down wood is prohibited. Fuel is sold in the parks for your convenience. (When considered a **hazard,** down wood is removed by park personnel.)

FIRES are permitted only in **facilities** provided for this purpose. This is necessary to prevent disastrous fires. Portable stoves may be used in designated areas. It is the responsibility of every visitor to use extreme caution with any burning materials, including tobacco. All fireworks are prohibited.

ANIMALS, including cats, may not be turned loose in park units. All animals, other than grazing animals, must be under immediate physical control. Dogs must be on a tended leash no more than 6 feet or confined in an

PhotoDisc, Inc.

ANALYZE INFORMATION

Why might the subheads in this document appear in boldface capital letters? What sort of information do these heads convey?

_____

_____

_____

_____

_____

_____

_____

_____

_____

_____

_____

_____

_____

_____

_____

_____

_____

VOCABULARY

hazard (haz′ərd) *n.:* dangerous condition.

facilities (fə·sil′ə·tēz) *n.:* places equipped for specific uses.

enclosed vehicle, tent, or pen. Unless posted to the contrary, dogs, other than those that assist the permanently disabled, are prohibited on trails, beaches, and wherever posted. Visitors with vicious, dangerous, noisy, or disturbing animals will be **ejected** from park units.

NOISE—ENGINE DRIVEN ELECTRIC GENERATORS which can disturb others, may be operated only between the hours 10:00 A.M. and 8:00 P.M. Loud disturbing noise is prohibited at all times, as is disturbing

40 those asleep between 10:00 P.M. and 6:00 A.M.

ALL VEHICLE TRAVEL must be confined to designated roads or areas. The speed for all vehicles is 15 miles per hour in camp, picnic, utility, or headquarters areas and areas of general assemblage. Parking is permitted only in designated areas. Blocking parking spaces is prohibited.

CAMPSITE USE must be paid for in advance. To hold a campsite, it must be reserved or **occupied.** To prevent encroachment on others the limits of each campsite may be regulated by the District Superintendent.

50 Checkout time is **12:00 NOON.** In order to provide for the greatest number of visitors possible the **CAMPING LIMIT** in any one campground is 30 days per calendar year.

REFUSE, including garbage, cigarettes, paper boxes, bottles, ashes, and other rubbish, shall be placed only in designated receptacles. Your pleasure and pride in your parks will be enhanced when they are kept clean.

PLEASE clean up after yourself so that others may enjoy the beauty of these parks.

60   **LEAVE ONLY FOOTPRINTS—**
TAKE ONLY MEMORIES

California State Parks: Rules and Regulations

Key Information Chart   Through public documents we might find anything: from how and where to vote to how we can help cure a disease in a developing nation. Fill out the chart below with five pieces of key information you found in "California State Parks: Rules and Regulations." Then, describe where in the document you found that information; for example, was it under a subhead, in a chart, or in a list?

SKILLS FOCUS

Reading Skills
Analyze information in public documents.

Key Information	Where Information Was Located

Skills Review

California State Parks: Rules and Regulations

VOCABULARY AND COMPREHENSION

A. Selection Vocabulary Write words from the Word Bank to complete the paragraph below.

The hikers stopped in the middle of the path, panting and out of breath. Leaning on their walking sticks, they read the warning sign: "HALT! This area has been (1) _____ by the State of California as off-limits to the public. Behind this fence is a landfill containing a health (2) _____. There are no restrooms, water fountains, or other (3) _____ there. The area is not fit to be (4) _____ by human beings, and any person found there will be (5) _____ from the park."

B. Reading Comprehension Answer each question below.

1. To find out whether it is legal to gather firewood in a California state park, under which subhead would you look? _____

   _____

2. Why is the gathering of down wood prohibited? _____

   _____

3. How early in the morning can you start your electric generator? Where did you find that information? _____

   _____

4. How many days a year can you camp in a California state park? What special feature is used to call out that information? _____

   _____

Index of Authors and Titles

Vocabulary Development

Pronunciation guides, in parentheses, are provided for the vocabulary words in this book. The following key will help you use those pronunciation guides.

As a practice in using a pronunciation guide, sound out the words used as examples in the list that follows. See if you can hear the way the same vowel might be sounded in different words. For example, say "at" and "ate" aloud. Can you hear the difference in the way "a" sounds?

The symbol ə is called a **schwa.** A schwa is used by many dictionaries to indicate a sort of weak sound like the "a" in "ago." Some people say the schwa sounds like "eh." A vowel sounded like a schwa is never accented.

The vocabulary words in this book are also provided with a part-of-speech label. The parts of speech are *n.* (noun), *v.* (verb), *pro.* (pronoun), *adj.* (adjective), *adv.* (adverb), *prep.* (preposition), *conj.* (conjunction), and *interj.* (interjection). To learn about the parts of speech, consult the *Holt Handbook*.

To learn more about the vocabulary words, consult your dictionary. You will find that many of the words defined here have several other meanings.

---

at, āte, cär; ten, ēve; is, īce; gō, hôrn, look, to͞ol; oil, out; up, fur; ə *for unstressed vowels, as* a *in* ago, u *in* focus; ' *as in* Latin (lat''n); chin; she; zh *as in* azure (azh'ər); thin, the; ŋ *as in* ring (riŋ)

Notes

Notes

Notes

Notes

Notes

Notes